Best Practice in
PROFESSIONAL
SUPERVISION

of related interest

Passionate Supervision
Edited by Robin Shohet
ISBN 978 1 84310 556 5

Creative Supervision
The Use of Expressive Arts Methods in Supervision and Self-Supervision
Mooli Lahad
ISBN 978 1 85302 828 1

Integrative Approaches to Supervision
Edited by Michael Carroll and Margaret Tholstrup
ISBN 978 1 85302 966 0

Enhancing Social Work Management
Theory and Best Practice from the UK and USA
Edited by Jane Aldgate, Lynne Healy, Barris Malcolm, Barbara Pine, Wendy Rose and Janet Seden
ISBN 978 1 84310 515 2

Being White in the Helping Professions
Developing Effective Intercultural Awareness
Judy Ryde
Foreword by Colin Lago
ISBN 978 1 84310 936 5

Good Practice in Supervision
Statutory and Voluntary Organisations
Edited by Jacki Pritchard
ISBN 978 1 85302 279 1
Good Practice in Health, Social Care and Criminal Justice Series

Systemic Supervision
A Portable Guide for Supervision Training
Gill Gorrell Barnes, Gwynneth Down and Damien McCann
ISBN 978 1 85302 853 3

Best Practice in PROFESSIONAL SUPERVISION

A Guide for the Helping Professions

Allyson Davys and Liz Beddoe

Jessica Kingsley Publishers
London and Philadelphia

Table 3.2 adapted with permission from Pearson Education
Figure 8.1 reproduced with permission from the author (Karpman 1968)
Figure 8.2 adapted with permission from the authors (Cornelius and Faire 2006)
Figure 10.2 reproduced with permission from Taylor & Francis

First published in 2010
by Jessica Kingsley Publishers
116 Pentonville Road
London N1 9JB, UK
and
400 Market Street, Suite 400
Philadelphia, PA 19106, USA

www.jkp.com

Library of Congress Cataloging in Publication Data
Davys, Allyson, 1952-
  Best practice in professional supervision : a guide for the
helping professions / Allyson Davys and Liz Beddoe.
     p. cm.
  Includes bibliographical references and index.
  ISBN 978-1-84310-995-2 (alk. paper)
  1. Social workers--Supervision of. 2. Social work administration.
3. Supervision of employees. I. Beddoe, Liz, 1956- II. Title.
  HV40.54.D38 2010
  361.3068'3--dc22
                                                        2009054068

British Library Cataloguing in Publication Data
A CIP catalogue record for this book is available from the British Library

ISBN 978 1 84310 995 2

Printed and bound in Great Britain by
MPG Books Group, Cornwall

Acknowledgements

We would like to acknowledge the generous support and assistance from many people in the preparation of this book. In particular Lisa Jones from the Curriculum Factory at Waikato Institute of Technology who developed the diagrams and models with us. We wish to acknowledge Dr Marie Connolly for the conceptualisation of the child protection system from her systems framework for reviewing child deaths. Our thanks are also due to Janet May and Vivianne Flintoff who kindly read chapters and gave expert advice and feedback. We also acknowledge the many practitioners who have attended our courses and who have contributed to our understanding and learning through their generous sharing of the challenges of, and excitement about, supervision. Finally Harold, Caitlin, David, Sebastien and Genevieve who have tolerated our preoccupation and absence from family life.

Contents

List of Tables and Figures

Tables

Figures

Chapter 1

The Context of Professional Supervision

INTRODUCTION

It is an unfortunate reality that, although it is relevant to all fields of human services and has become mandatory regular practice in many, the practice of professional supervision is contested and very differently understood and interpreted. We begin *Best Practice in Professional Supervision* by surveying its history and nature.

Supervision, which is believed by some to have its early antecedents in the seventeenth and eighteenth centuries, developed into the practice we recognise today over the past 120 years (Grauel 2002). The growth and refinement of supervision has been accompanied by an associated complexity (and richness) of definition and practice as different professional groups have adopted supervision as one form of professional development and accountability. The result, 'a malleable concept in search of precise definition' (Grauel 2002, p.4), aptly captures one of the key dilemmas for today's practitioners who are faced with a form of professional practice which, for all its similarities, is differently positioned within separate professions, and indeed for some professions differently positioned across international borders. Thus in some contexts supervision is exclusively the domain of the novice or student apprentice whilst in other contexts it is a lifelong process of professional critique and learning. In this book we have chosen to use the term professional supervision, not because we necessarily see this term as the 'best' term for what is a complex set of specific relationships and tasks, but rather it is our attempt to distinguish the practice of supervision from a plethora of other terms which describe similar activities but which do not exactly capture our meaning of supervision.

Ferguson (2005), in a multidisciplinary text on clinical mentoring and supervision in the allied health professions, provides a broad definition of supervision that works across disciplines and neatly manages to include the practice learning aspect of supervision and to encompass professional development:

> Professional supervision is a process between someone called a supervisor and another referred to as the supervisee. It is usually aimed at enhancing the helping effectiveness of the person supervised. It may include acquisition of practical skills, mastery of theoretical or technical knowledge, personal development at the client/therapist interface and professional development. (Ferguson 2005, p.294)

The past 15 years has seen an unprecedented number of publications on the topic of supervision in the helping and health professions. However, as Hawkins and Shohet (2006, p.76) observe, the volume of research on supervision has not kept pace with the conceptual material published on the topic. There remains little agreement as to what constitutes 'good' supervision and much of the evaluative research into the effectiveness of supervision has concerned student supervision or the supervision of interns. Here the distinction between training and supervision has not always been made and self report has been at risk of reflecting vested interests and assessment anxiety. Rich's observations that supervision is not accompanied by any 'single definition or theory…by which to describe its meaning, methods, or purpose' nor is there any 'coherent and succinct body of knowledge' (Rich 1993, p.137) remains valid. This lack of conceptualisation has, in the opinion of Milne *et al.* (2008), hindered the development of supervision.

In an attempt to address this lack Milne *et al.* (2008) reviewed 24 empirical studies of supervision and developed an 'evidence-based model' of clinical supervision. This foundation model, they argue, provides a base against which future research and hypotheses can be tested. The work of Milne and his associates is an important beginning to the process of drawing together the varied and various strands of supervision which straddle professional boundaries and claims a generic practice and theory base of its own.

A continuing problem in evaluating the effectiveness of supervision is the determination of appropriate evaluative criteria. Many schedules of criteria include some form of individual or parallel assessment by the supervisor and/or supervisee, or rates of staff satisfaction, and/or service user complaint. With regard to the two latter criteria, however, it may not be the effectiveness of supervision *per se*, but rather the organisational culture that ultimately wields the greatest influence over these factors. This is a topic we will discuss further in Chapter 4.

The difficulty of evaluating the effectiveness of supervision is compounded by the variety of definitions, the complexity of the activity, the multiple relationships and the variability of the context. Such complexity can become overwhelming not only for the researchers but also for the participants. Several recent studies point to effective supervision in the field of child welfare as having a positive impact on staff retention (DePanfilis and Zlotnik 2008; Yankeelov *et al.* 2009). Consistent with such findings, low supervisory support has been significantly related to the intention to leave (Nissly, Mor Barak and Levin 2005). Mor Barak *et al.* (2009) reported in a meta-analysis that the supervisory functions are positively and statistically significantly related to better outcomes for workers. Discussion of these factors will be expanded in Chapter 9. Recent literature thus continues to support the value of supervision and, through the mix of contexts and definitions, finds a common voice to support the practice of supervision and call for ongoing focused research. This progress and development of supervision is perhaps neatly captured by Bernard, who, on reviewing the past 25 years of supervision development confidently concludes that 'we have come from fledgling to robust' (Bernard 2005, p.17).

A BRIEF HISTORY OF SUPERVISION

Historically, professional supervision has been associated with the early development of social work during the latter part of the nineteenth century (Tsui and Ho 1997) and indeed it has been identified as 'social work's most important contribution to the helping professions' (Robinson in Grauel 2002, p.7). As O'Donoghue astutely observes, however, it is unlikely that such an activity should 'suddenly emerge from nowhere in the nineteenth century' and it is probable that the antecedents of supervision lie in much earlier social, spiritual and cultural arrangements of family and community (O'Donoghue 2003, p.43). In illustration of this Grauel (2002) identifies links between current supervisory practice and the seventeenth and eighteenth-century relationship between physicians and apothecaries.

Whatever the antecedents, the end of the nineteenth century saw the first application of supervision as it relates to current practice. As previously mentioned, this first stage of supervision development was introduced by social workers. At this time groups of volunteer social workers gathered around experienced leaders and, through a process which has been likened to an apprenticeship, learned through observation and instruction. Here the emphasis was on adherence to agency policy and concerned the 'appropriate' distribution of resources to those deemed to be in need and deserving of assistance (Munson 1993). Thus at the turn of the nineteenth century, when social work practice had begun to move away from the determination of who was deserving amongst the poor and become more interested in assessing the effect of poverty, so too did supervision cast a more critical eye on the broader aspects of practice. A shift of focus for supervision was recorded by Mary Richmond in 1917:

> Good supervision must include this consideration of wider aspects... Every caseworker has noticed how a certain juxtaposition of facts often reappears in record after record, and...this recurring juxtaposition indicates a hidden relation of cause and effect. (Munson 1993, p.50)

The relationship between models of practice and models of supervision has continued to be noted throughout the development of supervision practice (Gardiner 1989; Scaife 2001). The development of solutions-focused practice, for example, has led to the construction of a style of supervision held to be congruent with work with service users (Juhnke 1996; Santa Rita 1998). This supervision approach will be discussed in more detail in Chapter 2.

The influence of Freud and psychoanalysis in the early part of the twentieth century brought a new group of participants to supervision and also a shift of focus. Supervision was now concerned with client work and by the 1920s it had become a requirement of psychoanalytic training (Carroll 2007). The influence of new Freudian and psychoanalytic theories on existing social work practice and supervision was also evident (Pettes 1967). Within the supervision relationship, the psychoanalytic approach emphasised the authority and expertise of the supervisor and any difficulties experienced by the supervisee were identified as personal pathology and required remedy. The boundaries between the impact of personal factors on the practitioner's work and personal issues were blurred and supervision was, at times, hard to distinguish from counselling or therapy.

At this stage of supervision practice, where difficulties were deemed to reflect the failings, psychological or otherwise, of the supervisee, supervision was considered perhaps not surprisingly as the province of the new and uninitiated worker. Trained and experienced practitioners resisted the idea of supervision, considering it an insult and a suggestion of incompetence (Kane 2001). This is a theme that follows supervision on its journey in other professions as well, as will be seen below.

In the mid to late twentieth century, when psychotherapists and counsellors joined social workers and psychoanalysts in adopting supervision as an integral component of practice, Carroll notes the continued blurring between clinical practice with clients and supervision (2007, p.34). Carroll describes a new phase of supervision appearing in the 1970s. Now a clear distinction was made between counselling/therapy and supervision. Supervision became firmly focused on the 'work' of the practitioner and whatever affected or influenced that practice (p.34).

In the field of practice, however, an increased concern for accountability led to the development of task-centred models for some professions. This focus on accountability heralded the major ideological and political changes which affected social service provision during the 1980s and 1990s. The last decades of the twentieth century saw private sector management practices applied to the public sector, with considerable impact on schools, health care and social services where, formerly, professional status had determined decision-making power (Healy and Meagher 2004). We are all familiar with the requirements for measurable outputs, performance management and quality assurance systems.

One significant impact of the new preoccupation with accountability practices on supervision was the strengthening of the administrative function and an associated move away from in-depth review and critique of practice. For many, particularly those in social work, this period represented a time of challenge to the integrity of professional work as management demands took precedence in supervision (Payne 1994).

The socioeconomic influences of this time, however, did not have the same constraining effect on all professions. It was during the 1970s that counselling psychology in the United States established itself as a key developer and researcher of supervision theory and practice (Carroll 2007). It was here, according to Carroll, that 'the emphasis from within counselling psychology on the "reflective-practitioner" model as the best way to define a counselling psychologist gave supervision its credibility' (2007, p.34). This period also saw the development of other approaches to supervision which drew from theories of adult learning and development (Butler 1996; Loganbill, Hardy and Delworth 1982).

Supervision is currently in a new phase of change. Interest in career-long supervision has been shown by professions which traditionally only involved themselves in supervision as pre-service education. This revitalisation of supervision has, to a considerable degree, been led by changes in the nature of public services which have demanded increased scrutiny of direct practice. Two major factors have influenced this change. The first factor is the neoliberal preoccupation with systems of accountability mentioned earlier. The second factor is the impact of 'the risk society' and the concomitant public critique of professional practice (Beddoe 2010b). These features come together in a social trend described as a 'crisis of trust' in professionals (O'Neill 2002). Fear of failure, concern for public safety and a deep fear of public criticism (Stanley and Manthorpe 2004) on the part of government has led to more emphasis on compliance in oversight of professional practice and mandatory and continuous professional development.

SUPERVISION AND THE HEALTH PROFESSIONS IN THE REGULATORY CLIMATE

The introduction of supervision into health care professions has been an interesting journey, separate though at times parallel to that of social work, counselling and psychology. Traditionally health care professions have utilised supervision as a method of training students and/or as oversight for new practitioners. An example of the latter is the nursing profession's use of preceptors for new graduates or nurses commencing practice in a new role and function. Many health professions, however, have not historically required supervision for fully qualified practitioners. Supervision in these contexts has thus traditionally been regarded as something for those who are less expert or for those needing oversight. Research from these professions thus often reflects a supervision relationship which is characterised by student/expert dynamics and open to the anxiety and pressures of assessment.

As an exception, however, Fish and Twinn note that in the United Kingdom both mental health nursing and midwifery have had a process of supervision for qualified staff for many years (Fish and Twinn 1999, p.23). With regard to psychiatric nursing Fish and Twinn cite Swain (1995) who argues that psychiatric nursing has recognised the importance of supervision since the 1940s and note Barker's (1992) comment that 'such supervision in psychiatric nursing has two major aims, first to protect patients receiving care from nurses and secondly to protect nurses from themselves' (Barker 1992 cited in Fish and Twinn 1999, p.23). The requirement for regular supervision for midwives in the United Kingdom on the other hand has been laid down in statue since 1902. Whilst the mode of this supervision has changed over the years, it has remained essentially a model of ensuring competence and Fish and Twinn (1999) suggest that it has been primarily seen as a management function for the supervisor.

In the nursing profession in general, the early advocates of clinical supervision faced considerable resistance in the implementation of supervision programmes. Northcott reports that:

> clinical supervision entered the professional language of nursing…
> with a flurry of interest, uncertainty and suspicion, in part I believe
> a result of nurses' experience of appraisal. Was clinical supervision
> yet another attempt to control nurses, as one of my respondents had
> suggested? (Northcott 2000, p.16)

Nurses made links between clinical supervision activity and those measures associated with increased accountability: individual performance review, personal therapy, management and preceptorship (White *et al.* 1998, p.187). Butterworth, for example, suggested that 'clinical supervision should be seen as an activity that takes place in a wider framework of activities that are designed to manage, enhance and monitor the delivery of high quality services' (2001, p.320). One of the challenges facing proponents of supervision has been to reconcile the divergent discourses of personal professional development and managerial oversight. There is a sense that supervision attempts to ameliorate both perspectives, as Yegdich captures when she asserts that, on the one hand, when authors seek endorsement for supervision from clinicians for:

> 'new' concepts of clinical supervision as opposed to 'old' ideas of
> managerial supervision, they import the psychotherapeutic concept
> of supervision as an experiential teaching relationship. Nonetheless,
> they deviate from this model by their disinclination to differentiate
> the personal from the professional. (Yegdich 1999a, p.1201)

Yegdich notes, however, that there is subsequent irony when such proponents of supervision seek the endorsement of management and regulating bodies for clinical supervision, where they 'employ the connotations of supervision from ordinary usage (checking, overseeing) and abandon the radical idea of developing theoretical knowledge and practical skills in therapeutic nursing endeavour' (1999a, p.1201).

Allied to this blurring of functions in supervision, a significant issue identified in a review of the literature on supervision in the health professions is the nature of the relationship(s) between supervisor and supervisee. In 1998 White *et al.*'s research found that, in nursing, supervisors were often supervisees' managers, and this was a source of tension. 'Indeed, in one setting there was an intention to develop an organizational culture using such an arrangement, while in another setting it was argued that clinical supervision actually *"needed* to be hierarchical"' (White *et al.* 1998, p.188). This is a recurring theme in supervision literature, as demonstrated in a recent study by Williams and Irvine, which 'highlighted the precarious situation of the manager as clinical supervisor arrangement' (Williams and Irvine 2009, p.481). While the ideal type of professional supervision presents supervision as 'facilitative and supportive, interpretations of government directives rather promote supervision as directed towards consumer protection and safety' and this raises the spectre of surveillance (Beddoe 2010b).

THE CONTEMPORARY PRACTICE OF SUPERVISION

The last two decades have seen emphasis on managerial supervision in the public sector. Requirements for measurable outputs, rationalised service, efficiency, effectiveness, performance management and quality assurance created new priorities and tensions for managers and these features filtered into the supervision process. The new climate of accountability also brought increased public critique of professional practice, particularly focused on those operating at a threshold of risk such as child protection, mental health and the oversight of criminal offenders (Morrison 1997, 2001). Supervision thus became a locus for output and performance measurement and risk management, rather than a place for reflection and development.

Proving yet again its adaptability, supervision may be on the cusp of entering a further period of revitalisation. Supervision now has a significant mandate, as this section from a recent United Kingdom document demonstrates:

> If we are to deliver the very best services across adults' and children's services we need the very best workforces who are well trained, highly skilled and passionate about their role. We know from our research that the key to building this workforce is the support, guidance and opportunities we provide to our colleagues. High quality supervision is one of the most important drivers in ensuring positive outcomes for people who use social care and children's services. It also has a crucial role to play in the development, retention and motivation of the workforce. (Skills for Care and Children's Workforce Development Council 2007, p.2)

Changes in the organisation of professional practice have led to different emphases on the functions of supervision. In many instances, particularly in the health sector, these changes have followed increased stringency in requirements for professional registration and standards of competence of professional practice. This has resulted in a demand for increased accountability and risk management structures within organisations. For many services and in many different professional settings, this emphasis on accountability has been played out through supervision, with the result that the managerial function of supervision has been accorded priority over the other two functions – education and support. A by-product of this drive for accountability, however, has been that the new focus on supervision and best practice has created a renewed opportunity for debate, conversation and reflection about professional practice. In this post modern era the conditions of practice have significantly altered (Cooper 2001). Previous certainty and cohesiveness of professional practice have been dismantled and universal theories and practice have been replaced by pluralism of theory, practice and context.

Professional supervision, though buffeted in this period of major change, has retained its core functions of accountability, education and support (Bradley and Hojer 2009) and has emerged with increased diversity of styles and approaches to supervision (Cooper 2001). It seems likely that we may now experience a renewed focus on educative and supportive functions which may reflect long-standing concerns about retention of professionals (Healy, Meagher and Cullin 2009; Roche, Todd and O'Connor 2007).

In order to meet the supervisory needs of changing practice a variety of forms of supervision have emerged. These can be independent of each other or may be conceptually linked. A growing trend towards the development of a 'mosaic of strategies accessed in different configurations over time in response to educational, administrative and support needs' (Garrett and Barretta-Herman 1995, p.97) has introduced a range of options. These strategies include external supervision, internal supervision, peer supervision, line supervision, interprofessional supervision, individual supervision, team supervision, group supervision and cultural supervision. This list is not exhaustive but rather an indication of the responses of practitioners to the diversity of practice contexts and the consequent range of choices and decisions to be made around the practice of supervision. In recent years supervision has also faced critical scrutiny from those proposing to make matters of culture, world view and social justice centre stage in supervision practice. Hair and O'Donoghue argue that the 'leading social work supervision texts offer little to inform or encourage supervisors to integrate cultural knowledge with social justice... This absence is actually an example of how dominant discourse can influence knowledge production' (Hair and O'Donoghue 2009, p.74). In countries with indigenous populations such as Aotearoa (New Zealand) the imperative for culturally safe supervision, incorporating indigenous values and world view, has seen the development of indigenous approaches and models of supervision, including what is termed cultural supervision, which:

> creates a mode of supervision in which practitioners of a certain ethnicity are supported to practice within a supervision process that is grounded in spiritual, traditional, and coherent theoretical understandings congruent with a unique worldview. Culture becomes the overarching environment of supervision. (Beddoe and Egan 2009, p.414)

There is also a strong emphasis on social and cultural development in these cultural models (Beddoe and Egan 2009). Davys notes that such cultural models, however, often struggle to develop in organisations dominated by Western values, traditions and theory (Davys 2005a).

Given the certainty of change, the uncertainty of resource and the complexity of practice issues these last decades have required models of supervision to be sufficiently adaptable to adjust to a diverse range of practice contexts, to have the professional integrity to hold the unpredictability of practice content and the structure to respond to the tensions of change. In response to these challenges supervision models based on learning and reflexivity have been promoted (Carroll and Tholstrup 2001).

The view of supervision as a reflective learning process, rather than a process for direction and audit, represents a 'significant difference between teaching techniques as opposed to teaching a way of thinking' (McCann 2000, p.43). It is within this framework that we propose the Reflective Learning Model of supervision as the central model for this book (Davys 2001). We regard a reflective approach as essential to affirm practitioners' development, bringing together theory, tacit knowledge and transformative personal experience. This approach develops a more holistic understanding of the complexity of experience that practitioners encounter in their day-to-day work (Fook and Gardner 2007).

SUPERVISION BY ANY OTHER NAME: DEFINING SUPERVISION

Professional supervision is both context-dependent and context-specific. With no universally accepted definition many professions use the term 'supervision' interchangeably with activities which range across the scale of management tools and training requirements. Any text, article or research will therefore need to be considered within the terms defined by the authors and with reference to the professional and organisational context.

A useful model developed by Northcott identifies six performance management strategies, all of which are 'designed to optimise results, increase productivity and help ensure high quality service and activity of the organisation and individuals' (Northcott 2000, p.12). The determining factor in Northcott's model is 'who sets the agenda'. Thus disciplinary action, which sits at one end of the scale, has an agenda almost entirely determined by management. At the other end, Northcott positions clinical supervision in which the agenda is created by the practitioner. The beauty of Northcott's model is that it teases out those 'other' activities often lumped together with 'supervision'. Thus supervision is separated out from disciplinary action, management supervision, preceptorship, appraisal and mentorship.

Clinical supervision as thus defined by Northcott is clearly not remedial oversight for professionals whose practice has been assessed as impaired. Nor, we would argue, is supervision an activity confined to students and new professionals. Supervision in our context demonstrates an ongoing professional commitment to reflection, analysis and critique by professional practitioners who take individual responsibility to use supervision to renew and refresh their practice and ensure that they continue to work within the mandate for their work with other people. A commitment to supervision demonstrates a commitment to lifelong learning.

However, we cannot say that supervision is entirely voluntary and here is the rub. Within many professions, codes of practice and registration requirements prescribe a schedule of supervision which may vary with experience and qualification. Similarly there may be conditions on the form of supervision and the qualifications of the supervisor. For some practitioners supervision may only be recognised when provided by supervisors of the same profession, or by supervisors who are recognised by the registering body.

Organisations too may prescribe the type, duration and frequency of supervision and, indeed, in an increasingly regulated environment where professionals practice under a statute, supervision may be considered as mandated compliance with regulatory codes. Here supervision struggles to avoid becoming a risk-management tool, an indicator of practitioner competence and a process primarily designed to ensure consumer protection. Northcott's insistence that 'clinical supervision can only operate as a voluntary activity' is therefore an interesting challenge (2000, p.16). The reality is that for many practitioners supervision is not voluntary. Within this diversity of understanding about supervision there is, however, a continued focus in the literature on supervision as a process of in-depth reflection by practitioners on their work in order that they continue to learn and develop from their experiences.

We hope that this book will provide some guidance and inspiration to supervisors and supervisees alike so that supervision, regardless of whether it is compulsory or voluntary, will be a valued and welcome activity. This is well captured by Bernard:

> But at the end of the day, supervision was, is, and will be defined by the realisation of our supervisees that they understand the therapeutic process and themselves a tad better than when they entered supervision, and our own realisation that we have been players in the professional development of another. It is as simple and profound as this. (Bernard 2005, p.18)

OUR STANCE IN THIS BOOK

In 1990 the authors were asked to present a workshop on supervision to a group of probation officers. At the time both were experienced social work practitioners and supervisors who had considerable experience in providing workshops and training. We accepted this brief with enthusiasm and began to research the recent literature. This was the beginning of two decades of interest and excitement about supervision. The literature available to support education about supervision in 1990 was sparse and somewhat outdated. The early 1990s was probably a time when supervision was most profoundly at risk of management capture and in 1994 (Beddoe and Davys 1994) we echoed Payne's concern that supervision in social work was under threat (Payne 1994). Since that time we have seen an excitement and resurgence of energy for supervision within those professions where supervision has been a traditional aspect of practice and a growth of new ideas in professions where it has been introduced more recently.

Our own position on supervision has been influenced by the contexts of practice and teaching within which we have been engaged over the past 20 years. At the beginning, as providers of tertiary education, we delivered graduate supervision programmes to classes of social workers. We were, however, increasingly asked to provide 'workshops' to mixed groups of professionals, particularly from healthcare. Initially cautious about the boundaries of other professions, we soon discovered the generic core of supervision and also the strength of interprofessional learning (Davys and Beddoe 2008). For many years now we have delivered graduate and, more recently, postgraduate programmes to groups of professionals from a wide range of professions.

Also, as we engaged in our own practice, and as we accompanied other professionals on their practice journeys, we have recognised that at the heart of all practice is the ability to assess, reflect, adapt and respond. As discussed earlier in this chapter, certainty of practice no longer exists and practitioners today need to be able to examine critically all aspects of practice and adjust their responses and understanding accordingly. Professional supervision, therefore, is not about complying to ensure that the rules are followed, rather it is the application of professional skills, knowledge and principles to the variations of professional practice. As such, supervision provides the forum wherein practitioners can critically engage with their practice, reflect on their actions, review their decisions and learn. There are few 'right' answers but rather a choice of 'best'.

Supervision, therefore, for us is a forum for reflection and learning. It is, we believe, an interactive dialogue between at least two people, one of whom is a supervisor. This dialogue shapes a process of review, reflection, critique and replenishment for professional practitioners. Supervision is a professional activity in which practitioners are engaged throughout the duration of their careers regardless of experience or qualification. The participants are accountable to professional standards and defined competencies and to organisational policy and procedures.

OVERVIEW OF CHAPTERS

Chapter 2, 'Approaches to Professional Supervision', explores supervision as an expanding professional practice. It describes and differentiates between the functions and tasks of supervision and discusses four supervision models or approaches. These include developmental models, reflective models, post modern approaches and finally we present the newly developing practice of cultural supervision.

Chapter 3, 'The Supervision Relationship', examines how to negotiate the conditions of supervision and establish an effective supervision relationship taking particular cognisance of issues of power, authority and managing difference. Our approach to the supervision relationship promotes supervisee ownership and participation in supervision through developing trust and an orientation towards learning, and continuing professional development.

Chapter 4, 'The Organisational Context of Supervision', examines how supervision acts as a significant process within professional settings and within individual careers and explores professional learning in the organisational context.

Chapters 5, 6 and 7 focus on the 'doing' of supervision and the essential skills for supervisors. Chapter 5 introduces 'A Reflective Learning Model for Supervision', which draws from adult learning theory and understanding of reflective practice. This approach provides a detailed process for the conduct of supervision. It positions the supervisee as the director and the supervisor as facilitator of the supervision process. Chapter 6, 'Developing Expertise: Becoming a Critically Reflective Supervisor', explores the relationship between reflective practice, critical reflection, social justice and the core values of the helping professions and links these to ongoing reflective supervision, throughout professional careers. Chapter 7, 'Skills for Supervision', provides a developmental framework for assessment and development of essential skills for effective supervision within a reflective learning approach.

The next two chapters explore aspects of the emotional content of supervision and those elements of supervision that engage the functions of support and personal professional development. Chapter 8, 'Communication and Emotion in Supervision', explores difficult interactions in supervision processes and suggests interventions. This section will examine the place of strong emotion in professional practice and supervision and the relevance of this in understanding and responding to challenging moments in practice. Chapter 9, 'Promoting Professional Resilience', examines the development of professional resilience in practitioners in health and social care. We review the role of supervision in assisting professionals to manage stress in demanding and complex health and social care environments.

Chapter 10, 'Supervising Students in Clinical Placements', considers the particular issues and elements of supervising students in pre-service training and education for the social and health professions. The centrality of teaching and learning concepts is identified for this context of supervision practice. A variation of the Reflective Learning Model of supervision for students on clinical placements is outlined.

Chapter 11, 'Supervision in Child Protection', explores the contribution supervision can make to enhancing accountability, professional development and support of social workers in child protection. In particular we explore collaborative approaches to supervision that promote critical reasoning strategies. The development of group consultation approaches linked to effective assessment frameworks is outlined. The potential for the creation of communities of practice within and between health and social care organisations that have a common concern for child well-being is considered.

The authors have used a number of vignettes to illustrate the many challenges faced by practitioners in health and social care and how such situations may be drawn into the supervision encounter. We wish to declare that no one situation is real but, rather, all scenarios reflect a composite of the many events that have challenged us, both as practitioners and supervisors, and which we believe may resonate with readers.

Chapter 2

Approaches to Professional Supervision

There are many models and approaches to supervision. Bernard, however, in a review of supervision over the past 25 years, reports that during this time the development of models has been limited, and that what has occurred has been a refinement, exploration and testing of existing models (Bernard 2005, p.16). In some instances, Bernard notes, the introduction of an 'ideology' such as feminist supervision has transformed existing models whilst the introduction of new theory, rather than creating new models, has introduced new approaches. An example is the influence of post modern constructivist theory on the development of the 'strengths' and 'solutions focused' approaches to supervision. Research by Milne *et al.* 2008 (p.183) found that supervisors often 'employed more than one supervision method'.

Some models of supervision are highly detailed and structured, for example, the Developmental Model (Davys 2001; Loganbill *et al.* 1982). Others are based around a set of practice principles or theory and rather than providing a specific blueprint for supervision present an 'approach'. Rich (1993) developed an 'integrated' model of supervision whilst Milne *et al.* have constructed an 'evidence based, conceptually integrative' model of supervision (Milne *et al.* 2008, p.170).

In this chapter we begin with a discussion of the functional approaches to supervision, as we believe that it is here, within these basic parameters of supervision, that the supervision territory and framework is defined. Later in the chapter we will briefly consider four other models and approaches of supervision: the developmental, reflective, post modern and cultural models. Our choice of models presented here reflects those which have, in some part, been useful to or developed through our practice and teaching. This is not to say that omitted models are of less value or importance. Rather we refer readers to the original source where the authors are better able to do justice to their own ideas and work. One model that we do not address and yet has had particular value in our teaching and practice is the 'Seven-eyed supervision: process' model of Hawkins and Shohet (1989,

2000, 2006). We mention it here to note our appreciation of this very useful framework.

FUNCTIONS OF SUPERVISION

Traditionally, models of supervision have identified three key functions or tasks of supervision. Although differently labelled, these functions have remained fairly constant over the years. Pettes (1967) employed the terms 'administration, teaching and helping' whilst Kadushin (1976) described the functions as administrative, educative and supportive. The administrative function describes the practitioner and supervisor's accountability to the policies, protocols, ethics and standards which are prescribed by organisations, legislation and regulatory bodies. The educative function addresses the ongoing professional skill development and resourcing of the practitioner. The supportive function attends to the more personal relationship between the practitioner and the work context.

Inskipp and Proctor (1993, p.6) also identify the tasks of supervision under 'three main functional headings': the normative task, the formative task and the restorative task. This model, the 'Supervision Alliance Model' (Proctor 2001, p.25), which originates from counselling supervision, is commonly described in the nursing and health services literature on supervision. The normative task of supervision is the 'shared responsibility of the supervisor and (counsellor) for monitoring the standards and ethical practice of the counsellor'; the formative task of supervision is the 'shared responsibility for the counsellor's development in skill, knowledge and understanding' and the restorative task is the 'provision of space, or the chance to explore opportunities elsewhere, for discharging held emotions and recharging energies, ideals and creativity' (Inskipp and Proctor 1993, p.6).

Some functional models encompass only two functions (Payne 1994; Rich 1993). These models tend to differentiate between the administrative/managerial or normative functions and what is essentially an amalgamation of the educative/formative and supportive/restorative functions. Payne (1994) calls this amalgamation the professional function whilst Rich (1993), appears to be discussing a similar pairing which he calls the clinical function.

Morrison (2001, p.29) names four functions of supervision: 'competent, accountable performance/practice' (managerial or normative function), 'continuing professional development' (developmental or formative function), 'personal support' (supportive or restorative function) and 'engaging the individual with the organisation' (mediation function). The inclusion of the mediation function is an important and interesting addition. For Morrison (p.29) the mediation function is the negotiation of the different, and sometimes competing, aspects of the supervision encounter.

That there is tension between the functions of supervision and, accordingly, a need to negotiate this encounter is a theme which is identified and discussed throughout the literature (Carroll 2009, p.218; Hughes and Pengelly 1997, p.24; Proctor 2001, p.23). An excellent, and often repeated (Hughes and Pengelly 1997, p.24; Morrison 2001, p.29), observation from Middleman and Rhodes captures both this tension and the choices facing a supervisor. 'The supervisor–worker relationship is the key encounter where the influence of organisational authority and professional identity collide, collude or connect' (Middleman and Rhodes 1980, p.52).

Hughes and Pengelly identify three functions of supervision and propose a triangulated model which graphically captures the competing tensions of the supervision process. Linking the three functions of supervision to the participants of supervision (the supervisee, the supervisor and the service user or client), they describe the functions as managing service delivery, facilitating practitioners' professional development and focusing on practitioners' work (Hughes and Pengelly 1997, p.42). The functions are represented as corners of a triangle illustrated by Figure 2.1.

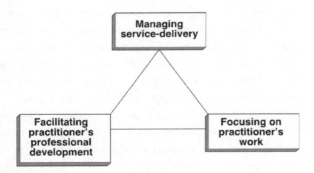

Figure 2.1 Triangle of supervisory functions
Source: Hughes and Pengelly 1997

In this model, 'managing service delivery' addresses the requirement of supervision to ensure that policies, procedures and protocols as defined by the agency (or by statute or regulation) are followed. It is also through this function that the 'quality and quantity of work' and the decisions and priorities of practice are addressed. The ongoing professional development of the supervisee takes place within the function of 'facilitating practitioner's professional development' whilst the third corner of the triangle, 'focusing on the practitioner's work' allows supervisor and supervisee to reflect upon and explore the practitioner's work with clients (Hughes and Pengelly 1997, p.42).

The depiction of each of the functions as a corner of a triangle neatly captures the tensions and decisions present in any supervision session. From this model Hughes and Pengelly identify three key issues: first, that it is difficult to address all three functions of supervision in any one session, second, that the interrelationship between the three functions means that they cannot be regarded separately and finally that supervision 'becomes unsafe if one corner is ignored or avoided for any length of time' (1997, p.43).

Failure to address issues at any one of the corners of the triangle is therefore not an option. The challenge or dilemma they believe 'lies in having the time, skill and experience to manage the difficult tensions' (Hughes and Pengelly 1997, p.46). They also warn of the 'deadly equal triangle' where rigid adherence to each corner can stifle the effectiveness of supervision work and not allow sufficient depth. There is, they suggest, no 'right' balance but supervisors are encouraged to view the model as a map by which they can review and check where time is spent in supervision and which corners are being avoided or neglected. In this way any imbalance can be challenged and addressed. A recent study by Bradley and Hojer (2009) (also referred to in Chapter 4), which reviewed social work supervision in England and Sweden noted that although each country addressed all three functions of supervision, each gave different emphasis. In England the managerial function received more attention whereas in Sweden it was the supportive. Bradley and Hojer also note that in Sweden 'each component of supervision is likely to take place in a different location' (2009, p.72).

Representation of the functions of supervision as a triangle is most effective. It graphically locates the intersection of each of the functions of supervision at each apex of the triangle and thus heightens the sense of tension inherent in supervision arrangements. The integrity of a triangle lies in these points of tension and the importance of holding them in balance is therefore apparent for otherwise the structure would distort or collapse.

Returning to Middleman and Rhodes' comment on how the profession and the organisation come together in supervision, we note from our own experience that some supervisors fall into a quandary of how to respond in supervision when faced with the tensions of these competing functions.

The choices, as Middleman and Rhodes (1980) remind, are between collision, collusion or connection.

Vignette – Jason

Jason was angry with the new requirement from the agency to limit the number of visits to patients in the community. In supervision, with a supervisor who was external to the agency, he expressed his anger and dismissal of the new process. The supervisor knew that Jason was a conscientious practitioner who liked to give his clients the best service.

Option 1 – Collide

The supervisor was clear and uncompromising. She reminded Jason that as this was a requirement then he had to comply. Yes, she understood that this might not be best practice, but he had no options. This was a sign of the times and a reality of current practice. Possibly he could review his time management – learn to work smarter. They could consider that in their supervision together. Jason left the session feeling angry and determined to avoid complying with the new process.

Option 2 – Collude

The supervisor heard Jason out and sympathised with his view of the situation. She shared her own practice experience in a similar situation and agreed that this policy was not in the best interest of patient care. When she asked Jason how he was going to adjust to this new policy, he replied that he had no intention of doing so and would still make the visits but not record his time. The supervisor warned Jason not to get found out. Jason left the session feeling justified in his decision to avoid complying with the new process.

Option 3 – Connect

The supervisor heard Jason out and sympathised with his situation. She shared her own experience and frustration with a similar situation. She asked Jason why he thought the new system was being introduced in his agency. What gains were being envisaged? Were there any benefits he could see in the long run? What support was being offered to assist staff and patients to accommodate the new system? She asked Jason to reflect on any similar past experiences he had had – what had he learned from that? What were his professional objections to the changes and were there other ways to address those? Jason left the session feeling heard and with a plan to approach his manager to discuss his concerns and to present a proposal which would give patients and practitioners some other options.

Middleman and Rhodes locate the tensions of supervision between the expectations of the organisation and the profession. Using Hughes and Pengelly's model we believe that the tensions are between all three functions and that the role of the supervisor is to manage the tension, and build relationships and an environment where connections can be made. Carroll describes this as holding the three tasks of supervision 'in creative tension, building and creating environments that sustain learning while still monitoring the professionalism of the work' (Carroll 2009, p.219).

One of the key differences between Hughes and Pengelly's model and other functional approaches is the explicit exclusion of support as a function of supervision. Support, they argue, is a means not an end. When support is identified as a function of supervision 'there is a danger of a collusive focus on the worker's needs for their own sake, rather than a focus on the worker in order to promote a better service' (Hughes and Pengelly 1997, p.48).

Support in supervision, we agree, is a core condition of supervision but not a function. Support is a central and necessary element in supervision for it is through an awareness of, and a confidence in, the 'supportive relationship' that the challenges of practice can be tolerated and accepted. Support in supervision has been 'conceptualised as the supervisor's provision of comfort, recognition, encouragement and approval' (Lizzio, Wilson and Que 2009, p.128). This provision of support is necessary whatever 'function' is being addressed. Supervisees' need for support in supervision, however, will vary. As supervisees develop in experience, competence and confidence the level of support they need changes (Lizzio *et al.* 2009). Too little support can create uncertainty and anxiety whilst too much support may be 'too permissive' and mean that issues of 'competence and performance' are not addressed (Lizzio *et al.* 2009, p.129).

The positioning of support as a condition rather than a function of supervision has a subtle but significant effect on the role of the supervisee in the supervision relationship. The supervisee is liberated 'from being the passive recipient of support' and instead is positioned as 'an active participant in a supportive supervision process which in turn is keenly focused on the provision of a better service to clients' (Davys 2005a, p.5). Supportive supervision encourages supervisees to express and explore their feelings and their work, not only so they will 'feel' better but also in order that they may 'know' their practice. We will discuss the place of emotions more fully in Chapter 8.

The relationship between supervision and counselling is often confused at this interface of supervision and support. The understanding of support to be a condition rather than a 'function' of supervision in our view helps to differentiate between these two activities. But this will not be sufficient unless all parties are clear about the boundaries between the two allied, but different activities of counselling (therapy) and supervision. Yegdich demonstrates this confusion when she describes the boundary between supervision and therapy in nursing: 'It may be inadequate simply to proclaim that supervision is not therapy, as ultimately, it is the techniques utilized, not the stated goals that determine the form of supervision, or therapy' (Yegdich 1999b, p.1266).

We argue that it is indeed the goals which distinguish supervision from therapy/counselling. The techniques of supervision do utilise the skills and interventions of practice but the goals of each are distinct and so shape how these techniques are employed. Fox (1989) provides a guide when he usefully describes the supervision relationship as therapeutic rather than therapy. He identifies two significant differences between therapy and supervision. The first is personal change which, he states, is the primary goal of therapy but occurs only as 'a by-product of the supervisory process' (Fox 1989, p.51). That is to say that the very process of exploration, reflection and learning which occurs in supervision (which we discuss in detail in Chapter 5) can lead to transformational change and inevitably to personal growth. The intent of supervision is, however, to develop a practitioner's professional not personal persona. The second difference arises out of the dictates of the professional and organisational standards, ethics and expectations which define the boundaries and accountabilities of supervision. 'The supervisor, unlike the clinician, does not suspend critical judgement' (Fox 1989, p.52) and therefore whatever is brought to supervision must be considered within these accountability frameworks.

It is well reported in the literature that supervision is the appropriate place for practitioners to express and explore the wide range of emotional responses they experience in relation to their work (Dwyer 2007; Lombardo, Milne and Proctor 2009; Smith 2000; Toasland 2007). This is both necessary and professionally responsible. It is important that neither supervisors nor supervisees confuse 'personal problems with quite appropriate emotional reactions to highly painful work or unsatisfactory work conditions' (Hughes and Pengelly 1997, p.48).

Incorporating the above, we propose our representation of the functions of supervision in Figure 2.2. Based on Hughes and Pengelly's (1997) model we have included on each side of the triangle, as a supervision task, the management of the tensions. This task involves making connections between the sometimes conflicting functions and accountabilities of supervision. Support, the core condition of supervision, sits in the centre of the triangle and includes validation, respect, the creation of a safe environment, conflict management and anti-discriminatory practice.

Figure 2.2 Functions and tasks of supervision
Source: Adapted from Hughes and Pengelly 1997

DEVELOPMENTAL MODELS

Developmental models of supervision can be traced to the 1950s and 1960s (Bernard and Goodyear 2009, p.89) and were particularly common throughout the 1980s (Hawkins and Shohet 1989; Ivey 1988; Loganbill *et al.* 1982). Bernard and Goodyear identify three categories of developmental models: those that offer linear stages of development, those focused on process development models and finally lifespan developmental models (2009, pp.89–97). The broad premise of these models is that practitioners follow a predictable, staged path of development and that supervisors require a range of approaches and skills to attend to each sequential stage as it is achieved by the supervisee (Brown and Bourne 1996; Hawkins and Shohet 2006). It is further implied that the process remains under the direction and control of the supervisor.

Most models of practitioner development consist of three to five stages which describe the progression of practitioner competence from student or beginning practitioner to mature and expert practice. According to Butler, practitioner competence is related to experience. It is developed by people who have been working in the same job or area for two or three years, is marked by the ability both to plan and strategise for the long term and to analyse complex problems (Butler 1996, p.278). Competence is, however, not the ultimate goal of his model. He describes five stages of performance development. The first *novice* (rule governed) leads to *advanced beginner* (seeking the external answer) to *competent* (personal analysis of each situation) to *proficient* (having the big picture in focus) and finally to *expert* (tacit understanding) (Butler 1996, pp.277–279). The supervision of a competent practitioner will be different from the supervision of a novice/ student. A novice practitioner will need 'rules and procedures to follow so that the performance can be done without experience', where as the competent practitioner centres his or her actions 'on a plan which is based on conscious, thoughtful, analytic reflection' (Butler 1996, pp.277–278). Expert practitioners, according to Butler 'have an accurate grasp of each situation' and do not waste time on 'a large range of unfruitful, alternative diagnoses and solutions' (1996, p.279). They are expert because 'personal knowledge is continually renewed by the uniqueness of some encountered events. Beliefs and assumptions are evaluated against the changing context' (p.279).

Developmental models have been subject to a variety of critiques, but, as Bernard and Goodyear (2009, p.101) note, little rigorous research. Bernard and Goodyear conclude with the somewhat lukewarm endorsement 'probably the safest conclusion at this point is that there is limited evidence to support some aspects of stage development models' (p.101). More specific comment has been offered by others. Gardiner (1989, p.11) warns of the prescriptive nature of developmental models which equate compliance to a norm with success and pathologises those who 'differ from…expectations of normal progress'. Hawkins and Shohet (2000) present their developmental model with the warning that too rigid an application of the stages may blind the supervisor to the uniqueness of the supervisee, the supervision context and the supervision relationship. Cultural bias and the associated assumptions implicit in developmental models must also be considered for 'the information they leave out, such as a person's experience due to race, class, gender or sexual orientation'

(Moffatt 1996, p.49) as much as for the information which they provide. Finally the influence on the supervision process of the supervisor's own developmental stage cannot be overlooked (Hawkins and Shohet 2006, p.74; Scaife 2009, p.135).

Nye (2007) offers a general and challenging critique of traditional models of development. Western models of development, she argues, typically describe a linear progression from novice to expert, from dependence to autonomy. Value is placed on the 'autonomous' 'expert' practitioner. Nye suggests that such models limit learning to the realm of 'actual development' as opposed to the 'potential development' of which a practitioner is capable 'or has access to in collaboration' (2007, p.90). Competence in these models is equated with 'knowing' whilst 'unknowing', associated with failure and shame, is often hidden or denied. Pack argues that the 'potential for shame' 'which leads to withdrawal from contact' (Pack 2009a, p.660) can result in supervisees acting on their own without consulting their clinical supervisor. This inappropriate and unsafe 'independence' can result in clinical errors with dire consequences.

Nye offers Vygotsky's developmental learning theory as a helpful framework by which to revalue and recognise 'dependence' on an *other* as 'essential to learning and development across the life course. For Vygotsky, this is not a process with an end point…something to be outgrown…[but] inevitable if learning and development are to occur' (2007, p.84).

Despite these limitations, developmental approaches are useful to supervisors as they provide a framework for thinking about how practitioners develop skills and competence over time and offer strategies for working with a range of practitioner experience and competence. Developmental models support supervisors to assess their supervisees against key professional competencies or dispositions and facilitate the growth of supervisees by enabling the supervisors to use interventions relevant to the supervisees' stage of development. Davys has suggested that if the developmental framework is considered as a dynamic, as opposed to a mechanistic structure, it can provide a useful conceptual framework from which to understand the difference of both relationship and dialogue which occurs between supervisors and students on the one hand and, more particularly, supervisors and competent practitioners on the other (Davys 2002, p.65).

Loganbill *et al.* (1982), in a classic formulation that continues to have influence, 'one of the 25 most-cited articles *The Counseling Psychologist* has published' (Bernard and Goodyear 2009, p.89), provide a framework for utilising a developmental theory in supervision. This 'Conceptual Model' is characterised by three stages and assumes that people will move through these stages over time. Loganbill *et al.* suggest that movement may occur as a natural progression of experience and awareness or it may follow a planned intervention on the part of the supervisor (1982, p.5). Two transition points are identified where particular interventions can be applied. An important characteristic of this model is that a practitioner 'may cycle and recycle through these various stages at increasingly deeper levels' (p.17). This circularity is evident where similarities are drawn between the characteristics of a 'new' practitioner and one who is 'burnt out' and stuck. The identification of ten critical issues (themes which recur in practice) provides supervisors with a template against which to assess practitioner development and the ability to create a profile of the practitioner's progress. Such a profile will display areas where integration has been achieved and highlight those areas still to be developed.

REFLECTIVE APPROACHES TO SUPERVISION

A recent review of the supervision literature, which summarised the models and concepts used in supervision, found that 82 per cent of the studies reviewed 'described outcomes consistent with the experiential learning cycle of Kolb (1984)' (Milne *et al.* 2008, p.183). This, as Milne *et al.* suggest, indicates the centrality of experiential learning to the practice of supervision. Reflection, one of the four phases of experiential learning, is embedded as a process in many supervision approaches and has been considered an approach in its own right.

Fook and Gardner see a reflective approach as affirming other ways of knowing, such as personal experience and its interpretation, by supporting a holistic understanding of the complexity of experience that practitioners encounter in their day-to-day work. 'A reflective approach tends to focus on the whole experience and the many dimensions involved: cognitive elements; feeling elements; meanings and interpretations from different perspectives' (Fook and Gardener 2007, p.25). Such an approach facilitates the discovery of the kinds of knowledge relevant to the unpredictability of modern day practice. According to Fook and Askeland reflective learning is a process that seeks to unsettle assumptions in order to change practice and helps us to understand the connections between our public and private worlds (2007, pp.522–523).

Butler's Model of Human Action (1996, pp.270–271) explains these connections clearly. Two contexts, the *social* (which comprises public knowledge and professional practice) and the *self* (comprising personal knowledge and world view) are connected by reflection. In this model 'public knowledge' is 'all that abounds outside the self in the form of theories, formal knowledge, policy directives, research results, quality assurance processes, hints and folk lore, community expectations', whilst professional practice is 'informed by beliefs, undertaken to achieve important goals in particular contexts'. World view which 'influences all thoughts and actions' is formed largely through an individual's 'culture and traditions'. And personal knowledge is 'knowledge and understanding attained through lived experience'. Reflection, positioned at the centre of these contexts, 'is the open, active communication channel between the outside social context, and the inner self' (pp.270–271).

World view, Butler notes, seeks to remain stable, however 'to be effective it must be continually revised' (p.271) and it is through the process of reflection that an individual's world view is challenged and this revision occurs. We will return to consider how reflection is crucial in effective supervision in Chapter 5, where we discuss the Reflective Learning Model (Davys 2001) and in Chapter 6 where we examine the role of the critically reflective supervisor.

POST MODERN APPROACHES TO SUPERVISION

Post modernism, described by Ungar as a 'collection of interpretations made about the world that are constantly changing' (Ungar 2006, p.60) has influenced approaches to supervision, just as it has influenced practice in many professions. Post modernists try to avoid imposing organising ideas about how the world (and practice) should be but rather focus on interpretations made by participants in social processes, through the language and narratives and the search for meaning. Post modernism influences the helping professions in its advocacy of in-depth consideration of the language of the encounters between workers and clients. In post modern thinking there is a fundamental shift from the 'grand narrative' of science and positivist approaches to an emphasis on the social construction of meaning in professional life. 'Post-modernist approaches focus on strengths rather than deficits, potential rather than constraints. In social constructivist practice it is held that there are multiple perspectives instead of universal truths' (Edwards and Chen 1999, p.351). The strengths-based approach which has been applied to the supervision process over the last two decades has been referred to by a variety of names such as 'solution-focused' and 'solution-oriented'. All share the movement away from assessment of deficits and problems, characteristic of the medical model, to reflect a post modern view of human-systems interaction.

Post modernism has had an influence on practice and supervision, and in particular stresses the importance of language in encounters (Edwards and Chen 1999). Edwards and Chen discuss two meta-frameworks for strengths-based supervision: a post modern view of human systems interaction, and an understanding of the isomorphic nature of the supervisor/worker/client relationships. Post modern supervision brings to the forefront issues of identity, stories and the language of supervision encounters. Ungar asserts that supervisors bring into supervision relationships their identities as individuals, professionals and supervisors, along with the expression of different culture, gender, ability and so forth. Thus, 'starting with such a plurality of possible selves, when we encounter supervisees we have much to draw on and much to account for' (Ungar 2006, p.60). For Ungar, a post modern supervisor 'accentuates aspects of his or her identity in order to participate with supervisees in a co-construction of the supervisees as competent in their practice' (p.60). Collaborative relationships in supervision are also emphasised by Edwards and Chen (1999). Ungar identifies six roles in supervision, each imbued with meaning by the participants: supporter (to the supervisee), case consultant, trainer/teacher, colleague and advocate (for both the client and/or the supervisee) (2006, p.61). In summary, post modern approaches imbue supervision with social constructionist ideas and:

- advocate careful consideration of the language of the encounters between workers and service users and workers and supervisors

- posit an approach to supervision which emphasises the way the participants in professional encounters construct meaning

- focus on strengths rather than deficits; potential for change rather than constraints and barriers to change

- acknowledge that there are multiple perspectives instead of universal truths

- are less hierarchical and focus on establishing collaborative approaches and co-constructing solutions

- avoid labelling people in ways that emphasise their differences as deficits or pathological in some way.

Social work and counselling in particular have strong links to 'social constructionist' approaches in which the social circumstances and power relations are examined and where social justice ideals are central. Applied to supervision, a social constructionist perspective 'invites supervisors to shape a supervisory relationship that encourages transparency, collaboration, and an exchange of ideas' (Hair and O'Donoghue 2009, p.76). Noble and Irwin argue that applying a constructionist lens requires supervisors to 'explore and reflect on the way the supervisors, the supervisees and the agencies work with the service users/clients' thus ensuring that 'practitioners' actions and those of the organization are more explicit and conscious' (Noble and Irwin 2009, p.354). Noble and Irwin cite O'Donoghue (2003), whose earlier work explicitly explored the relationships and the process of supervision from a social justice perspective. Noble and Irwin point to O'Donoghue's movement away from the 'more traditional atheoretical notions of the separate functions of supervision towards a social constructionist approach' (Noble and Irwin 2009, p.354).

In a recent publication Hair and O'Donoghue note the differences between social constructionist and traditionalist approaches to supervision. These differences include: the recognition of plurality and diversity of knowledge; an emphasis on collaboration; the acknowledgment that supervisees have agency in a co-constructive process; the engagement in various relational forms such as dyadic, group, and in-session supervision; increased sensitivity to power and the politics of empowerment and disempowerment in supervision; and the explicit recognition of the influence of the social and cultural context within which supervision is immersed (Hair and O'Donoghue 2009, p.77). Hair and O'Donoghue's social constructionist perspective suggests supervisors include the following process:

- 'Ask "curious" questions about idiosyncratic descriptions of local community knowledge of the supervisees and clients, including the influence of dominant sociopolitical and economic contexts such as national laws, tribal expectations, and spiritual understandings' (p.78).

- Develop supervisory conversations which 'consider structural barriers such as poverty, legislative policies, and suitable housing alongside clients' relational conflicts and distresses' (p.78).

- Acknowledge barriers to enable 'supervisors and supervisees weave multiple strands into a comprehensive, time-bound snapshot of culture' (p.78).

- Ensure dialogue between supervisors and supervisees includes 'the exploration of their own cultural narratives over time' (p.78).

- Note that those educated in the dominant Western practices supervision require 'continual critical self-reflection about the use of taken-for-granted authority and privilege, so that domination over others is not silently reinforced' (pp.78–79).

Reflective questions encourage collaborative practice and, Hair and O'Donoghue argue, perspectives that have been marginalised may surface and 'ideas and values can be prevented from forming rigid "truth" that inevitably means ascendancy for a select few persons and tyranny and oppression over others' (2009, p.79).

Strengths-based supervision

Strengths-based supervision has its roots in strengths-based practice, post modern counselling and family therapy practice and is underpinned by the same principles and ideas. Isomorphism, which implies a similarity of process from one system to another, can be used to influence change. In strengths-based work, supervision centres on the development of supervisee-focused and directed supervision. Essentially this approach is a 'way of being' with supervisees, where attention is given to power 'with' rather than power 'over', and the environment is such that both supervisor and supervisee contribute their expertise to the relationship. Strengths-based supervision seeks to address the hierarchical nature of supervision by favouring the co-construction of ideas with those supervised (Edwards and Chen 1999, p.351).

The key principles of strengths-based supervision are as follows:

1. All practitioners possess strengths that can be activated – supervision is future focused and assumes success, 'rather than problem-saturated talk' and the potential for further competence of the supervisee to build further competencies (Presbury, Echterling and McKee 1999).

2. Supervisees are experts about their own practice – a supervisor encourages comfort with uncertainty and rather than assuming expertise, is open to the many ways people construct experience with a focus on utility (what works) (Edwards and Chen 1999, p.352).

3. Supervisors need to suspend their beliefs and assumptions (Thomas and Davis 2005, p.192) in order to be open to hearing the supervisee's story.

4. Supervisors support their supervisees' goals (Santa Rita 1998) and enable their strengths to be present in the work. This approach also incorporates and encourages talk about challenging issues in a safe process which is initially negotiated at the outset of the supervision contract.

5. Supervisors need to be respectful, hopeful and the language used needs to avoid pathologising explanations (Edwards and Chen 1999, p.354).

The supervisor does not assume a normative approach and attempt to 'correct' or dominate the supervisee's aims or views but will work to create a strengths-based supervision with a future focus on potentials, possibilities and multiple perspectives. In doing so the supervisor models an ideal of practice that is service user driven and empowering.

Edwards and Chen in their framework for strengths-based supervision see supervision moving to what they call 'co-vision' and 'co-created' vision (1999, p.353) where the 'co-visee' is expected to be the expert in what is happening in his or her work. Their experience in the supervision context will be carried over to the counselling context (p.353). Edwards and Chen (1999) identify six supervision contexts for use in training counsellors:

1. 'Symmetrical voices': rather than provide a directive monologue where one narrative dominates, the supervisor supports the supervisee to explore options for working with client problems and emphasises the supervisee's competence (p.353).

2. 'Competence focus': a supervisor must model the values they want the supervisee to demonstrate with their clients. By focusing on strengths and successful interventions, supervisees will feel more competent. This is also reflected in the non-pathologising language used when talking about clients (pp.353–354).

3. 'Client-participated supervision': by including clients in the supervision or imagining they are present in the room, the tone of the supervision changes from one in which their deficits are analysed, to one of respect, curiosity and hopefulness (p.354).

4. 'Unassuming transparency': supervisors will share their own professional struggles with their supervisees which enable them to more readily take on a 'not-knowing position' (p.354).

5. The 'reflecting team': live supervision in therapy contexts where group input offers a resource for the generation of new ideas (p.355).

6. 'Tag-team group supervision format': a supervisee describes then role plays a service user they are working with, assigning roles to other members of their training class – one from the rest of the class will take the role of counsellor until 'tagged' by another observer who takes over from where the previous one left off. This allows for different perspectives to inform discussion and reflection (p.355).

The solution-focused model of practice developed by de Shazer (1985) also applies the principle of isomorphism to the context of supervision (Santa Rita 1998, p.129). Solution-focused supervision has some distinctive features and is underpinned by four basic assumptions (Santa Rita 1998, pp.129–133). First, supervisees inevitably cooperate with their supervisors, and have a range of cooperative responses (p.129). Second, supervisors identify and *amplify* supervisee exceptional behaviour in order to highlight positive productive experience and the challenges present in the work (p.130). A third assumption is that supervisors will only use interventions that have been effective previously and will actively try new approaches when supervision gets stuck (p.131). Finally, solutions-focused supervision assumes that the supervisee will define the learning goals in the supervision process, with the supervisor acting as guide. Solution-focused supervision aims to encourage the supervisee to set small achievable goals for each session (p.132) and noticing and highlighting achievements builds morale (Presbury *et al.* 1999, p.150).

A variety of interventions from solution-focused therapy are utilised in solution-focused supervision. While these essentially philosophical principles underpin the strengths-based/solution-focused approach to supervision, a range of tools and techniques, especially questions, have been developed to assist the supervisor in her or his facilitation. Supervisors familiar with strengths-based practice will recognise these as similar to techniques in client work, refocused on the thinking of the practitioner and her or his experience. Supervisors use 'pre-suppositional' language (Presbury *et al.* 1999, p.152) to promote confidence and self-efficacy now. Presbury *et al.* (1999) argue that there is a vast difference between using subjunctive language (supposing a possibility) and using pre-suppositional language (assuming an actuality). Pre-suppositional questions avoid yes/no answers and reflect positive expectations of change:

'What has really worked well in your practice since we last met?'

'Tell me about your best work this week?'

'As you get better at dealing with (this situation) how will you know you have become good enough?'

'If you are feeling more confident what will you be doing differently?'

'What would I notice if I was watching you working more confidently with these service users?'

'How will you have changed?'

The beliefs underpinning these questions are that: there are always exceptions; there will be circumstances that hold promise of the alleviating problem and it is important to provide the opportunity and encouragement to recall a time of greater confidence (Presbury *et al.* 1999, p.148). Scaling questions (de Shazer 1985) can be used to help supervisees determine their progression toward pre-identified time specific goals:

'At the onset of our supervision relationship you indicated a goal of being able to appropriately use authority and power when working with high risk situations, on a scale of 1 to 10, with 1 indicating little progress toward this goal and 10 indicating completion of this goal, what score would you give yourself?'

Presbury *et al.* suggest the use of scaling questions to help to establish small realistic goals and engender expectations of success, for example: 'On a scale of 1 to 10, with 1 being that the problem is at its worst, and 10 being that the problem is completely solved, where would you say you are today?' After the worker offers their estimate, 2, the supervisor says 'when you are on your way to 3 how will you know?' (Presbury *et al.* 1999, p.151).

'What will have changed?'

'When you are on your way to (next highest number) how will you know?'

'What will be different about how you handle the situation...?'

'What will have changed in your practice?'

Using these techniques the changes identified become the supervision goals. To identify a time specific goal a supervisor might ask, a 'miracle question' (de Shazer 1985), for example, 'if a miracle happened just before your next family meeting, and you have become the fantastic nurse you want to be, what would be the first thing you would notice suggesting your increased confidence and skills?'

Developing strengths-based approaches: reflections for supervisors

- How do I notice and celebrate success with my supervisees?

- How do we talk about service users in supervision? What am I modelling about expectations of success and change?

- Does our supervision model match the way we approach our professional practice?

- How often do we highlight what is working well and the times of exception to problems?

- What different kinds of power do I utilise in this relationship and what is the impact of this? How important is it for me to be expert? How do I invite feedback from supervisees and respond to it?

- How do we talk about challenging issues?

- How do I reflect on my own supervision process? What goals do I set for myself?

(adapted from Thomas and Davis 2005, p.195)

SUPERVISION AND CULTURE

Both supervisor and supervisee take into the supervision process their own attributes and aspects of their personal identity: their gender, sexuality, age, educational background and culture, religious beliefs and values. Tsui and Ho (1997) have emphasised that within the context of supervision are ideas and practices determined by cultural considerations, the context of supervision and the prevailing culture informing it. Tsui and Ho have challenged the traditional approach to supervision as being influenced most by the organisational context and drivers. Rather, they argue that any model of supervision is shaped by the cultural system in which it occurs. Beddoe and Egan note that the influence of culture is relevant to consideration of agency purpose and goals, the supervisor's roles, style and skills, the supervisee's working experience, training, and the emotional needs including those of service users (Beddoe and Egan 2009, p.414).

Active recognition of the practitioner's culture is best considered as an essential condition and function of effective supervision, as this 'legitimises and anticipates the tensions which will arise from different value bases and perspectives within the work context' (Davys 2005a, p.7). In New Zealand the practice of 'cultural supervision' has developed in recent decades (Eruera 2007; Mafile'o and Su'a-Hawkins 2005) but this is not the same as the recognition of culture within the supervision process and relationship. Rather it represents a new and 'independent contribution to supervision' (Davys 2005a, p.7). In New Zealand, where development of cultural supervision is being pioneered (Hair and O'Donoghue 2009), Eruera's work articulates the uniqueness of some of these developments in differentiating *kaupapa* supervision (representing a Maori world view) from cultural supervision. Kaupapa supervision can be defined as:

> an agreed supervision relationship by Maori for Maori with a purpose of enabling the supervisee to achieve safe and accountable practice, cultural development and self-care according to the philosophy, principles and practices derived from a Maori world view. (Eruera 2007, p.144)

The development of explicitly cultural approaches to supervision is, as Hair and O'Donoghue (2009) have stated, closely tied to the broader social development of indigenous and minority cultures. Developing local models has been an important response to the social inequalities experienced by oppressed communities and involves 'the active engagement of Maori and *Pasifika* [Pacific Island nations] social workers in the elevation of their own indigenous ways of knowing. These configurations demonstrate how dominant discourse and emerging local narratives intersect to shape culturally relevant practice' (Hair and O'Donoghue 2009, p.82). Cultural supervision practice such as described by Eruera (2007) supports practitioners with supervision 'grounded in spiritual, traditional and theoretical understandings that are congruent with their worldview. Culture becomes the overarching environment of supervision' (Beddoe and Egan 2009, p.414). Cultural supervision is thus linked to 'personal, family, community, cultural and professional domains... Cultural supervision is also about supporting Pasifika social workers to operate in predominantly non-Pasifika contexts' (Mafile'o and Su'a-Hawkins 2005, p.120).

Arkin (1999) identifies two common tendencies in attempting to meet the challenges of cross cultural supervision of students that have utility in considering all supervision: minimising cultural differences and magnifying cultural differences. Arkin (1999) argues for the training of supervisors in 'multicultural' competency based on four dimensions:

1. The awareness dimension – 'the supervisor must be aware of his/her own cultural and personal values, stereotypes, prejudices and biases, as well as the differences between the supervisor and supervisee in terms of values, styles of communication, cognitive orientations and emotional reactions' (p.12).

2. The knowledge dimensions – 'facts and information about the… political, social and economic history…research, world views, cultural codes, (differences in) verbal and non verbal language and emotional expression' (p.12).

3. The relationship dimension – 'this requires examination of supervision in cultural terms…cultural identification, expectations, criticism, initiative, passivity, roles' (p.12).

4. The skills dimension – it is important to develop 'the ability to intervene in a culturally sensitive way without detracting from the quality of the professional training…the culture must be legitimized by showing a keen interest in it and by respecting the practitioner's own cultural identity and group membership' (p.12).

There are limitations in multicultural approaches to supervision. Multicultural approaches don't always address power and authority issues nor the structural inequalities, roles and status of minority cultures within mainstream institutions. There is often an assumption that the supervisor's knowledge of practice is superior, and the biases of Western thinking may be underemphasised. There is a danger that the minority students/ supervisees' differences are still pathologised – to be worked around and accommodated. There are often assumptions that the minority person is always the student or supervisee – what if he or she is the supervisor? How does this impact on power in the relationship if there are hidden agendas or racist assumptions? What strategies could be used to reduce these oppressive elements of the multicultural approach? Table 2.1 outlines some key requirements for the development of positive cross cultural and multicultural supervision relationships.

Table 2.1 Requirements for non-oppressive supervision practice

Awareness	of the holistic and dynamic nature of culture in human life and how these influence our thinking as service users, supervisees and supervisors
Conceptual frameworks	applied to understanding the cultural and social construction of knowledge for practice
Understanding	of the way the dominant culture is maintained through policies and practices
Removal of barriers	that limit the utilisation of knowledge from other cultures in decision-making and critical reflection
Insight	into one's own self and how one perceives and values alternative views
Ability	to culturally deconstruct dominant 'group think' in the practice context and in supervision
Respect	for rituals of encounter and engagement that may be essential for safety within practice
Capacity	to honour, respect and develop perspectives derived from other world views and knowledge bases

CRITERIA FOR EVALUATING APPROACHES TO SUPERVISION

Given the importance of considering the social and cultural contexts and practices of supervision that we have explored in the preceding sections of this chapter, it is useful to consider the development of criteria for evaluation. Whatever approach to supervision is chosen it will be influenced by professional and personal preference, cultural considerations, and the context within which supervision takes place, whether this be large governmental agencies, smaller non-governmental organisations, or private practice. The following structure may provide a useful starter guide:

- structure
- attention to 'relationship'
- attention to 'process'
- attention to context
- underlying theoretical orientation
- technical or clinical detail
- evidence for success
- applicability and utility across professions
- focus on the supervisee's development
- attention to issues of power and influence
- cultural aspects and values
- issues of difference
- time.

Table 2.2 Comparison of key features of four supervision approaches

Evaluation criteria	Developmental	Reflective Learning	Strengths-based	Cultural
Structure	Developmental stages Transition points for interventions	Action–reflection cycle	Not prescribed	Follows cultural rituals of engagement and encounter
Purpose	Assists supervisees to move from novice to expert Recognises key points of transition between stages	Facilitates supervisees to find solutions within themselves through reflection on their experience and actions	Facilitates supervisees to find solutions within themselves based on their existing strengths and prior positive experiences	Supports supervisees through a process that is grounded in spiritual, traditional and theoretical understandings that are congruent with their world view
Attention to relationship	Reflects progression through developmental stages (supervisee and supervisor)	Trust and safety Collaborative	Trust and safety Collaborative	Negotiates and affirms cultural roles and responsibilities
Attention to process	Uses a range of interventions suited to supervisee developmental stages and transitions between stages	Follows the steps of action–reflection cycle	Language critical to address strengths Isomorphism requires supervisor to model strengths-based interventions	Close adherence to processes which are culturally explicit, i.e. beginning with a prayer/ reflection, acknowledgement of kin and community connections
Attention to context	Based on supervisee's level of experience	Based on supervisee's actual experiences and responses – past, present and future	Based on supervisee's 'reality'	Personal, family, community, cultural and professional domains
Underlying theoretical orientation	Developmental theory	Adult learning theory, reflective practice and experiential learning	Post modernist ideas about language and meaning Social constructionism Isomorphism	Holistic orientation Spiritual and traditional knowledge

Technical or clinical detail	Supervisor led with input from supervisee 5 interventions: prescriptive, confrontative, conceptual, catalytic and facilitative	Mainly supervisee's agenda Cyclic process of reflection, exploration, analysis, experimentation and review	Supervisee's agenda Construction of narratives based on exploration of strengths and reframing old 'stories'	Reflects cultural practices and understandings of participants who share a similar world view
Utility across professions	Can be applied to any profession	Can be applied to any profession	Can be applied to any profession	Can be applied to any profession
Attention to power	Supervisor's authority assumed Supervisee's authority develops with expertise	Collaborative to develop supervisee's self-awareness and learning	Collaborative: reframing to empower supervisee and raise self-efficacy	Consideration of the power of the dominant culture and the position of cultural minorities May include explicit hierarchy related to cultural roles and responsibilities
Cultural aspects	Assumption of homogeneity Traditional Western determination of stages of development	Exploration of context and content	Understanding of social constructionism of ideas, values and beliefs that underpin practice	Validation and support for cultural identity Explicit links to cultural and social development
Issues of difference	A developmental issue	Values and recognises individual perceptions and differences	Recognises and values individual differences and strengths	Homogeneity is important and deliberate Status is recognised Recognises impact of dominant culture Isomorphic
Time	Stages are recycled over time at deeper levels as practitioners develop in their experience and competence	Uses past and present to measure change and access experience and to bring to the fore for future action and understanding	Presupposes the actuality of success	Time is imbued with cultural meaning and often linked to traditional knowledge and ways of 'knowing'

In Table 2.2 we have used the criteria listed above to summarise the four models presented here.

SUPERVISION: AN OVERVIEW

This chapter has explored the functions, tasks and core conditions of supervision as well as various approaches and models. The following is a list of the characteristics of supervision which have been shared by the participants of our supervision training courses. It is not definitive nor exhaustive but rather a reflection of the complexity of this very personal professional practice.

- It is an interpersonal, negotiated relationship in which both parties have rights and responsibilities.

- It is accountable – to the organisation, the profession and to the service user.

- It is ethical.

- It is confidential.

- It is ongoing and regular (a process rather than an event).

- It has boundaries.

- It has power dynamics.

- It is a forum for reflection, learning and professional growth.

- It is educative (but not education).

- It is managerial in that it relates to organisational standards and policies but it is not management or appraisal.

- It is supportive but it is not counselling.

- It is a safe place to express and explore emotion.

Supervision provides the chance to stand apart from our work and to reflect on what we do, the context of what we do and the impact that this has on ourselves as people (in particular, as professional people). This reflection brings a greater objectivity and personal understanding to our work. It is an opportunity to evaluate our practice in terms of both progress and challenge and it allows us to develop and learn from our experiences. The development of a safe environment encourages mistakes and vulnerabilities to be examined as learning opportunities and not disciplinary occasions. Supervision recognises the stress and vicarious trauma of those in the helping professions and aims to support practitioners so that they remain healthy in their job.

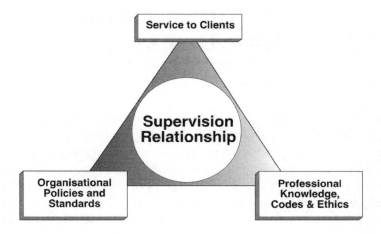

Figure 2.3 Overview of supervision

In summary, our view of supervision can be represented by Figure 2.3. Here we see that supervision is primarily to develop an improved service to clients. It is a practice which is accountable to organisational policy and associated legislation. It is underpinned by the knowledge, skills, competencies and codes of practice and ethics of relevant professions. These three elements provide the framework for supervision. Within this framework sits the supervision relationship which is the medium through which all else is accomplished.

Chapter 3

The Supervision
Relationship

Within the diversity of ideas about supervision the one least contested is the significance of the supervision relationship. The quality of the relationship between supervisor and practitioner has been identified as the most powerful determinant of the success or quality of the subsequent supervision relationship, and is perhaps best summed up by Bernard: 'Relationship factors continue to be where the action is, literally. Everything else resolves around it' (Bernard 2005, p.15). That this is a complex relationship is also noted in the literature and considered by at least one author as 'perhaps one of the most conceptually ambiguous and challenging topics in the supervision and professional development literatures' (Lizzio et al. 2009, p.128). For most supervisors and their supervisees this relationship commences with the first meeting and the subsequent negotiation of the supervision contract, which is sometimes referred to as the supervision alliance or working alliance (Proctor 2001). It is here that a working supervision relationship can begin. Expectations can be laid out, boundaries mapped, differences identified and negotiated and goals established.

For some, this relationship is considered by to be central to good practice (Tsui and Ho 1997). One study, which found a significant connection between the supervisee's perception of the supervision relationship and the client's perception of the therapeutic relationship, concluded that the supervisees 'are taking the knowledge they are gaining in supervision about building and maintaining relationships and applying it to the relationship with their client' (Patton and Kivlighan 1997, p.113). Given this connection between good supervision and effective practice others have questioned why this connection is not highlighted in practice. In response Ash suggests that the answer lies in the fact that the supervision relationship is 'an aspect of supervision for which it is most difficult to legislate, which exists outside procedural frameworks and which centres on the actual interchange between supervisor and supervisee' (Ash 1995, p.20).

The ability to establish and maintain the supervision relationship is a core requirement of a supervisor. Honesty, disclosure, respect and thus the effectiveness of supervision will all be affected by the quality of this relationship which in turn rests on the supervision contract. The supervision relationship can be considered as four stages as outlined in Table 3.1.

Table 3.1 Stages of a supervision relationship

Preparation – personal audit	What does each participant bring to the relationship and what does each person want?
Beginning – the process of contracting	How are the differing needs and expectations of supervision articulated and agreed?
Middle – developing the relationship	Doing the work of supervision and maintaining the relationship
End – finishing the relationship	Review and tying up the ends

PREPARATION: PERSONAL AUDIT

A number of inventories have been compiled which list the qualities that supervisors need to possess in order to be a 'good' supervisor. Our favourite is that complied by Loganbill *et al.* possibly because of the richness of the language and the strong sense of personal engagement and commitment to the supervision process. The list includes: genuineness, potency, optimism, courage, sense of time as a gift, sense of humour, capacity for intimacy, openness to fantasy and imagery, respect and consideration (Loganbill *et al.* 1982, pp.28–29).

Subsequent inventories of supervisory competence have located supervision more firmly as a practice of the twenty-first century with its concomitant tensions around power and discrimination and diversity. As a forum for learning and development, supervision operates in practice settings which are buffeted by change and uncertainty. Hawkins and Shohet's list of attributes, which is based on the work of Gilbert and Evans (2000), includes flexibility, room to view many perspectives, a working map of the discipline in which they supervise, the ability to work transculturally, the capacity to manage and contain anxiety, openness to learning, sensitivity to the wider contextual issues, the ability to handle power appropriately and, finally, humour, humility and patience (Hawkins and Shohet 2006, p.50).

In a study conducted by one of the authors which explored 'good' supervision as experienced by a group of supervisees, the following list of supervisor characteristics were identified:

- competence and knowledge as practitioners
- competence and training as supervisors
- an ability to challenge in a supportive manner
- an openness to feedback and an ability to be self-monitoring
- an ability to provide support and containment for a range of situations and emotions
- an ability to manage power and authority
- they received and valued their own supervision.

(Davys 2005b, p.16)

We think that it is significant that training for supervision is included in this list. Personal skills and attributes are important but are not a substitute for specific training for supervisors and there is a strong voice within the fields of supervision practice for supervisors to receive focused education and training (Bernard and Goodyear 2009; Hawkins and Shohet 2006; van Ooijen 2003). Recent research by Bradley and Hojer found that a 'persuasive minority' of supervisors asserted that training for the supervisory role 'should be more challenging and linked to individual professional development and not a one-off short programme provided in the early phase of their supervisory career' (2009, p.81).

All too often progression to a supervisory role appears on professional or career development plans as a rite of passage, a role for which practitioners are deemed to be equipped by dint of years of experience and practice breadth. Or, increasingly, we meet practitioners who are assigned supervisor roles by managers who are seeking to comply with changing codes of practice and legislative requirements. These, often reluctant, supervisors may have never experienced supervision themselves and are catapulted into supervising 'colleagues' who are understandably suspicious of a new process which has been thrust upon them. In these situations, where there is no tradition of supervision, what ensues is often a process of managerial oversight rather than of reflection and learning, which serves to reinforce negative perceptions about supervision. Such arrangements are at the best unhelpful, at the worst dangerous, to the practice of supervision, to the supervisees and to the ultimate users of the service provided.

The lack of training for the supervisor role is not new, nor is the call for it to occur. Thirty years ago Westheimer expressed this clearly when she said, in relation to social work supervision:

Preparation and training for this influential role is essential. There is no automatic way in which a social worker of today can become a supervisor by tomorrow. If social service departments aim for effective supervision, the training programme should include preparation for potential supervisors. (Westheimer 1977, p.16)

With or without training there are other ways in which practitioners can prepare for supervisor roles. One useful activity is a personal audit.

Such an audit involves a review of the supervisor's practice. A supervisor's professional history, supervision history, personal strengths, weaknesses and interests will all influence who that supervisor is in the supervision relationship and what he or she offers. Before entering into any supervision relationship it is important to have some clarity about who you are, where you are in your professional career, what theories, ideas and values shape your practice, and to be able to articulate your view of the profession and how you understand the role of supervision in your work and the work of others.

Supervision is a two-way relationship. It is important for supervisors and supervisees alike to ask themselves the question 'How open and prepared am I to engage in my side of this relationship?' The questions in Table 3.2 may be useful to help supervisors to shape this audit.

CHOICE

Good supervision relationships are mutually developed and require effort from both parties who 'act as guardians of the supervisory relationship' (Jones 1997). The choice, or lack of choice, of supervisor is therefore of significance when we consider the negotiation and the subsequent quality of the ensuing supervisory relationship. For many 'having a real choice of who to see as a clinical supervisor is essential to building a working alliance' (Bond and Holland 1998, p.204).

A range of suggestions has been made about ways to optimise the supervision process: matching of gender, culture, sexual orientation, age and physical disability (Brown and Bourne 1996; Howard 1997), consideration of learning styles (Scaife 2009), whilst Clare (2001) considers supervision matches across the continua of specialist/generalist, learning/teaching styles, local/cosmopolitan dimension and professional/ anti or non-professional dimension. In an extensive literature review of the effect of individual, cultural and developmental differences within the supervisory relationships (which specifically included difference of race, gender and sexual orientation), Bernard and Goodyear, however, conclude

Table 3.2 Supervisor audit

Who are you? Personally	Who are you? Professionally
• Where are you in your own life? • Are you looking for a change? • Are you in a process of transition – partnership, parenting, empty nest? • Are you at a period of rest or consolidation? How do any of the answers to these questions impact on how you might view your profession and the professional careers and professional development of people you supervise?	• What is your professional experience to date? • What have been the highlights? • What have been the greatest learning situations? • Where are your interests? • What are your strengths? • What are your weaknesses? • What areas of practice do you not enjoy? • What is your current learning edge? • What are your current professional goals/plans? How will the above impact on your supervision of other practitioners?
Experience of supervision	**Supervisor's supervision**
• What is your experience of receiving supervision? • Who, or what, has had the most influence on your supervision to date? • How has this affected your supervision practice? • What training have you had to prepare you for the role of supervisor? • How do you articulate your own approach to supervision? • What are your values and beliefs about supervisees? • What are your expectations of supervisees? • How good are you at giving feedback? • How good are you at receiving feedback?	• In your own supervision how do you contribute to the supervision relationship? • Are you receiving the sort of supervision you need at this point of your career? • What are your current questions or dilemmas about the practice of supervision? • How much of your own supervision time is spent on your role as a supervisor (as opposed to other roles such as clinician or manager)?

Source: Adapted from Davys 2007 with kind permission from Pearson Education

that 'regardless of the cultural differences within the supervisory triad, it is the supervisor's cultural competence and openness which will dictate whether the experience is positive' (Bernard and Goodyear 2009, p.147).

The desirability, and the feasibility, of supervisees making a choice of supervisor is discussed in the literature (Bond and Holland 1998) with some of this discussion becoming entangled with arguments concerning the role of authority and control and the relationship between line management and supervision (Johns 2001; Morrison 2001). The benefit to supervisees of choosing their supervisor is supported by such statements as 'the greater the opportunity to choose, the more likely the supervisee will positively anticipate engaging in the supervisory process' (Scaife 2009, p.19). Cooper and Anglem (2003) report supervisees' dissatisfaction with the lack of choice of supervisor and their supervisor's availability and Sloan (2006) found that supervisees placed less value on internal supervision because they were not able to choose the supervisor. In a study by Davys (2005b) the ability of supervisees to choose their supervisors was highlighted as an attribute of good supervision. In this study supervisors and supervisees alike saw the benefits of choice as including the ability to both enter and to leave the relationship. These acts of choice, which included deciding to continue in the relationship, were considered by the participants as reinforcing the ultimate commitment to the relationship.

Caution, however, has to be exercised as it is 'quite possible that effective supervision is not always the most satisfying supervision' (Ladany, Ellis and Friedlander 1999, p.453).

The question arises as to 'whether supervisees choose that which is good for them or that which makes them feel good' (Davys 2005b, p.17). This question was posed by participants themselves in the research cited above. One respondent wondered if her choice of supervisor reflected an easy, less challenging relationship (Davys 2005b, p.17) whilst a supervisor pondered the possibility that she was chosen because she provided 'a cosy support system' (Davys 2005b, p.17). These reflections, we believe, highlight the importance of an awareness of the processes of supervision rather than a need for greater or less choice. In all supervision arrangements where the focus is on learning and the professional development of supervisees there will be an element of challenge. This challenge, which can provoke anxiety, discomfort or defensive self protection (Lizzio *et al.* 2009, p.129), will occur whether or not there has been a choice of supervisor. It will need to be acknowledged and managed as part of the supervision process. 'The struggle inherent in learning may not always be experienced as the most satisfying' (Ladany *et al.* 1999, p.453). Supervision which is deemed 'good' by the supervisee may in fact be attending to the supervisee's comfort and reinforcing the 'known' rather than encouraging development and change by challenging the practitioner's growing edge.

It is our contention that frequently the issue of whether or not a supervisee, or supervisor for that matter, can choose his or her supervisor (or supervisee) assumes an importance which distracts from the issue at hand. The key issue is how to develop a supervision relationship which will enable both parties to attend professionally to the review and development of the work of one of them (the supervisee). Supervision does not occur in a professional vacuum and all good supervision contracts include, or should include, a process for complaint and review. Further, the majority of supervision relationships occur between 'professionals' who know about relationships as their work includes, or depends upon, a relationship with others. Is it possible that preoccupation about choice becomes an end in itself and detracts from the core ability of competent practitioners (and supervisors) to get on with it and develop the best relationship possible for the given period of the supervision arrangement? It is certain that many of us have experienced supervision where there has been no choice of supervisor and which we would not have chosen. We have developed skills to extract the best we can from the supervision partner, or we have used the processes available to challenge and, it is hoped, constructively move on. What is important is for there to be a clear process for review which does allow supervisees to remove themselves from destructive relationships. The supervisee who embraces supervision and takes an active role in making supervision work opens an opportunity for learning and professional growth. A wise mentor once said 'the best therapist is the one who pushes your buttons – because all your issues will be to the fore'. Is there possibly a parallel truth here for supervision? Do we always choose the right supervisor?

It is worthy of note that many practitioners are employed in public organisations within health, social service or justice systems. The clients of these practitioners, unlike fee paying consumers of private practitioners, have no choice of their practitioner. Isomorphism, the 'matching between the form of supervision and the form of practice' (Edwards and Chen 1999, p.352, citing Kerlinger 1986) would suggest that there is an appropriate parallel between the limited choices in the supervisor/supervisee relationship and the practitioner/client relationship. Be that as it may, it is a useful, and important, exercise to clarify what, ideally, we want from a supervisor at any given time regardless of whether or not we have a choice in the matter. If we know what we want from supervision we are better equipped to ask for it. We are in a good position to discuss with our supervisor whether he or she is able to meet all of our needs and to identify how any gaps can be filled in other ways outside of the relationship. In this manner a supervisee can take active responsibility for their role. Whilst we may not all be able to choose our supervisor we do have choices about how we conduct ourselves in supervision.

Increasingly as supervision has developed as a profession (Bernard 2005, p.16; Carroll 2007, p.35), or professional activity (Lizzio *et al.* 2009, p.127; van Ooijen 2003, p.22), in its own right it is practised across a range of professions in a range of organisational and private settings. From this, debate has arisen as to whether or not a supervisor should share the same profession as the practitioner (Davys 2005b; O'Donoghue 2004; Townend 2005). Many professional and regulatory bodies address this issue directly and prescribe the qualifications and experience necessary for supervisors. Bernard and Goodyear (2009), whilst observing that many professionals are supervised outside their profession, note that one of the limitations of this arrangement is the absence of the 'socialisation function' of supervision to assist, particularly new, practitioners to create a sense of professional identity (Bernard and Goodyear 2009, p.10). They also warn of the 'cuckoo' effect where, like the cuckoo laying her egg in another nest, a novice practitioner is socialised into the practice 'mores' of another profession, thus losing some of the uniqueness of their own (Bernard and Goodyear 2009, p.11).

Research conducted by the authors (Davys and Beddoe 2008) into interprofessional learning contexts for supervision also contributes to this debate and adds another perspective. Four findings in particular are significant:

1. The mix of professions in the training groups increased an appreciation of the range and breadth of supervisory practice (Davys and Beddoe 2008, pp.63–64).

2. Communication between practitioners from different professions improved the quality of communication and expression of ideas as it required an avoidance of jargon and clarity of thought (p.64).

3. Respondents recognised that assumptions are commonly made between members of the same profession and these assumptions can limit communication and problem solving. Unconstrained by the implicit limitations and agreements which can exist between members of the same profession, a person from another profession can question and challenge a greater range of practice. There was less collusion and less self-congratulation (p.64).

4. When the development of professional insights, learning and responsive practice are considered to be a primary function of supervision, then supervisors require higher order skills which transcend the day-to-day task focus of profession specific practice (p.66).

An identification of what a practitioner wishes to achieve from supervision, it has been suggested (Lynch *et al.* 2008, p.181), is more productive than a debate about whether the supervisor should share the same profession as the supervisee. We believe that when supervision is considered as a forum for learning, critique and reflection, supervision from a supervisor from a different profession can be very beneficial. When the supervisor does not share the same work context it allows the practitioner to have the benefit of an outside perspective which is free from some of the unspoken assumptions within professions. The supervisor is indeed a true naive enquirer whose need to understand requires an explanation which in turn prompts consideration of those often 'taken for granted' practices so often accepted without critique when practitioners and supervisors share a knowledge base. This exploration can bring forward new ideas and challenge practice which has previously been accepted without question. A supervisor from another profession may also introduce a new and extending range of skills and perspectives. Some authors have stated a belief that competence as a supervisor is more important than a shared professional base (Cassedy *et al.* 2001, p.198).

There are, we believe many benefits to cross-profession supervision, however, care does need to be taken to ensure that profession-specific skills and protocols are not compromised. This may lead to a distinction between professional supervision and clinical oversight. One important consideration is the practice experience of the practitioner. The student practitioner, the new practitioner, or the practitioner who is new to a particular role, has different supervision needs to the experienced practitioner who is familiar with his or her role. For these 'new' supervisees, there is often a need for explicit profession-specific clinical knowledge or guidance. This is knowledge which would not be held by a 'generic' supervisor and it is important that all practitioners have formal access to a person who understands the detail of their professional clinical practice and procedures. If the supervisor does not share the same professional base as the practitioner, we stress that it is important that some other form of 'professional critique' and evaluation of clinical practice is organised in order to ensure safe practice.

BEGINNING

Supervision is 'strongly influenced by infrastructure and relationship variables. In other words, the performance will be as good as the attention that has been paid to these seemingly extraneous variables' (Bernard 2005, p.9).

There is general agreement that the supervision contract underpins and defines the parameters of any supervision arrangement and provides a structure for the relationship (Scaife 2009; van Ooijen 2003).When a practitioner knows what he or she wants from supervision then he or she is in the best position to negotiate a supervision contract which delivers that which is needed.

As with all relationships the opening engagement is critical to create common understanding, shared expectations and thus ensure that the ongoing supervision meets the needs of both parties. As Clare notes, this is a task which requires 'skills in negotiating difference' – managing an ambiguous 'authorities relationship' (Clare 2001, p.73). For the practitioner and the supervisor this engagement occurs with the formal process of negotiation of what is variously called the supervision contract, supervision agreement or working alliance. Morrison (1996, p.29) has defined the supervision contracting process as 'a means of making explicit the aims of the parties to work towards agreed goals in agreed ways'. In subsequent work Morrison makes the proviso that a contract will not guarantee a successful supervision relationship, but it will provide the best beginning place from which a 'good' relationship can grow (Morrison 2001, p.114).

The contract document is the record of those conditions of supervision which are prescribed by organisational and professional policy and contains the agreements and goals which have been independently negotiated by the supervisor and supervisee. The process of negotiating this contract is however as, if not more, important than the content. Pack describes the necessity of 'becoming acquainted with one another' at the beginning of the supervision relationship (Pack 2009b, p.74) and identities several key prerequisites to the creation of a safe and productive environment. Discussion of these issues lays a foundation of understanding from which to discuss and agree the ultimate content of the contract. The prerequisites noted by Pack include an acknowledgement of the power differential between supervisor and supervisee; a clear understanding of the boundary between supervision and therapy; where assessment is a factor this needs to be clearly defined; confidentiality and privacy and their respective boundaries need to be clearly understood and finally a shared understanding of the purpose of supervision must be reached (Pack 2009b).

By declaring and discussing the expectations of supervision both the supervisor and the practitioner are able to acknowledge the constraints, the opportunities and the possible areas of difficulty of their working alliance. 'The process, of discussing, and establishing both general principles and the nitty gritty of the alliance, is the vehicle through which an intentional and unique relationship is initiated between this particular practitioner and this particular supervisor in this particular context' (Proctor 2001, p.31). It is, however, not always the experience of practitioners that the supervision process begins with discussion, often supervisees are simply presented with a formatted contract to sign as a fait accompli. Whilst it is readily accepted that a prepared 'contract' is expedient in terms of time and ensures that basic organisational and professional requirements are explicit and equivalent for all practitioners, it is important that the piece of paper does not become a substitute for the opening relationship-building conversations which take place between supervisor and practitioner.

In general the conditions which need to be specified in a supervision contract include:

- the aims of supervision

- frequency

- duration

- cost (if any)

- confidentiality (and its limitations)

- accountability to professional or registration bodies and organisational policy

- interruptions

- issues of safety

- limits to clinical accountability (particularly if the supervisor is not from the same profession)

- record keeping

- preparation

- agenda setting

- feedback and review

- processes for dealing with conflict and complaint

- the relationship of supervision to performance management, appraisal and counselling

- the degree of access the supervisee has to the supervisor

- missed appointments.

Negotiate a supervision contract or working alliance

The negotiation of the supervision contract, as we continue to stress, is a process as much as it is a task. Proctor (2001, p.29) identifies two levels of engagement when negotiating what she terms the 'working agreement'. First there is the level of practical clarification and negotiation. This is the clarification which will occur through discussion of the checklist above. It is however our contention that the second of Proctor's levels, that of shared information, is the more significant and potent. Information is shared verbally and intuitively and it is during the process of sharing of this information that the core conditions of trust, openness and respect begin to develop. Others are no doubt referring to this level of negotiation when they refer to the psychological contract (Carroll and Gilbert 2005; Scaife 2009).

> The psychological contract refers to the agreement (on a more implicit level) that the supervisor is committed to co-creating with the supervisee a safe and facilitative environment in which work can be discussed and evaluated. (Carroll and Gilbert 2005, p.26)

Carroll and Gilbert (2005) reinforce the importance of making explicit any assumptions and/or expectations because, they warn, unless these expectations and assumptions are explicit the potential for 'misunderstandings and disappointments' is high. The acknowledgement of power in the supervision relationship and a clear definition of the boundaries around power is a necessary conversation to avoid such misunderstanding.

Traditionally hierarchical in nature, the supervision relationship confers considerable authority on the supervisor. From this authority is derived various types of power which are exercised through the filter of organisational, professional, cultural and personal values, beliefs and norms (Bond and Holland 1998; Brown and Bourne 1996). Supervisors are frequently uncomfortable with this power and at times their failure to exercise their authority can amount to collusion with the supervisee and result in poor and unsafe practice (Morrison 2001). A focus during supervision negotiations on mutuality and the 'shared' two-way relationship can, on occasion, lead to a mistaken belief that the supervision relationship is an equal relationship. It is important that supervisor and supervisee alike are clear about power in the relationship and have a candid discussion about the defined boundaries and possible consequences of any exercise of power by the supervisor. This is not to be confused with threats or disguised control. On the contrary it is to avoid misunderstanding and to ensure that the parameters of the relationship are explicit.

Typically a conversation about power in supervision will cover legitimate power. This includes the responsibilities of the supervisor as defined in the policies and protocols of the organisation and in the codes of practice and codes of ethics of the professional or regulatory body. Where a supervisor has power to reward or withhold reward, which often occurs when the supervisor also holds a line management responsibility or, in the situation with a student, where the supervisor has an assessment role, these conversations need to include a discussion about the effect that this power will have on trust and disclosure.

Equally important, but sometimes more difficult, are conversations about personal power. These conversations require more disclosure on the part of both supervisor and supervisee and are thus more likely to be overlooked. Finally, we come to charismatic power which is possibly the most complex form of power and harder to define. Charismatic personalities can be associated with relationships which are characterised by acceptance and or rejection – the in crowd and the out crowd. Charismatic power from community or cultural status, on the other hand, can at times create genuine difficulties of divided loyalty for supervisees whilst Eurocentric models of practice can play out the assumptions of dominant cultures and can render supervisees voiceless (Hair and O'Donoghue 2009). How will a supervisee give critical feedback to a supervisor who holds status as an elder in a particular cultural structure? Or in cultures where gender and age have specific status how will that be accommodated in supervision, particularly if it is the supervisor who, in cultural terms, has less status?

In a more general sense, through the process of sharing information and negotiating the expectations of supervision, similarities will be discovered and differences uncovered. The supervisee will be making assessments as to how safe he or she feels in the relationship with the supervisor and the supervisor will be assessing how the supervisee is likely to respond to challenge and how much support might be needed. During this process of negotiation respect can be demonstrated and trust begins to be established. 'Often, to make the deepest changes the relationship between supervisee and supervisor needs to be based on a high level of mutual trust and confidence' (Owen 2008, p.63).

The establishment of that trust is a complex process in supervision. Paradoxically, one of the ways to begin to establish trust is to take risks through the willingness to be open. The discussions which take place during the negotiation of the supervision contract provide a key opportunity where, at the beginning of the supervision relationship, openness can be modelled and beginnings of trust seeded. Lizzio *et al.* highlight the significance of the supervisor in this process. 'If a supervisor is perceived as not being open, the supervisee may in turn, not trust their supervisor sufficiently to be open themselves' (Lizzio *et al.* 2009, p.136). Openness for the supervisor begins by knowing his or her own strengths and the limits of his or her abilities and knowledge and being willing and able to articulate these with the supervisee. It includes a supervisor knowing what he or she expects from supervisees and saying so. A supervisor's openness contributes 'to a virtuous cycle of trust building between supervisor and supervisee' (Lizzio *et al.* 2009, p.136) which will continue to grow with the supervision relationship.

The establishment of the supervision relationship begins with the discussion of the contract. It requires both the supervisor and the supervisee to accord the time to have these conversations and to withstand the pressure to get on and 'do' supervision before these fundamentals are discussed. It requires the supervisor and the supervisee to both value and respect the 'other' so that needs and expectations can be heard, middle ground defined and creative options developed where there are differences.

Essentially, the negotiation of the supervision contract or working agreement can be considered as the process of working through three key questions:

1. Who are we?

2. Where do we want to go?

3. How will we get there?

Like many documents and processes the supervision contract is a living document (Owen 2008, p.61) which needs to be reviewed and renewed on a regular basis. Many supervision arrangements have an initial review process three months after being signed and thereafter they are reviewed annually. As supervisees develop in skill and confidence what they require from supervision changes. Supervision activities and focus will change accordingly and it may be necessary to revisit and redesign the contract. Where third parties are involved in the supervision negotiation, such as an organisation, it is important that they too are included in both the negotiation and the review. The challenges of external supervision are explored further in Chapter 4.

Morrison in his most useful four-stage process for negotiating the supervision contract includes a stage which he calls 'acknowledging ambivalence' (Morrison 2001, p.107). This is the stage where the supervisor and the supervisee identify possible blocks which can occur during a supervision relationship, discuss how these blocks may be recognised when they occur and negotiate ways of dealing with them. Morrison identifies three possible areas to be considered:

- the potential effect of the 'work' on the supervisee and the personal expectations the supervisee may have around resilience and coping

- the general feelings the supervisee may have about the supervision process and its benefit

- the potential effect of 'difference' between the supervisee and supervisor.

(Morrison 2001)

An exploration of ambivalence and resistance provides an opportunity to pre-empt difficulties which can arise as the result of difference. When a supervisee and her or his supervisor identify that they have different experience, around any of the difference continua of practice, values or beliefs, they can anticipate possible difficulties and negotiate how best to deal with them if they did arise. It might be that they agree to engage a third person to act as a mediator or advisor to assist understanding or resolution of disagreement. Situations where the supervisee may be unable to voice his or her discomfort, disagreement or point of view are also usefully identified. Conversations can be undertaken to explore how the supervisor might notice this difficulty or withdrawal on the part of the supervisee and how best to assist the supervisee to convey his or her concerns. Once again these conversations require honesty and disclosure. Where supervisors have encouraged and invited supervisees 'to have a voice' it has been found that there is a reduction in 'resistant behaviours' and an increased 'willingness to receive feedback' (Lizzio et al. 2009, p.136). Unfortunately these honest conversations, which can be uncomfortable, are often hurried, superficial or overlooked.

Middle

Thus far we have described and discussed the preparation for the establishment of the supervision relationship, and given some consideration to the selection of a supervisor and to the negotiation of the conditions for conducting this alliance. In this next section we wish to consider the development and maturation of the supervision relationship.

Traditionally the role of the supervisee has been portrayed as passive and indeed the very construction of the language of supervision places the supervisee in the role of a recipient. The supervisor is active – he or she 'supervises' whilst the supervisee's role is defined by passivity – he or she 'is supervised'. The ultimate quality of the supervision relationship is dependent, therefore, on the development of a mutual exchange. The supervision contract and the process of its construction and negotiation sets the scene for the manner in which this relationship will mature. One factor which will influence the manner in which the relationship evolves is the developmental progress of the practitioner.

Models of practitioner development have been discussed in Chapter 2 and we refer to those models here only to provide a framework to consider how the supervision relationship will be altered according to the level of supervisee development.

Where the new practitioner depends largely on rules and structures the experienced practitioner organises his or her work around 'more conscious, thoughtful, analytic reflection' (Butler 1996, p.278) Lizzio *et al.* (2009, p.129) note that supportive behaviour in supervision may be more beneficial in the early stages of the supervision relationship when practitioners are more anxious about their professional role and the supervision relationship. As the practitioner develops in competence and experience the level of support in supervision lessens and, consistent with a wish to reflect upon and critique practice, the experienced supervisee seeks challenge through corrective rather than confirmatory feedback (Lizzio *et al.* 2009, p.129).

A developmental framework for supervision may thus depend, not so much on the adaptation of approach and skills of the supervisor, but rather on adaptation and changes within the relationship between the supervisor and the supervisee. As the relationship changes so will our understanding of mutuality within the relationship. As the supervisee moves from novice to expert and beyond he or she will, at each stage, attend to a different level of him or herself. So will the supervisor respond from a different place within him or herself.

We believe that there are three qualities which are fundamental to a good supervision relationship: authenticity, respect and positive regard and mutual investment in or openness to learning. When a supervisor is present, open and authentic and conveys genuine interest and regard, supervisees are encouraged to trust and share their work. There is an exchange of energy and enthusiasm which becomes a cyclical process. The supervisees' honesty and their willingness to share material reinforces the regard and respect from their supervisor. This regard and respect are the conditions required by the supervisees to continue to share. This process of sharing we believe defines the supervisory space and it is within this space that transformational learning can take place for both supervisor and supervisee. 'The personal connection that results from openness related strategies...appears to have the strongest influence on keeping supervisees engaged in the learning process' (Lizzio *et al.* 2009, p.136).

Freshwater, in an interesting exploration of what she calls the interactive field in supervision, suggests that in order for there to be mutuality in the supervision relationship, the supervisor needs to be open to be 'infected and affected' by the supervisee (Freshwater 2005, p.40). Freshwater suggests that throughout the supervision relationship there is a state of 'uncertainty'. In what she describes as the middle phase of the 'alliance' she identifies a period of reduced 'uncertainty' which is however accompanied by such control strategies as 'the illusion of knowing' (p.40). Freshwater's challenge is for supervisors and supervisees to give up 'knowing' and enter a creative space where both can be transformed. Ultimately Freshwater questions whether, given the accountabilities of supervision, there can be a true mutual relationship and suggests rather that there are glimpses of the possibility of oneness. She concludes 'all the more reason to pay attention so as not to miss the few opportunities that present themselves' (p.42).

We define mutuality differently to Freshwater and suggest that it encompasses shared goals and a commitment to a shared process of relationship which will have different outcomes from both parties but which requires an authentic presence, respect and a willingness to create and explore the supervisory space into which the supervisee places his or her work. To move into this supervisory space requires courage and trust and a knowing that both parties may emerge with new learning and be possibly altered. Not all supervision arrangements and relationships achieve this level of learning.

REVIEW AND ENDINGS

Given the amount of attention paid to the establishment of the supervisory relationship it is interesting that so little attention is paid to its end. In this section we will consider the process of review and consider how to conclude a supervision relationship.

Explicit in the supervision contract should be a schedule for review. Typically supervision is reviewed annually and this provides an opportunity for the participants to take stock and reflect on the relationship, the process and the outcomes of supervision. Some questions need to be considered:

- How often will supervision (and the contract) be reviewed?
- What will the process be?

In supervision the contract can become the focus for this review and the questions itemised in Table 3.3 can be discussed between the supervisor and supervisee.

Table 3.3 Reviewing supervision – a supervisee's perspective

For the supervisee

- Is the supervision meeting the stated goals?
- What needs to be added or removed from the original contract?
- At the end of this period of supervision what learning have you made about your practice?
- How has this made a difference to the way you work?
- How has the process of supervision affected your learning?
- What do you like about the supervision process?
- What would you like to change?
- What feedback would you like to give your supervisor?
- What areas of feedback would you like to receive from your supervisor?
- What are your current goals for practice and are they reflected in your supervision plans?

For the supervisor as the 'facilitator' of the supervision process Table 3.4 sets out a series of particular questions which he or she may explore with the supervisee.

The supervision relationship may end for one of several reasons:

- The contracted period for supervision has finished.
- The supervisor or supervisee is leaving the organisation or the role.
- There has been a breakdown in relationship and the contract is terminated.
- It is time for a change.

Whatever the reason it is useful to consider how we finish this relationship. In a parallel with practice we recognise the importance of review and consolidation at the end of a piece of work where the client or patient together with the practitioner reviews the achievements and details the work still to be done.

Table 3.4 Reviewing supervision – a supervisor's perspective

For the supervisor

- Does the supervisee feel heard?
- Is supervision supportive?
- Do I assist the supervisee to reflect?
- If I hold a dual role (supervisor and line manager) is there a clear boundary?
- Is the contract still relevant?
- Do I do things the supervisee doesn't want me to do?
- Does the supervisee feel safe?
- Am I approachable?
- Do I impose my culture or values on the supervisee?
- Do I facilitate a learning environment?
- Does the supervisee feel that on leaving supervision his/her goals have been met?
- What areas need to be improved upon?
- Does this relationship work?
- What feedback do I want to give the supervisee?

At the end of a supervision relationship it is important to take the time to review and honour the time spent together. If this has been a relationship where significant moments of practice have been shared then the relationship may hold deep and sometimes painful moments of the practitioner's professional history. The ending of supervision relationships, as we have suggested above, occur for a number of reasons. Sometimes these are mutually timed and agreeable to all concerned. In other circumstances the timing may not suit one, or both parties and the very ending may create discomfort and ambivalence. What is important is that time is allowed for either party, but particularly the supervisee, to express his or her response to the change and to come to terms with the consequences. Marris (1974) cited in Ford and Jones (1987, p.149) identifies three tasks in response to change. When confronted with change people need to: have an opportunity to react, to articulate their ambivalence and to work out their own defence of it.

In supervision, time needs to be allocated to allow these processes to occur. Particularly where change has not been the choice of the supervisee it is important that the supervisee is given time to accommodate the implications of, and responses to, the impending change. Time must be allowed for the supervisee and supervisor to review and reflect upon the relationship and any significant development and learning which has occurred. Where relationships have been more problematic it is even more important for opportunity to be given for any unfinished business to be aired and if possible put to rest before the relationship finishes.

Chapter 4

The Organisational Context of Supervision

Supervision is one significant component in the complex system of professional and organisational processes designed to ensure competent practice in health and social care. In the twenty-first century most helping professionals work in highly bureaucratic, organisational contexts and increasingly fewer can truly claim to be fully able to control their own work, or even their own knowledge. This is particularly so where their profession exists under the control of central government or local authority controlled services (Bierema and Eraut 2004). The nature of the climate in any given workplace has a major impact on the effectiveness of supervision and learning in that workplace. 'For supervision to work well within an organisation, its culture needs to be favourable. If the culture is unhealthy it is likely that the supervision will be affected accordingly' (van Ooijen 2003, p.221). This chapter examines the way organisational culture in workplaces supports or hinders supervision and the professional development of staff. The nature of workplace cultures will also be examined with consideration of external societal influences.

So what constitutes organisational culture? Schein defines 'culture' as a 'Set of basic tacit assumptions about how the world is and ought to be that a group of people share and that determines their perceptions, thoughts, feelings, and, to some degree, their overt behaviour' (Schein 1996, p.11). Most descriptions of organisational culture define it as the whole of the traditions, values, attitudes, work practices and policies that constitute an all-encompassing context in which the work of the organisation is carried out (Hawkins and Shohet 2006, pp.194–195). A commonplace definition is 'it's the way things work around here', and at its simplest it is grounded in the everyday life of a workplace: it may be about greetings, breaks, meetings, celebrations, welcomes and farewells. In its more complex dimensions it concerns the way workers relate to each other, the interpersonal dynamics and histories and the hierarchies, visible and invisible, that determine informal roles in the agency. Significant elements are found in the manner in which 'workplace relationships are developed and maintained and how boundaries between work and private life are constructed. At a deeper level culture will include the taken for granted and shared meanings attributed to actions in the agency, and the values and beliefs which underpin those actions' (Beddoe and Maidment 2009, p.82).

Hawkins and Shohet (1989, 2000, 2006) have provided an often cited typology that delineates the impact of dysfunctional workplace cultures on the supervisory climate. It is clear that the best and worst features of the organisation often accompany the participants into supervision. Hawkins and Shohet (1989) described five common 'cultures' and their impact on supervision in their first edition of *Supervision in the Helping Professions*, adding a sixth cultural type, the addictive organisation, in their second edition (2000, pp.174–175). Their optimal culture is the learning and development culture (Hawkins and Shohet 2006, pp.202–203) in which there is a high degree of congruence between organisational polices, staff development goals and the actual day-to-day work practices which impact on staff.

As we have seen in earlier chapters contemporary authors have presented models and approaches to supervision in health and social services which strongly ground supervision within learning and development policy and practice. These approaches to supervision have been influenced significantly by ideas about how professionals learn in practice (Butler 1996; Eraut 1994; Schön 1987). Professionals are not empty vessels to be filled. From their own lives they bring to the practice context their beliefs, culture, values and relevant prior experience. Competence in professional practice requires practitioners to form 'judgements through a process of negotiating shared meanings' (Jones and Joss 1995, p.29). Individuals are constantly adding to their store of knowledge, where their formal knowledge, skills, experience and intuitive wisdom are augmented and refined through contact with colleagues, other professionals and of course patients and service users. In addition to ideas derived from knowledge about individual learning, another set of ideas has been employed from the study of organisational learning (Garratt 1986; Marsick and Watkins 2002; Senge 1990). The site of learning is of increasing importance and distinct accounts of learning for professional practice are identified in the workplace (Eraut 1994; Schön 1987; Wenger 1998). Health and social care service organisations do not exist in a vacuum; they are shaped by history, government policy, requirements of regulatory bodies and broad social trends. As we have noted in Chapter 1, the 'risk society' and conceptualisations of danger and vulnerability of service users and communities we work with occupy our thoughts as we interact with each other and make decisions (Fawcett 2009; Warner 2008).

Bradley and Hojer argue that 'the worker/supervisor relationship may be constructed and viewed as an integral and interdependent part of a broader dialogue within the organisation and beyond, one that actively seeks feedback, interaction and improvement that is less reliant on the more usual form of hierarchical communication' (Bradley and Hojer 2009, p.82). To achieve its aims supervision must be held as a central component of a culture that nurtures learning. In an ideal workplace, in which the prevailing approach is the fostering of a 'learning and development culture', one would expect to see the following practices in place:

- greater engagement of frontline staff in determining local and personal professional development goals (Beddoe 2009)

- recognition of the emotional impact of constant exposure to illness, distress and trauma with effective processes to mitigate any deleterious effects (Cox and Griffiths 1996; Hughes and Pengelly 1997)

- professional learning as continuous throughout careers and including learning within practice activity (Schön 1991)

- facilitative, learning-focused supervision which is valued, supported and well resourced (Hawkins and Shohet 2006, p.202)

- all staff members, including the most senior, participating in supervision and professional development (Hawkins and Shohet 2006, p.202)

- reviews of mistakes and problems to provide opportunities for learning with a focus on practices and potential improvements, not on finding scapegoats (Green 2007, pp.405–406)

- good practice based on a balance in a cycle of learning – action, sharing stories of success and failure, reflection, experimentation, evaluation, planning and renewed approaches to problems (Davys 2001)

- individuals and teams making time to review their effectiveness (Hawkins and Shohet 2006, p.203)

- provision of ongoing feedback including 'immediate comment on aspects of a task or a role given on-the-spot or soon after the event by a co-participant or observer' (Eraut 2006, p.114)

- informal conversations away from the frontline of service delivery via supervision or formal mentoring; formal appraisal a more formal and less frequent process (Eraut 2006, pp.114–115)

- opportunities for feedback between the levels of the organisation (Hawkins and Shohet 2006, p.203)

- room for professional autonomy and discretion and practice which is not dominated by rule-bound proceduralism (Cooper 2001; Franks 2004).

Health and social care organisations frequently promote policy statements exhorting that they are 'learning organisations'. The rhetoric, however, is sometimes not matched by evidence of what really happens. Genuine commitment to cultural change in organisations creates 'spaces for generative conversations and concerted action. In them, language functions as advice for connection, invention, and coordination. People can talk from their hearts and connect with one another in the spirit of dialogue' (Kofman and Senge 1993, p.6). Similarly supervision policies can be acceptable on the surface but not meet their promises in reality. Gardner found that participants in a critical reflection process felt that there were problems with their supervision. Among the problems were: 'Supervision that's confusing, not clarifying', poor quality of supervision that does not help develop skills, a lack of direction, inconsistency, and the 'rules of supervision – that do not meet needs of team' (Gardner 2009, p.184).

Peach and Horner comment that low levels of public and political tolerance of mistakes in contemporary human services and health organisations mean that the main purpose of 'supervision is in danger of becoming the elimination of risk through the micro-management and surveillance of practitioners and their outcomes' (Peach and Horner 2007, p.229). This is far from the idealised nurturing restorative process in which supervision is the 'quiet profession' (Alonso 1985) focused on the provision of reflective, supportive, yet challenging facilitation of the supervisee's professional development. As Jones asserts, 'the nursing literature concerning clinical supervision is consequently anything other than quiet. There is a burgeoning discussion concerning many complexities of clinical supervision' (Jones 2006, p.579). What research tells us is that often the reality of the organisational culture is such that supervision is not happening in practice, or is under pressure (Stanley and Goddard 2002; Stevenson 2005). It is also the experience of many that supervision time or focus is inadequate or that it does not occur (Hunter 2009).

Reference is often made to supervision when practice is reviewed following child abuse tragedies. The Laming report on child protection practice, for example, includes supervision explicitly as a practice to be fostered:

> Regular, high-quality, organised supervision is critical, as are routine opportunities for peer-learning and discussion. Currently, not enough time is dedicated to this and individuals are carrying too much personal responsibility, with no outlet for the sometimes severe emotional and psychological stresses that staff involved in child protection often face. Supervision should be open and supportive, focusing on the quality of decisions, good risk analysis, and improving outcomes for children rather than meeting targets. (Laming 2009, p.30)

Health and social care agencies have faced many decades now of escalating demands, an adverse climate of scrutiny and public criticism. Such a climate is corrosive of core values of helping professions and undermines public confidence. The significant of these concerns is discussed in further detail in Chapter 11, where we explore supervision in child welfare and protection practice.

LEARNING AND WORKPLACE CULTURES

Workplace cultures can exert positive and negative influences on the attitudes of staff and their motivation to participate fully in learning activities, including supervision. Unhappy workplaces in health and social care organisations can be unduly bureaucratic and stifle innovation, or become crisis-driven, without time for reflection. They can be risk averse, with high levels of anxiety, or highly competitive environments which lead to severe overworking (Hawkins and Shohet 2006, pp.196–201). In the case of a 'workaholic' culture managers may collude with unsafe working conditions rather than challenge the leadership. Often dysfunctional workplaces have faced significant or continuous change that has placed many key processes beyond the control of professional leaders; for example, where the external decisions of funders and policy makers create a highly competitive environment that imposes targets (and sanctions) on individuals, teams or sites. Burke suggests that restructuring and downsizing have contributed to:

the crisis conditions conducive to workaholism. As organizations strive to become more entrepreneurial, support for workaholism is fostered. Organizations rarely discourage such behaviors; some take pride in developing cultures where long hours and sacrifice are seen as requirements for success and advancement. (Burke 2001, p.639)

Casey describes how decades of change, manifest in such features as continuous or repeated organisational restructuring, downsizing, the introduction of flexible employment practices such as temporary jobs and changes to working hours have impacted on the nature of working life. She notes that 'many of these developments occur in conflict with other social and cultural aspirations, such as for secure employment, social inclusion, community development and quality of working life' (Casey 2003, p.622).

Awareness of the impact of organisational culture on learning, reflection and supervision practices has been informed by consideration of research and development happening in the broad fields of organisational development and lifelong learning. The past decade has seen a movement towards greater recognition of the importance of work cultures with regard to both pragmatic concerns about productivity and competence and to more altruistic efforts to ensure worker happiness and empowerment (Koppes 2008). Table 4.1 sets out features of dysfunctional workplace cultures and their impact on learning and development and contrasts this with features of resilient organisations. Developments in positive psychology (Collins 2008; Luthans 2002; Wright and Quick 2009) are encouraging workplace leaders to reassess and affirm values (Gardner 2009), and foster learning in order to promote resiliency and retain committed professional staff. In addition Western governments have placed commitment to post-school learning as a significant feature of economic and social development in the past few decades. There is sustained political support for whole societies to be engaged in continual learning and development. Policy driven terminology such as 'lifelong learning', 'the learning society' and 'the learning organisation' has entered everyday language in health and social services. In particular the ideal of the 'learning organisation' has taken firm hold.

Table 4.1 Contrasting the features of organisational cultures

Organisational type	Common themes	Impact on learning and development	Resilient organisations
Blame and shame culture dominates (Hawkins and Shohet 2006)	Defensive practice Risk averse Scapegoating Focus on identifying individual deficits Staff cover up any difficulties	Fearfulness about admitting mistakes. Surveillance dominates supervision (Peach and Horner 2007) Failure to reflect and change practice Supervision resisted and undermined Supervision focus on surveillance Low support for reflection	Collective responsibility for problems and mistakes Supervision and group consultation processes embed culture of collaboration (Jones 2008; Lietz 2008; Lindahl and Norberg 2002 and Lohrbach 2008)
Efficiency model dominates	Rigid hierarchies High on task orientation and low on personal relatedness (Hawkins and Shohet 2006)	Efficiency valued over communication (Cooper 2000) Audit processes create additional overload and limit learning activities Stifles innovation – seeks standardisation and routine Supervision focus on targets and output	Recognition that professionals in health and social care use their own personal emotional resources in the work and these resources need care, oversight and 're-stocking'
Perpetual crisis dominates (Hawkins and Shohet 2006)	Constant state of stress and vigilance Low social connectedness Little planning Problem solving focus	Little space for understanding, stories, reflection and exploration Supervision focus on debriefing and 'survival'	Hardy organisations (Collins 2008) foster hope and optimism (Koenig and Spano 2007) Strengths-based, positive approach (Luthans 2002)
'Workaholic' culture (Burke 2001; Hawkins and Shohet 2006)	Enthusiasm and commitment warps into 'missionary' zeal Denial, collusion or reward for overwork (Burke 2001)	Climate is overtly politicised or highly competitive Supervision and support for the 'needy' and less heroic Professional development support may be a reward not a right	Work–life balance and empowerment (Koppes 2008) Collaborative decision making and space for reflection

THE LEARNING ORGANISATION

The concept of 'the learning organisation' developed in the 1980s is often cited in supervision literature. The rise in prominence of this concept has been attributed to Peter Senge whose influential text, *The Fifth Discipline: The Art and Practice of the Learning Organisation* (Senge 1990) has gained a place on the bookshelves of many managers in health and social care. The origins of the learning organisation are found in the work on organisational development undertaken by Argyris and Schön in which organisational learning was viewed from a systems perspective (Argyris and Schön 1974, 1978). Senge's prescription for a learning organisation requires the mastery of five core disciplines: self-mastery, shared vision, team learning, mental models and systems thinking (Senge 1990). Common features include a systemic view of organisational learning and development, a cycle of continuous critical reflection on the business of the organisation, empowerment of individuals within the work world, emphasis on communication and the harnessing of knowledge and energy through commitment to teamwork. The learning organisation's influence beyond the business sector is indicated by articles that refer to it in professional contexts such as health, social services and education (see for example Eraut 2004; Gould and Baldwin 2004).

'Lifelong learning' and 'learning organisations' are interesting features of contemporary society as, on superficial examination at least, it seems that government policy and organisational practices are rather well aligned with the professional values of the helping professions, 'on the surface what could possibly not be "good" about "lifelong learning"?' Is there a dark side? (Beddoe 2009, p.724). Recent research finds that practitioners in social services were highly conscious of these 'discourses' and their impact on the workplace, but that they were rather cynical. Beddoe (2009) identified several problems in a study of social workers' ideas about continuing education. First, learning discourses are acknowledged as influential but practitioners recognise personal costs and may experience this as yet further encroachment of work on their time (p.728). Second, learning organisations aspire to foster learning from mistakes, however, practitioner perspectives suggested that feedback loops were unlikely in low trust environments (pp.728–729). Lastly, the social workers in this study felt that health and human services organisations were far too unstable to manage continuous improvement (Beddoe 2009, p.731).

A critical examination of the learning organisation suggests that it is vital to retain a sense of the value of learning for its own sake, where it is self-directed and free from manipulation by short-term political agendas

(Beddoe 2009). Other kinds of knowledge, cultural, transformative and personal, are valuable and contribute to the professional knowledge base. Knowledge is enriched by critical reflection and the wisdom uncovered by examining practice over time and its replacement with technologies of learning and practice (Reich 2002). These approaches risk objectifying both service users and the nature of the work by assuming that assessment tools and limited 'system' responses create sufficient skill to keep disasters from occurring and effect good enough practice. Again, the Laming report clearly identifies the importance of embedding regular time for reflection, supervision and peer learning:

> There is concern that the tradition of deliberate, reflective social work practice is being put in danger because of an overemphasis on process and targets, resulting in a loss of confidence amongst social workers. It is vitally important that social work is carried out in a supportive learning environment that actively encourages the continuous development of professional judgement and skills. (Laming 2009, p.30)

At the time of writing this book, announcements were being made about the development of extensive training for supervision, to ensure that the recommendations of the Laming report can be met. In examining various accounts of 'managed' implementation of supervision strategies, there are often problems with top-down approaches, see for example Froggett (2000). One enterprise, reported in Davies et al. 2004, described how a 'computerised auditing system is being used to track the occurrence of supervision and the nature of any events which prevent supervision from taking place' (p.41), perhaps indicating a concern that compliance might be patchy.

It is also important to consider the significance of the mediating capacity of supervision and its potential to contribute to multiple levels, and direction, of feedback within health and social care (Morrison 1996). Failure to communicate, anxiety and lack of trust within organisations can lead to poor or unsafe practice. Supervisors can assist through creating a conduit for feedback or what Morrison (1996) described as the mediation function of supervision within organisations. Austin and Hopkins (2004) cited in Kaiser and Kuechler (2008, p.78) have described this mediative function as having three parts: 'managing down' (transforming the vision of the administration into action); 'managing up' (advocating for the needs of clients and staff) and 'managing out' both in the agency (dealing with tensions between diverse professionals in an agency) and in the community (addressing the interests of and pressures from multiple agencies who might be involved in client services). Table 4.2 suggests some questions which may assist supervisors to consider the context of their particular organisation.

Table 4.2 Organisational context

Considering organisational context

- Power – who decides the learning goals in this organisation?
- Collaboration – what processes are used to elicit employee ideas about learning needs?
- Do managerial interests dominate decisions about supervision?
- Are there opportunities to learn in groups?
- Is the use of group supervision or consultation used to tap collective learning power?
- Is there a continuous improvement strategy and, if so, does it focus only at the micro level, ignoring macro problems that frontline health and social care workers can't control?
- Is there room for honest reflection and evaluation of supervision and professional development to guide the organisation in its decision-making about development and improvement?

WORKPLACE LEARNING

It is part of a professional's personal obligation to remain competent. Increasingly this shifts workers' study time to their non-work hours and into their home life. As we saw in Chapter 1, many professional bodies have now embedded these expectations within requirements for annual practising certificates. One of the problems is that there is still a great deal of work to be done to understand how professionals do continue to learn during their careers and how to motivate practitioners who struggle to participate because of time constraints, costs and personal responsibilities. In reality most practitioners are learning all the time whether this is conscious or not! For most practitioners in the health and social services professions, their professional work is carried out within group and agency settings. Informal learning is constant, 'everyday' and sometimes accidental.

Much of this development of everyday knowledge occurs informally through trial and error, observation, discussion and sharing stories as well as more formal guidance and mentoring. Supervision is most effective when it is led by the supervisee's agenda and is learning focused. This makes practitioner narratives significant and locates learning centrally in the work context and not remote from practice. This does not mean that professional development via external training, study towards higher qualifications and practitioner research do not contribute to learning, but all these are likely to be more successful and lead to change and improvement if supervision provides a conduit for their support. Dirkx argues that 'learning and change are conceptualized largely as cognitive, decontextualized, individualistic, and solitary processes' (Dirkx, Gilley and Gilley 2004, p.36). A consequence of learning activities being located in the world external to the practitioner's employing agency is that distance is created between the educational institution and the site of practice. This distance is unhelpful and limiting and does not align with practitioners' accounts of their learning.

Dirkx expresses this distance clearly:

> Practitioner stories suggest that lifelong learning and change in continuing professional development reflect an ongoing struggle to keep the rational deeply connected with the richly felt experience of practice.... From this perspective, the knowledge we use to inform our practices evolves in an ongoing way from dialectical relationships that involve the relevant technical or scientific knowledge, the sociocultural context of practice, and the practitioner's self. (Dirkx *et al.* 2004, p.36)

Table 4.3 suggests some questions which may assist supervisors to consider how the culture of their particular organisation affects learning.

Table 4.3 Organisational learning reflections

Organisational learning exercise

- What are the particular strengths in your workplace?
- What particular expertise do team members have?
- How do the learning activities in the workplace facilitate sharing of expertise in this workplace?
- What supports or hinders innovation in your workplace?
- What would you like to strengthen in 'learning' in your setting?
- What would you like to discard?
- What would you like to develop or create which is currently missing?

Supervision, given its location closer to the workplace, often in peer and professional relationships, offers considerable potential for promotion of a more practice-grounded learning. In considering the links between supervision and career-long learning, it is important to note an emerging agreement that professionals learn in the job through a combination of work experience, clinical practice, clinical or professional supervision and in ongoing post-qualifying learning. Good facilitation though is needed to ensure that reflection and critical review assist professionals to turn this collected information into enhanced practice.

In an ideal health and social care organisation, supervision is valued and training and ongoing support encourages and maintains excellent communication amongst supervisees, supervisors and managers alike. The desire to build 'continuous conversation', reflective practice, feedback loops and time to share ideas and concerns in health and social care workplaces (Beddoe 2009) is increasingly leading to the examination of group and collaborative approaches to supervision (in nursing Lindahl and Norberg 2002 and Jones 2008; in social work Lietz 2008 and Lohrbach 2008). Group approaches are developing strength as organisations strive to create more participatory cultures. Baldwin 2008, for example, utilised cooperative inquiry methods working with social care workers to explore how the organisation could best foster innovation.

MANAGERIALISM, 'THE RISK SOCIETY' AND SUPERVISION

A survey of the supervision literature of the last two decades produces a gloomy view of supervision in which the impact of the current fiscal policy environment in health and social services has weakened the focus on the formative and restorative aspects of supervision (Hawkins and Shohet 2000; Hughes and Pengelly 1997; Morrison 2001; Payne 1994). Economic rationalism, managerialism and the growth of management as a new and distinct profession, the emphasis of outcome and output led service delivery, contracting, and consumer advocacy have all had an influence on the organisational contexts in which supervision occurs. At the time of writing this book, health and social care organisations around the globe nervously watch for spending cuts.

More recent discussion emphasises the links between the revitalisation of supervision and the impact of 'the risk society'. The term 'the risk society' is used to describe a society that is organised in response to risk (Beck 1992) and preoccupied with safety (Giddens 1999, p.3). We live in a world in which there is a belief that we must keep and be kept safe (Fawcett 2009). One of the consequences of this heightened awareness of risk is that professionals are expected to take particular responsibility for identifying, managing and reducing risks to which patients and service users are exposed. Risk features at all levels. Individual practitioners are recommended to develop a personal safety plan, whilst in health and social care organisations risk assessment of intake procedures and fiscal accountability require organisations to identify the potential for costly risk. As we will examine further in Chapter 9, this concern extends to the role of supervisors in identifying the potential for supervisees to be harmed by their work and assisting in prevention.

The raised awareness of public accountability and the desire of governments and other health and social care organisations to avoid exposure to reputational and other risks has, in a rather paradoxical manner, led to a revitalisation of supervision. In 1994 Beddoe and Davys asked 'what is the future for social work supervision in crisis-driven bureaucratic agencies?' (p.21) as involvement in providing supervision training for probation officers had suggested that supervision had become captured by the gathering of information about case management and there was little room for practitioners to focus on their practice issues and even less to think about their professional development. Supervision had become a 'checklist' exercise that was essentially a managerial tool.

Payne suggested in 1994 that supervision was a practice in danger of becoming captured by 'unthinking adherence to politically and bureaucratically defined roles' (p.55). Payne's hopeful view was that there might be a reconciliation of managerial and professional supervision models through the increased focus on quality (pp.54–55), and indeed the extension of professional supervision as a practice which developed in social work, counselling and psychotherapy is very much underpinned by the risk-averse cultures within contemporary health and social care. Beddoe (2010b) argues that the revitalisation of supervision emerges during a period in which risk comes to occupy central stage in health and social care. Supervision has not always been welcomed as a consequence of this association with risk culture and the preoccupation with audit that has characterised much of the change in health and social services over recent decades.

The current preoccupation with 'quality' and the numerous mechanisms to interrogate professional practice has clearly strengthened the mandate for supervision. The links between quality assurance and clinical supervision have often been used to support and protect supervision. Recently a concern has emerged that this emphasis may threaten the integrity of supervision as a worker-centred and learning-focused activity. In social work Peach and Horner have cautioned that because of low tolerance of mistakes in contemporary human services and health organisations, 'the sole goal of supervision is in danger of becoming the elimination of risk through the micro-management and surveillance of practitioners and their outcomes' (Peach and Horner 2007, p.229). Statutory social work in particular has a high public profile and is especially vulnerable to political scrutiny and public criticism. Supervisors in statutory child protection work face major challenges. They need to manage the expectations of multiple stakeholders in a high stress environment and yet find the time, skill and emotional energy to provide supervision to frontline workers. Bogo and Dill, in a study of child welfare supervisors, reported that 'walking the tightrope' was the metaphor for a significant theme of struggle in their supervision practice:

> One side of the tightrope relates to their relationship to the workers they supervise and indirectly to the workers' clients... They struggle to achieve enough trust about their workers' competence and practice so that they can share power with these workers. The other side of the tightrope refers to their relationship with those senior to them, their managers, the agency director, and the government ministry that decrees new legislation and policy. (Bogo and Dill 2008, p.151)

Chapter 11 will examine more closely the importance of supervision in child protection services.

Clouder and Sellars (2004) provide an interesting counter to the problematising of supervision as a spectre of increased surveillance. Their paper is described as a pragmatic response to Gilbert's important critique of supervision in which he argues that clinical supervision can be shown to operate as a 'mode of surveillance disciplining the activity of professionals' (Gilbert 2001, p.199). Clouder and Sellars argue that, rather than a consequence of new work practices, 'surveillance is ubiquitous and an inevitable concomitant of the social practices in which professionals engage', citing the numerous public encounters health professionals have with colleagues, managers, patients and others and which means that 'professionals are constantly in the spotlight under which competence is being evaluated' (Clouder and Sellars 2004, p.264). Indeed at work we 'are under constant surveillance, whether or not we are consciously aware of it or its effects on us, because we are social beings operating within a system of social practices' (p.265). Supervision can at the very least allow, albeit briefly, the doors to be shut, the noise to be reduced and a quiet space for satisfying professional conversation.

As outlined in Chapter 3, the quality of the supervision relationship is a significant factor in determining the effectiveness of supervision. A review of the literature identifies the range of managerial elements in the relationship between supervisor and supervisee. The linking of supervision and managerial concerns has been a significant issue for nurses but it is contested in other professions as well. Social work has a longer tradition of supervision and in practice has always included some managerial or administrative functions.

EXTERNAL SUPERVISION: THE DEBATES

To a large extent this current climate encourages the individualist response which characterises the shift towards external supervision (Cooper 2006). External supervision is a term often used as synonymous with non line-management supervision. Points in favour of external or privatised supervision generally focus on the importance of supervisee choice and direction and the negative influence of power differentials in the supervisory relationship. Supervisee choice, especially in relation to group membership and professional identity, was reported by Davys (2005b) as a major indicator of satisfaction. Matching of supervisee and supervisor characteristics particularly in relation to ethnicity, culture, gender, age and professional and theoretical orientation are also considered to be important. It is expected that with an external supervisor, where power and authority issues have less impact, supervisees will have greater freedom to express concerns and frustrations about organisational issues.

External supervision, located as it is outside the agency, allows more intensive focus on clinical issues and personal professional development rather than organisational concerns. In addition this external supervision arrangement may improve the likelihood that supervision actually does take place. In busy agency settings supervision can often be neglected or deferred to accommodate the latest crisis unless it is made a high priority by management.

While these arguments are valid, there remains some justification for a degree of scepticism about the efficacy of external supervision arrangements. The following questions are pertinent:

- How effective is the unchecked stream of ventilation about organisational issues that can sometimes preoccupy external supervision sessions?

- To what extent can the external supervisor be an advocate for stressed and troubled workers when their mandate is ambiguous?

- Does the absence of organisational authority in the supervisor lead to a lack of real challenge?

- What do supervisors do to check out other perspectives?

- How do supervisors assess clinical practice and ensure safety?

- To whom is ultimate loyalty and confidentiality owed when a third party is paying for the supervision?

We are aware that these questions may reflect the authors' grounding in social work models of supervision which has long reflected the organisational context. Nevertheless, it is a reasonable assumption that other approaches may be influenced by traditional assumptions about context. Counselling and psychotherapy supervisory approaches are frequently based on a private practice structure which is strongly predicated on a set of assumptions about the relative autonomy of the individual practitioner. The private or semi-private (group practice) practitioner may make choices based on reputation, therapeutic or theoretical orientation, style and of course more pragmatic concerns such as cost, access, professional accreditation requirements and third party funding bodies. The private supervisor will be able to determine the length and nature of the supervision process and will largely self-monitor and evaluate his or her interventions. These conditions are likely to be replicated in the supervision arrangements.

Disadvantages of external supervision

There are a number of pitfalls in the separation of supervision from clinical accountability:

- There may be an ambiguous mandate for dealing with issues of poor performance where supervisors become aware of performance matters but have no mandate or clear contract to address these.

- Unhealthy collusion can occur where there are grievances in the practitioner relationships with line managers.

- Separation may deepen the experience of the gulf between 'management' and 'practice' and thus reduce the flow of information between the layers of the organisation.

- There is a tendency to rely on reported performance rather than 360 degree information collected through day-to-day interaction and observation of performance in teams, case consultations, etc.

- There is the potential for unhealthy triangulation of practitioner, line manager and clinical supervisor if there is not sufficient attention paid to clarity of mandate.

- The line manager may be relived of responsibility to ensure that anti-oppressive polices are satisfied, including cultural support for particular staff, addressing conflict between team members, and the monitoring of personal and practice safety issues in the workplace.

- Duty of care issues can remain unclear and yet be vitally significant when things go wrong.

- Dissonance between organisational goals and the focus and direction of supervision may remain unaddressed.

In a recent article Bradley and Hojer compare English and Swedish approaches to supervision of social workers. It is noted that in Scandinavian countries the practice of supervision provided by external consultants is 'combined with a system of internal, method-oriented supervision, from the line manager to the social workers. This latter aspect of supervision focuses on the management of cases and may be seen to be within an administrative model (Bradley and Hojer 2009, p.75). Bradley and Hojer cite Bernler and Johnsson (1985) when suggesting seven criteria that form the basis for supervision in social work (p.75). These are (1) that supervision should be a continuous activity, (2) it should assist the integration of all integrate all aspects of their work, (3) the process should encourage reflection on the use of self and feelings, (4) ideally it should be a non-linear organisational relationship between supervisor and group of practitioners, (5) supervisors should be responsible for the process of the supervision, not for the supervisee's direct work with client, (6) *all* social workers should have supervision, and finally (7) the supervisor should have expertise in social work (theoretically as well as practically), education in supervision theory and method, and cultural competence in the specific area of practice (p.75). Table 4.4 identifies a list of questions through which to consider external supervision from the perspective of the external supervisor, the manager and the supervisee.

Table 4.4 Reflections on external supervision

Reflections on external supervision
If you are an *external supervisor* what can you do to support the full professional learning of your supervisees? • Could you influence your supervisees' organisations? • How can you ensure you get good information? • How do you influence in both directions and *should you?* • What arrangements are in place for you to provide feedback to your supervisee's manager?
If you are a *manager* or *professional leader* and your team members have external supervision: • How do you negotiate the lines of accountability and feedback on supervision issues and process? • What arrangements do you have to liaise with the supervisor if you have concerns about your practitioner's work performance? • What agreements are in place if the supervisor has concerns about the practitioner and/or the work context?
If you are a *supervisee* with external supervision: • What should you do to ensure that your supervision is accountable to your manager/workplace? • What are the boundaries of confidentiality that you think important?

CONCLUSIONS

Supervision has a major role to play in safeguarding practitioners in health and social care in a process which can assist them to cope with their emotions, manage uncertainty and to continue to grow and learn professionally. The culture of the organisation will shape the manner in which supervision is valued and accepted within that organisation. Organisational culture will also filter the effects of public and legislative surveillance and ultimately determine how effective supervision can be in promoting learning and renewal of practice. In the organisational setting supervision practice is 'at the intersection of the personal and professional, where "dangerousness" may be a fear and optimism may be muted' (Beddoe 2010b) and, whether supervision is internal or external, there are inevitable difficulties of balance. Stanford's study of social workers' reflections on practice intervention supports supervision as providing a place for the rekindling of hopefulness:

> Recognition of hope and the possibility of change, alongside a commitment to care therefore need to become directives, as opposed to incidentals, of practice. Supervision is a site in which this orienting

framework could be mutually explored and supported by managers and practitioners. (Stanford 2007, p.257)

To retain critically reflective practice, exploration of practitioners' emotions and their understanding of risk and uncertainty need to be given a central space in supervision (Parton 1998). Moral reasoning and a more nuanced exploration of emotional responses and concerns can strengthen supervision practice. We will explore this in more detail in Chapter 8.

Contemporary professional practice is scrutinised, audited and open to the public gaze. Most professionals do much of their work in crowded, noisy, public and stressful environments where meaningful dialogue and reflection is impossible. Supervision can at very least allow, albeit briefly, the doors to be shut, the noise to be reduced and a quiet space for satisfying professional conversation.

Chapter 5

A Reflective Learning
Model for Supervision

*The assumption is that the [supervisee] is always in the process of
'becoming' what is required by the ever changing parameters of the
learning context. (Butler 1996, p.265)*

The fundamental proposition and underlying premise of the Reflective
Learning Model (Davys 2001) is that supervision is first and foremost
a 'learning process'. This process is driven from the experience of the
learner (the supervisee) rather than from the wisdom and knowledge
of the supervisor. The model was first developed by one of the authors
(Davys 2001) and has been the basis of an interprofessional supervision
programme taught at the University of Auckland. Over the years it has
been adapted and updated. Supervision models based on learning and
reflexivity offer the flexibility needed for practitioners to adjust theory and
practice to the ever-changing and messy shapes of the modern practice
context. When supervision is regarded as a reflective learning process, a
shift occurs which moves the supervisor from an 'expert' to a 'facilitator'
in the supervision forum. As a facilitator the supervisor's role becomes
one of ensuring the space and context for learning. McCann (2000, p.43)
has described this role as one of co-explorer. The supervisee defines the
problem and is responsible for his or her own learning as generated from
this co-exploration with the supervisor. The Reflective Learning Model of
supervision promotes a way of thinking rather than a blueprint for doing.
Solutions which emerge from the supervision process are discovered and
owned by the supervisee rather than 'taught' by the supervisor.

As discussed in Chapter 2, however, supervision is not practised in
a vacuum and boundaries of accountability which accompany both the
mandate and the role of supervisor require both participants to understand
and respect the limits of exploration. This means that in given situations
such as safety or crisis the supervisor may, and indeed should, assert
appropriate authority. These, however, are the exceptions.

Reflection as described by Johns and Freshwater (2005, p.2) is 'a fusion of sensing, perceiving, intuiting and thinking related to a specific experience in order to develop insights into self and practice. It is vision driven, concerned with taking action towards knowing and realising desirable practice'. Reflection in professional practice may be a solitary event or, as Johns and Freshwater suggest, may require guidance. Supervision is one occasion where reflection is 'guided' and so new learning may occur.

Beliefs and values within each individual person's world view determine what is perceived, and so influence not only what experience is offered for reflection, but also the outcomes of the reflective process (Butler 1996). In the nature of homeostasis, perception acts to reinforce an individual's world view. Thus discrepancies and events which could disturb that world view will be filtered out and only those that reinforce and confirm the position of the practitioner are available for reflection (Butler 1996, p.275). For this reason it can be difficult for any individual to 'critique' his or her world view.

Carroll reinforces this when he observes 'my own work and experience have taught me that I cannot learn some things on my own. I need others' (2009, p.213). In the supervision process a practitioner's work is presented for consideration by both the practitioner and the supervisor and it is here that the practitioner's world view may be identified. Opportunities for new options and ideas are uncovered when different 'filters' are applied to a situation and so, with the assistance of an 'other', transformational learning can take place. Learning, Carroll concludes 'is as much between people as it is within people' (Carroll 2009, p.213).

The Reflective Learning Model of supervision combines the closely related ideas of reflective practice and adult learning. The model is underscored by our belief that supervision is about learning. 'The key to learning and development lies in the ability to engage in, and make use of, the worker's experience' (Morrison 2001, p.57) and reflection is central to this learning. The model assumes that supervision and learning are lifelong processes in which a practitioner engages from the beginning of formal training until retirement from practice.

Reflection as a learning process is not new and can be traced to Aristotle's 'distinction between technical, practical and theoretical forms of reasoning' (Kondrat 1992). In more recent times John Dewey's 'reflective activity in learning' has been influential (Boud, Keogh and Walker 1985, p.11). Dewey determined that the boundaries to 'a complete act of reflective activity' were 'a perplexed, troubled, or confused situation at the beginning and a cleared-up, unified, resolved situation at the close'

(Dewey 1998, p.139). For Dewey failure was instructive and he argued that 'the person who really thinks learns quite as much from his failures as his successes' (p.142). According to Kolb the increased demand for change and versatility of response in the workplace in recent times has emphasised the very challenges which Dewey's approach was designed to address (Kolb 1984).

Whilst Dewey led the way, it is Kolb's 'experiential learning model' which is probably the best known model of adult learning. Kolb's definition of learning is 'the process whereby knowledge is created through transformation of experience' (Kolb 1984, p.38). Kolb's model has four stages beginning with a 'concrete experience' in which the learner is 'fully' involved. In other words something happens and the learner, or person involved, not only notices that it has happened but also places value on the moment. Without this noticing and valuing no learning can occur. 'It is not sufficient to have an experience to learn, for the experience may be suppressed, denied or rejected as irrelevant or of no significance' (Morrison 2001, p.137).

When it is noticed and valued, 'experience' can then be observed and 'reflected' upon in order to establish its impact on the 'learner'. There follows a 'conceptual analysis' of the experience to determine the implications and meaning of this experience in terms of theory and context. Finally a new action plan is formulated on the basis of the assimilation of the reflection and analysis and the cycle is ready to be repeated with new experience or action. We are not the first to incorporate Kolb's experiential learning cycle into supervision and others have offered their own descriptions of the stages. Bond and Holland (1998) have added 'What? So what? Now what?' and Carroll and Gilbert (2005) 'Activity-Reflection-Learning and Application'. Figure 5.1 illustrates these interpretations.

Where Kolb's model lays the basis for experiential learning, reflective practice has been moulded by the seminal work of Donald Schön (1983, 1987). Citing Schön's work, Gould and Harris comment that 'knowledge is directly constructed through engagements with problems encountered in the field, and built through successive stages of hypothesising, testing and reflection' (Gould and Harris 1996, p.224).

In order to learn from reflection the practitioner must examine the effect of events, actions and interactions on him or herself. Consideration must also be given to how the practitioner impacts on those same events, actions and interactions. The practitioner must locate him or herself in the situation in order to understand fully what has occurred. Learning is not the application of rules and theory but, rather, the uncovering and

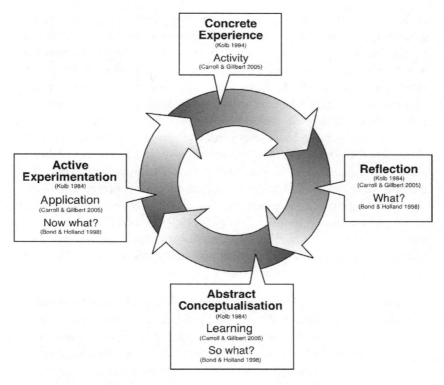

Figure 5.1 The Reflective Learning Cycle

understanding of the intuitive wisdom which underpins practice (Gould and Harris 1996). Such examination also encourages practitioners to notice and to value their intuitive response. 'At the same time' (Moffatt 1996, p.53) warns, 'intuition is one of those 'moments of knowing' which should be open to inquiry to ensure that it is used in a responsible manner'. Hence the process of learning from reflection requires more than intuition. Intuition must be critiqued and considered alongside thoughtful analysis and concrete data.

In a similar vein, Kondrat argues that:

> critical reflexivity involves the practitioner-knower in the process of making explicit the knowledge that is implicit in action so that it becomes available for both critique and enquiry. The effort called for includes, but goes well beyond, the task of outcome evaluation. (Kondrat 1992, p.250)

Reflection, thus, does not uncover the 'ultimate' truth, but rather a subjective truth relative to time, place and person. It allows practitioners to examine dissonance between espoused theory and theory in action, that is, what they intend or say they do, as opposed to what they actually do (Argyris and Schön 1974). Reflectivity requires a subjective examination of experience which includes engagement with and respect for 'the emotional world of self and others' (Papell 1996, p.14). Such views offer contradictions and inconsistencies and thus, importantly, reflectivity also offers the possibility of a number of perspectives. The possibility of plural views equips practitioners well for the changing perspectives and the uncertainties which characterise current practice contexts. The rate of change of these confusing practice contexts far outstrips the possibility of 'right' answers and responses. The possibilities of practice are therefore more certain than the 'rules' of practice. For some practitioners, however, a desire for clean solutions wrestles with the anxiety and challenge of choice. And of them Schön observes:

> many practitioners, locked into a view of themselves as technical experts, find nothing in the world of practice to occasion reflection. They have become too skilful at techniques of selective inattention, junk categories, and situational control, techniques which they use to preserve the constancy of their knowledge-in-practice. For them, uncertainty is a threat; its admission a sign of weakness. (Schön 1983, p.69)

These may well be the practitioners we need to challenge and monitor as they seek to impose stability onto an ever-changing and evolving landscape of practice.

Schön's work on reflective practice identified two central forms of reflection, reflection 'in action' and reflection 'on action' (Schön 1987). 'Reflection in action' relates to conscious considerations, evaluation and decision-making which occurs during the performance of a practitioner's daily tasks. 'Reflection on action' is the consideration, analysis and evaluation of a situation or event after it has occurred. Both forms of reflection lead to new understandings and new knowledge of practice.

The role of supervision in this creation of new understanding and learning is to focus on, and develop, the process of *reflection on action*. In this manner supervision provides the foundation for effective *reflection in action*. By internalising the supervision process the practitioner is able to access the reflective process more readily when engaged in practice. The reflective process in supervision can therefore be considered as a transportable learning process which can be internalised and accessed at the worker–client interface.

OVERVIEW OF THE MODEL

The Reflective Learning Model of supervision follows the cycle of experiential learning with specific tasks at each stage for both supervisor and supervisee. As with all models, it has a beginning and an end and in between is a cyclic process of reflection, analysis, experimentation and evaluation. This cycle is repeated for each item which is placed on the supervision agenda.

The structure of the model: beginnings and endings

We have noted elsewhere the importance of acknowledging the beginnings and endings of a supervision session (Davys 2001). Unless an appropriate space and context is defined the 'work' of supervision is at risk of being undervalued or discarded. If we truly wish to invite our supervisees to reflect upon and consider those hidden and sometime painful intuitions and details of practice then the supervision 'space' must reflect respect, regard and trust. Both parties need to be 'present' if the truths of practice are to be considered. Supervisors and supervisees who have completed a thorough initial contracting process will have agreed on the manner in which each session will start. The form will vary from dyad to dyad. In some situations a ritual of prayer, song or reflection may start the session and reflect cultural responses. In other situations it may be the offer of refreshment or simply a brief hello and 'How are you?' Whatever the form, it is an important moment where both parties can tune themselves to the rhythms of the other and focus on the task and relationship at hand.

The 'end' of the session will also vary from dyad to dyad and may include individual or cultural rituals. Once again the 'process' is important and an analogy can perhaps be made to knitting. When the knitter has finished the garment unless she or he casts off, the work is at risk of unravelling. Good beginnings set the shape of the session and good endings assist the learning to be contained, valued and transported into practice.

AGENDA SETTING

When supervisor and supervisee are sufficiently present it is time to build the agenda for the session. Different models of supervision have varying expectations about the setting of the agenda. It is our contention that the agenda for supervision is primarily the responsibility of the supervisee.

Supervision is the 'learning' and 'reflection' time for the supervisee and hence it is he or she who needs to have primary responsibility for setting the agenda. That said, it is important to recognise the limitations of 'supervisee knowing' and awareness and at times supervisors will need to lead.

Developmental approaches to supervision (Loganbill *et al.* 1982) remind us that supervisees do not always know what they do not know and, within the tensions and roles of supervision, there may be agenda items which the supervisor has a responsibility to draw to the supervisee's attention. It is therefore important that the supervisor also has an opportunity to contribute to the agenda. When a supervisor does place items on the agenda the process of supervision is subtly altered. It is therefore important for the supervisor to monitor his or her contributions. If the 'learning' is dominated by the supervisor the session risks becoming hijacked as one of instruction and control rather than of reflection and discovery.

As the agenda determines the content and focus of supervision it is important that adequate time is given to the setting of the 'agenda'.

Scenario 1 (a)
Marsha arrived at supervision directly from a service user interview. It had been a difficult session which had challenged her skills and patience. When she entered the supervision room she was delighted to give full vent to her recent experience. Her supervisor heard her story with interest and encouraged her to review and consider the interaction. Marsha left the supervision session feeling buoyant and good about her morning's work, but also troubled. She was aware that she had not dealt with any of the pressing issues she really wanted to discuss with the supervisor. The morning's visit had hijacked the supervision time and she was aware that whilst she appreciated the opportunity to reflect on that visit, it was not the priority of her caseload at present.

Priorities for discussion need to be considered regardless of the seemingly pressing items which arrive with the supervisee.

Scenario 1 (b)
Marsha arrived at supervision directly from a service user interview. It had been a difficult session which had challenged her skills and patience. When she entered the supervision room she was delighted to give full vent to her recent experience. Her supervisor heard her story with interest but stopped her after several minutes and asked if this was where she wanted to spend her supervision time. The supervisor was aware that Marsha was an enthusiastic practitioner who engaged strongly with her work and wanted to be sure that this issue was actually the best use of their time together. Marsha appreciated the intervention. She was able to table the 'other'

supervision issues and prioritise so that when she left she knew she had covered the most pressing concerns.

A cyclic structure

The Reflective Learning Model of supervision describes a four-stage cycle of supervision. These stages comprise the Event, the Exploration, the Experimentation and the Evaluation stage, illustrated in Figure 5.2.

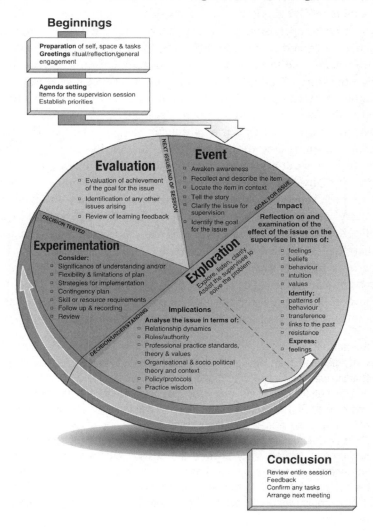

Beginnings

Preparation of self, space & tasks
Greetings ritual/reflection/general engagement

Agenda setting
Items for the supervision session
Establish priorities

Evaluation
- Evaluation of achievement of the goal for the issue
- Identification of any other issues arising
- Review of learning feedback

DECISION TESTED

Experimentation

Consider:
- Significance of understanding and/or
- Flexibility & limitations of plan
- Strategies for implementation
- Contingency plan
- Skill or resource requirements
- Follow up & recording
- Review

DECISION/UNDERSTANDING

NEXT ISSUE/END OF SESSION

Event
- Awaken awareness
- Recollect and describe the item
- Locate the item in context
- Tell the story
- Clarify the issue for supervision
- Identify the goal for the issue

GOAL FOR ISSUE

Exploration
Explore, listen, clarify
Assist the supervisee to solve the problem

Impact
Reflection on and examination of the effect of the issue on the supervisee in terms of:
- feelings
- beliefs
- behaviour
- intuition
- values

Identify:
- patterns of behaviour
- transference
- links to the past
- resistance

Express:
- feelings

Implications
Analyse the issue in terms of:
- Relationship dynamics
- Roles/authority
- Professional practice standards, theory & values
- Organisational & socio political theory and context
- Policy/protocols
- Practice wisdom

Conclusion
Review entire session
Feedback
Confirm any tasks
Arrange next meeting

Figure 5.2 The Reflective Learning Model

THE MODEL

Event: awareness of experience

The first stage of the supervision cycle considers the item on the agenda which the supervisee identified as being the most important.

The cycle begins with the identification of the goal for the issue or item which the supervisee has placed at the top of the agenda. The supervisee is asked to explain why he or she wishes to discuss this item. What does he or she want to resolve about the issue? How does the supervisee want to work on the issue in supervision? In order to answer this question the supervisee may need to spend some time reviewing the 'event' or 'experience' and identify, define and locate it in context. For some this process may lead to 'telling the story'. Through this 'telling' the supervisee may reawaken the thoughts and feelings which have been aroused by the situation and thus bring to the fore useful material for supervision.

For the supervisor this can be a difficult stage to manage. The task is to assist the supervisee to 'describe' the situation in order to reconnect with the events but not to become so immersed that he or she is unable to identify why this situation is worthy of supervision time. There is a risk that the supervisee (and the supervisor) will become so involved in the 'story' that they lose focus of what it is that the supervisee wishes to resolve. Keeping a tight focus on the goal clarifies the real issues and avoids the narrative 'swamping' reflection with detail. We have noted that it is the 'experience of many supervisees that they leave a supervision session with a sense of achievement but still carrying the same issue they brought to the session. The supervision time, useful though it may have been, has not been focussed on the problem at hand' (Davys 2001, p.92).

Scenario 2 (a)

Bert presented a list of four prioritised agenda items at the start of supervision. Starting with the first priority he and his supervisor launched into a detailed and thoughtful discussion of the service user situation. The supervisor encouraged Bert to explore the relationship and Bert was pleased with the new insights he gained. As time was running on they moved to the next items on the agenda. When Bert left supervision his sense of achievement diminished. He had really enjoyed the session but, despite the useful conversation and insights he had gained, he was leaving supervision with the actual problem still unresolved. The supervision session had moved in a direction which was very useful but not where Bert was seeking immediate assistance.

An engaged and competent supervisor will identify many issues which can be discussed in any situation placed before him or her. The importance, however, is to identify what the supervisee has identified as the problem. The core of supervision is to assist supervisees to identify and resolve their problems. This of course is not to deny supervisors the opportunity to broaden the supervisees vision of the situation but rather it is to ensure that supervisees are encouraged to learn to pinpoint their own issues and identify where they need particular assistance.

Scenario 2 (b)

Bert presented a list of four prioritised agenda items at the start of supervision. Starting with the first priority he launched into a detailed account of the service user situation. After a few minutes the supervisor stopped him and asked him 'What he wanted from the session. What was the issue he wanted to deal with in supervision concerning this service user?' Bert realised that part of the problem was that he didn't really know what he wanted. The supervisor encouraged him to consider this 'What would he need to have resolved in order to feel that the session had been useful?' 'How would he know he had got what he wanted?' and importantly 'How did he want the supervisor to assist him?' Bert realised that what he wanted was to review his interventions to date and plan for discharge. He wanted the supervisor to confirm whether or not he had covered the necessary ground and he wanted the supervisor's feedback on his discharge plan. He was interested in the supervisor's ideas but wanted to explore his own first – he did not want advice. When Bert left supervision he felt a great sense of achievement. He had really enjoyed the session and was leaving feeling affirmed for his work to date and with a clear plan for the coming weeks of work with this service user. His supervisor's feedback and comments had also given him some very useful insights which he valued and wanted to take away and reflect upon.

When the supervisee has clarified what he or she wants to get from supervision in relation to the issue presented the session can move to the next stage.

The task of clarifying 'the issue' for supervision is a valuable exercise for all supervisees and is vital in positioning the supervisee as an active, rather than a passive, participant in the supervision process. When a supervisee names the issue, identifies what sort of outcome he or she would like and is able to articulate the 'type' of assistance from the supervisor then the supervision process becomes one of joint responsibility and collaboration. Each participant has clearly defined separate roles and functions but has an equal responsibility to achieve a 'good' outcome from supervision. In this manner a more 'passive' supervisee is challenged to be accountable to the process and outcome of the session and joint ownership of the problem solving discussion is promoted. As supervisees become familiar with this process of establishing a clear question for supervision it becomes incorporated into their preparation and they arrive at supervision with clearly formulated goals. This not only saves precious supervision time but also often means that smaller supervision problems are more easily resolved leaving time for the more difficult dilemmas.

Supervisee passivity or disengagement may at times be disguised as autonomy and independence (Nye 2007). In an interesting exploration Nye notes that these practitioners bring solutions, answers or old rehashed cases to supervision. The supervisor has therefore 'limited access to the supervisee's on-going work or the supervisee's learning process' (Nye 2007, p.82). This stance on the part of the supervisee, Nye suggests, may be in response to cultural models which promote independence and autonomy as desirable traits and dependence as shameful. Using Vygotsky's model which promotes ongoing 'dependence' as necessary for learning and development throughout one's professional career, Nye translates this into the supervision arena and recommends supervisors to find an 'appropriate balance between dependence and independence' (p.96). By positioning the supervisee as co-explorer the Reflective Learning Model encourages ownership by the supervisee of both the problem and the solution.

Exploration

With a clear goal established for the agenda item the supervisor and supervisee can move on to the next stage of the cycle. Here, with knowledge of the supervisee's purpose or issue, the supervisor is able to focus his or her listening and ensure that the supervisee's question or dilemma is addressed. Just as it was the supervisee's role to identify the problem so it is for the supervisee to solve his or her own problem albeit with the assistance of the supervisor. The supervisor's role is to listen, explore and clarify. Whilst there is always a place in supervision for the supervisor to share ideas, practice wisdom and knowledge, premature sharing of this may prevent the supervisee from discovering his or her unique solutions. Hence, before creating new options, it is important for the supervisor and supervisee to start at the place where the supervisee stands so that they both understand and acknowledge what has already been done, what has been considered and how this has been experienced. Some supervisors approach supervision with a belief that they must 'solve' the problem for the supervisee. Such an approach not only creates stress and undue expectations on the performance of the supervisor but also diminishes the supervisee's role and responsibility for the session. Supervision is at risk of becoming a competitive sport where the supervisor attempts to resolve the supervisee's problems and the supervisee measures the success of supervision according to the supervisor's performance. In this situation independent growth and learning is problematic for the supervisee and there is considerable potential for game playing.

The exploration stage is divided into two parts: Impact (reflection) and Implications (conceptualisation).

The exploration stage is the place where the 'work' of supervision takes place. In order to undertake this work and to fully examine, understand and learn from a situation there needs to be balance between the emotive/ personal and the cognitive. The supervisee is thus encouraged to explore and examine the issue from two perspectives. The first is from a personal perspective: 'impact'. The second is from an analytical perspective: 'implications'.

'IMPACT'

Effective exploration of any supervision issue involves the consideration of that issue in terms of its impact or affect on self. The boundaries between 'self' and 'other' are important and supervision is a forum where these boundaries can be reviewed in order to identify and prevent any blurring or breach of this separation.

The supervisee is invited by the supervisor to locate him or herself in the situation. What impact has he or she had on the situation and how has he or she been affected by the situation? Feelings, beliefs, attitudes, behaviour and intuitions are considered. The supervisee's personal assumptions and expectations of his or her own reactions to the surprises and challenges of practice can be explored. 'Messy' feelings can be allowed to surface. Patterns from the past can be identified and transference acknowledged. From the place of 'knowing' what has occurred the supervisee has the opportunity to consider what could be different and to uncover what is not known. The supervisor's role is to create the space within which the supervisee can explore the possibilities of his or her own behaviour and feelings and those of the 'others'.

Scenario 3

Jackie was bothered by a situation she had encountered with the mother of a client with whom she was working. Her goal for supervision was to identify why she felt uncomfortable and to plan how to approach this woman in her next session. As the supervisor listened to her story he noticed that Jackie began to minimise the situation and to list reasons why she should just close the case. The supervisor pointed this out to Jackie and asked her what sorts of feelings she had about the situation and if this sort of situation had occurred before. Jackie was initially surprised but on reflection identified feelings of incompetence and inadequacy. These were old feelings which she associated with her very competitive and successful older sister. With her supervisor's assistance Jackie explored the transference with her sister and was readily able to recognise how those old feelings were intruding on, and undermining, her sense of competence in the present situation. She was surprised to recognise that her first response in these situations had been, and continued to be, one of withdrawal.

This stage of exploration also provides an opportunity for supervisees to express the emotional impact of their work. In a safe and trusting environment the emotions and feelings which inevitably accompany practice can be expressed, acknowledged and validated. The importance of the validation of the 'personal self' is well captured by Horney:

A healthy integration is a result of being oneself, and can only be attained on this basis. If we are sufficiently ourselves to have spontaneous feelings, to make our own decisions, and to assume responsibility for them, then we have a feeling of unity on a solid basis. (Horney 1970 cited in van Kessel and Haan 1993, p.9)

For professional practice, however, expression, or knowledge, of the personal self is not sufficient in itself but must be understood in the context of the 'professional' role:

Through this integration of personal competence and the professional role profile, the professional worker comes to acquire the different facets of the required professional ability in such a way that they are united in a whole of a higher order and s/he can function as a professional self. (van Kessel and Haan 1993, p.9)

In order to assist the development of this integrated 'professional self' the 'exploration' stage of supervision includes consideration and review of external points of reference from the broader fields of practice.

'IMPLICATIONS'

In the implication stage a wider consideration of the supervision issue occurs. There is an opportunity to balance the emotive with the cognitive. The supervisee is encouraged to consider the supervision issue from the perspectives of professional practice, values and theory, policy and protocols, and sociopolitical contexts. The broader value base and assumptions of practice and policy can be examined and tested for congruency whilst roles, plans and interventions can be scrutinised for effectiveness and viability. There is a potential here for intellectual rigour and for meaningful debate which tests professional values, assumptions and theory. In an active supervision relationship meaning can be made of the connection between theory and practice and new ideas and practice can be germinated. Discussion may also identify areas for development with regard to knowledge, skills or resources and ways in which these can be addressed. For newer practitioners links can be made to the key theory and research that underpins their practice or the supervisee can be guided to search for recent evidence. This is the place where the supervisor may share knowledge and experience in order to assist the supervisee to broaden his or her own knowledge base and so arrive at new possibilities and solutions. It is, however, important for the supervisor to ensure that the sharing of wisdom and knowledge is to enhance the supervisee's practice rather than to dictate action. In specific situations of safety and policy there may be reasons for supervisees to be 'directed' to take a course of action but these should be rare. The task of supervision is to develop the repertoire of the supervisee not to clone the supervisor.

Scenario 4

With the insights gained in the first part of the session Jackie and the supervisor considered how Jackie could change her response in future sessions with the mother. The supervisor encouraged Jackie to review the purpose of her work with the client, the contract which had been drawn up between her and the client and to identify how the mother contributed to that work. They considered Jackie's position as therapist in the situation and discussed issues of power and control. From this Jackie was able to clearly articulate her role with the client and the boundaries of that work. She was able to define where the mother fitted into that work and understood the limits of her authority as a therapist and potential areas of conflict. The next step, she decided, was to organise a meeting with the mother to clarify their different roles.

The exploration stage is the place where the supervisee is assisted to arrive at new understandings or actions and to do so with an accompanying clarity of his or her own self and actions.

Experimentation

When a supervisee has reached some form of decision or understanding it is important that this is tested to determine if it is possible and realistic and whether there are sufficient resources available for the decision to be successfully implemented. Thus the task for the supervisee in the experimentation stage is to examine the solutions or understandings she or he arrived at and to determine whether or not they are viable in practice.

When the identified outcome of supervision is in the form of an activity or strategy it is important that the proposed action is considered and tested. What are the possible consequences of the proposed action(s)? How might these plans be sabotaged and by whom? What contingency plans are possible? What strategies can be identified to address any resource deficiency? Future scenarios can be identified and significant conversations rehearsed and/or role played so that new roles, approaches and interventions can be trialled in a safe environment.

The importance of this stage of the supervision cycle is that it allows the 'solution' to be examined and tested to ensure that it is robust and that the supervisee is confident and has the required skills and knowledge to implement the plan. The detailed examination of the 'plan' or 'solution' not only tests its viability but also provides an opportunity for the supervisee to integrate new learning into his or her practice repertoire. This integration is vital if the supervisee is to be successful in the implementation of new skills and methods. When a supervisee is familiar with an action plan, has identified strategies to deal with possible obstacles and has a contingency plan of action should the original plan fail, the supervisee is able to move forward. Many excellent strategies and plans are lost when the supervisee leaves supervision without the confidence, clarity or skills to follow through the next step.

In some situations, particularly in the supervision of experienced practitioners, the exploration of an issue may bring insight and understanding rather than an 'action plan'. In these situations the experimentation stage allows these understandings and insights to be considered and integrated into practice theory and wisdom. Supervisees are encouraged to review their new understandings against established practice, existing ideas and theories and to identify where they may need to make adjustments. As with 'action plans' new 'understandings' can also be sabotaged, particularly if the new understanding or insight is accompanied by feelings of discomfort.

Scenario 5 (a)

Sandra has had a good supervision session. She had brought two issues to supervision and she and her supervisor had clarified and established a clear goal for each issue starting with the first priority. They had reflected on the impact of the situation and Sandra's role and interventions to date and through discussion Sandra had determined a course of action. Sandra was pleased with this and they moved on to the next issue. When she was on her way home, however, Sandra began to have doubts as to the usefulness of the agreed action. She could think of several things which could go wrong and in view of her busy workload doubted that it was worth the effort.

When the supervisee has ownership of a strategy and through practice or discussion has integrated this into his or her repertoire then follow-up action will be clear and can be approached with confidence.

Scenario 5 (b)

Sandra has had a good supervision session. She had brought two issues to supervision and she and her supervisor have clarified and established a clear goal for each issue starting with the first priority. They have reflected on the impact of the situation and Sandra's role and interventions to date and through discussion Sandra has determined a course of action. Sandra is pleased with this and suggests that they move on to the next issue. The supervisor, however, suggests that before they move on they spend a bit of time on establishing how Sandra is going to carry out the agreed course of action. 'What is the next step?' 'How and when and where is she going to do it?' 'What could go wrong and what would she do then?' The supervisor encourages Sandra to formulate how she is going to raise the issue with the person concerned and Sandra and the supervisor engage in an impromptu role play. As she seeks to find the 'right' words Sandra becomes increasingly clear about her stance and the issue she wants to convey to the other party. When she was on her way home Sandra felt very confident about her ability to follow through with her plan. She had identified what she needed to do. She knew she could do it and had considered her options if it all turned to custard.

It is important to clarify how the supervision issue will be recorded and reviewed. This not only establishes accountability but also provides additional encouragement to the more tentative or reluctant supervisee to follow through on the action. This process in the supervision cycle also provides the opportunity for any identified gaps of knowledge or skills to be recorded and linked to specific training opportunities.

Evaluation

The evaluation stage of the cycle marks the completion of the 'work' on the 'issue' which has been under discussion. The questions posed are 'Has the issue raised by the supervisee been addressed and resolved? Has the supervisee got what he or she wanted from supervision regarding this issue?' The supervisor and the supervisee may reflect on the 'process' of the discussion and identify specific learning and any additional issues which have arisen as a result of the discussion and identify future action. There is an opportunity for feedback. This opportunity for the supervisee to review whether he or she has met the identified goal allows space for reflection and prevents both the supervisor and the supervisee from prematurely moving on to the next issue.

The supervisor and the supervisee will then return to the agenda and address the second item, repeating the cycle once more.

The conclusion

The supervision session ends when the agreed time has elapsed or when all agenda items have been addressed. As noted earlier, good beginnings create the space for learning and good endings enable the learning to be retained and integrated for future use. The conclusion of the supervision session is very important, creating an opportunity for both parties to attend to the ongoing supervision relationship. As we discussed in Chapter 3, the medium through which supervision is conducted is the supervision relationship. The conclusion of the supervision session allows the time spent together to be considered as a process from start to finish. It is an opportunity for each party to reflect on the session and to give and receive feedback. This can be conducted in a formal structured manner or through informal review. What is important is to ensure that over time both supervisor and supervisee have the opportunity to comment on each other's participation, the usefulness of time spent, techniques used and to identify any changes which would improve the sessions. This review allows the supervision relationship to grow as well as the individual participants. Lizzio *et al.* refer to this process when they promote a regular monitoring of the supervision relationship 'to prevent or at least mitigate misunderstandings and assumptions' (Lizzio *et al.* 2009, p.137).

The conclusion is also the time for the nuts and bolts of the session to be noted. The confirmation of any tasks set, time frames for completion, issues for follow up and the date of the next meeting. Increasingly supervision dyads comprise practitioners and supervisors who come from different ethnic or cultural backgrounds and for some the session may end with a ritual. Rituals of beginning and ending are often the time where difference can be respected and acknowledged and where the supervision space can be affirming of the 'professional self'.

Professional practice in the current practice climate of the twenty-first century is experienced as uncertain, ever changing and anxiety laden. To survive the practitioner requires a strong professional self and an ability to critically analyse and assess themselves in a range of diverse situations. The old 'truths' of practice no longer apply and professionals are being called upon to make rapid decisions and take action in ever-changing professional landscapes. The Reflective Learning Model of supervision provides the basis for supporting and developing critical awareness. When a supervisee internalises the processes of reflective learning these can be accessed as a tool for 'in action' reflection.

Developing Expertise: Becoming a Critically Reflective Supervisor

Supervision is an inquiry into practice. It is a compassionate appreciative inquiry… In supervision we re-write the stories of our own practice… supervision interrupts practice. It wakes us up to what we are doing. When we are alive to what we are doing we wake up to what is, instead of falling asleep in the comfort stories of our clinical routines. (Ryan 2004, p.44)

Chapter 6 will address the development of supervisory expertise and explore the role of supervision in promoting reflective practice, critical reflection, social justice and the core values of the helping professions. This chapter will explicitly promote career-long critical reflection on practice, with supervision as one means to facilitating this. This is not to assume that supervision alone can enable ongoing professional excellence. It needs to be accompanied by other means of professional renewal: postgraduate study, research mindedness, a spirit of critical inquiry and so forth. Five topics will be explored in this chapter: six key tasks of becoming a supervisor; supervising ethical practice ethics; exploring critical reflection; culture and diversity in supervision and fostering supervisory expertise in interprofessional learning.

BECOMING A SUPERVISOR

When we first began teaching supervision to social workers in the early 1990s we were surprised at the lack of material which clearly identified skills for supervision. As Schindler and Talen (1996, p.110) expressed it, 'the prevailing assumption [was] that new supervisors knew how to supervise because they had been supervised. Learning supervision by osmosis seems to have been the underlying belief'. The literature rather uniformly focused on the rationale for supervision, the state of supervision during a period of rapid change and the development and critique of 'models' of supervision that were about functions rather than process. Students rightly criticised the traditional literature as assuming much more benign and well-resourced health and social care services than were a reality by the late 1980s. This situation has improved in recent decades as a number of authors have contributed useful perspectives which acknowledge the impact of the organisational climate (Bond and Holland 1998; Brown and Bourne 1996; Hawkins and Shohet 1989; Hughes and Pengelly 1997). Publications addressing supervision have rapidly grown in both numbers and professional orientation.

How do supervisors learn? How do they integrate new knowledge and incorporate new skills into the practice of supervision? A brief review of the international literature on supervisory training reveals a significant emphasis on developmental models of supervisory competence (Brown and Bourne 1996; Heid 1997; Hess 1986). A study of counselling supervisors found little evidence that supervisors improved greatly with experience alone (Worthington 1987). It seems that supervisors need training and good supervision for themselves in order to continue to grow in their practice. In essence these approaches all represent an extrapolation of developmental theories of practitioner development to the building of competence in new supervisors (Hess 1986; Loganbill *et al.* 1982; Watkins 1997).

Neukrug discusses the stages of theoretical integration for practitioners in the human services. This framework can be usefully recounted here as it incorporates many aspects relevant to the development of new supervisors. Neukrug describes a four-stage developmental process where practitioners begin at Stage 1 with *Chaos*, where practice is informed by rapid and haphazard responses and decisions (Neukrug 2008, p.80). New supervisors often feel pressured to attend quickly to supervisee concerns. Stage 2 of worker theoretical development is characterised by *Coalescence*, where theory is learned and one particular theoretical perspective may be favoured with the integration of techniques from other approaches. For beginning supervisors comfort may be gained from developing a thorough knowledge of one approach to supervision and being able to practise it. At Stage 3 practitioners demonstrate *Theoretical Integration*, where one theory or approach is predominately used with the integration of one or more alternative approaches. At this stage the supervisor becomes at ease with an integrated approach and their practice is more fluid. The fourth and final stage of this process is characterised by *Metatheory Analysis*, where practitioners have an 'appreciation of many theories and begin to explore the underlying commonalities and themes' (p.80). At this stage workers seek to understand the connections and effectiveness of combining discrete parts of differing theoretical perspectives to inform intervention strategies (pp.80–81). So too will supervisors draw from a range of approaches in their repertoire, being able to flexibly change approach to meet supervisee needs.

In our experience new supervisors initially focus on the anxiety provoking aspects of the supervisor role. There is ambivalence about the power and authority inherent in the role and the dominant question is 'will they like me?'. Table 6.1 sets out some common preoccupations and associated behaviours of new supervisors. Echoing Neukrug's formulation, supervisors experience a middle stage where they aim to adopt changes in their practice and experiment with new approaches, settling where there is a fit with their practice orientation. Finally, their own unique style develops as they integrate new learning, build their own practice wisdom and, like Hawkins and Shohet's 'process-in-context-centred' stage of development (2006, pp.73–74) supervisors have applied their 'helicopter skills' (p.73). Here supervisors are able to be 'with' the supervisee but simultaneously be thinking about promoting learning and supporting practitioner resilience. The phases of learning are summarised in Table 6.1.

Table 6.1 Phases of learning for new supervisors

Phase	Preoccupations of supervisors	Supervisory behaviours
Becoming a supervisor	• Ambivalence about taking responsibility • Focus on role rather than process • Hoping to impress and be in control • Fear of supervisee's critical gaze • Focus on relationship building • Focus on own competence *'Will they like me?'*	• Uncertainty about readiness • Focus on facts and premature problem solving • Avoidance of *or* over-reliance on authority • Limited range of interventions but enthusiastic about learning • Focus on own world view and style

Phase	Preoccupations of supervisors	Supervisory behaviours
Making connections	• Less emphasis on maintaining control • Anxiety about supervisee competence • Recognition of cultural differences • Adoption of the supervisory approach with best fit for their own theoretical orientation and practice style • Deepening skill in supervision process *'Do they respect me and am I helpful?'*	• Increasingly consistent handling of power and authority • Greater range of interventions and willingness to experiment • Active curiosity about different world views
Integrating theory and style, promoting change	• Critical reflection on own practice • Learning to trust judgement and practice wisdom • Conscious monitoring of cultural maps of self, supervisee and clients • Finding courage to work with difference • Seeking deeper learning *'Are they practising ethically and are they learning?'*	• Use of relationship to intervene and explore clinical issues • Awareness and comfort with own limits • Authority used appropriately within ethical domain • Greater ability to contain and interpret supervisee distress • Utilisation of 'helicopter' skills to use process effectively

THE DEVELOPMENT OF EXPERTISE IN SUPERVISION: SIX KEY TASKS

There are six key tasks facing a new supervisor. The first is to develop the ability to work with the perceptions and reactions of the supervisee forming much of the content and keeping the service user focus at arm's length. A second is to recognise the centrality of teaching and learning in supervision if supervision is to be effective. A clear separation of the process of supervision from the role of supervisor forms a further early focus in supervision and a third key task. The fourth task is to manage the new authority that comes with the role, and explore the importance of power in supervision. The fifth is to facilitate the safe expression of emotions in supervision. The sixth and final task is to maintain a balance in supervision with respect to risk.

Task 1: Working with the service user at arm's length

The process of becoming a supervisor involves developing the ability to stand back from using one's own knowledge and skills with clients and instead to facilitate this transformative learning in the supervisee. There are benefits for both supervisor and supervisee in this process. Urdang (1999) provided an interesting account of the experience of a group of social work practitioners as they began to supervise students on placement. This study found that supervisors' self-esteem increased both through mastery of a new skill and the validation, through teaching and supervising the student, of their own knowledge base and practice. Most supervisors indicated that supervising increased their self-awareness and capacity to analyse their own work, much of which had become automatic (Urdang 1999). When the supervisor identifies the clear boundaries between his or her awareness of knowledge and the supervisor's role in assisting the supervisee to develop his or her own unique and separate professional knowledge, the supervisor must consider the task of teaching and learning in supervision.

Task 2: Knowledge for supervision practice

The acquisition of formal knowledge for professional practice is considered to be a prerequisite for expertise and in supervision a new supervisor often calls upon his or her practice experience plus formal professional or disciplinary knowledge. As Valkeavaara puts it, 'the knowledge which we all have about our own profession, and which lies behind how we function but which we have difficulties in conceptualizing explicitly, has been termed as tacit knowledge' (Valkeavaara 1999, p.178). Citing Argyris (1991), Valkeavaara notes that 'learning to be an expert in one's own domain takes more than a string of successes, it also requires problematic situations in practical settings which trigger the processes of the construction and reconstruction of expertise' (Valkeavaara 1999, p.178).

Expertise comes from repeated instances of encountering problems for which routine solutions and responses do not exist. Solving problems in professional life includes various phases of examining and defining the problem, finding and implementing potential solutions, trying these in action and evaluating the outcomes. Engagement in such processes, of course, does not occur in a vacuum as practitioners work in complex social, cultural and organisational contexts, which are rich in both resources and challenges. In the twenty-first century the protocols surrounding many professions require discussion, reporting, evidence and a return to formal knowledge, before action is taken. Knowledge for practice is in this way transformed. Supervision that contributes to effective utilisation of research findings, for example, develops research-minded practice by modelling the spirit of inquiry and not slavishly repeating the 'what works' mantra.

The professions vary in terms of their degree of focus on formal knowledge, the utilisation of research findings, critical inquiry and the extent to which theory forms part of the supervisory process. We have seen in Chapter 1 that there is consistent inclusion of education in the major definitions of supervision, but interpretation of this is wide-ranging. Certainly in the supervision of pre-service professional education, learning is paramount. Here there is commonly an explicit focus in supervision on the integration of theory and 'practice' in a clinical or practical setting and considerable agreement that supervisors should model the integrated approach. Baxter argues that the oft described theory–practice gap in nursing means that 'if students do not have theory-based practice modelled for them then it may actually result in 'de-professionalization' (Baxter 2007, p.104).

Task 3: Defining process and role

The third task facing a new supervisor is to distinguish between the process of supervision and the role of the supervisor. In many organisational settings this is made difficult because of the blurring of clinical supervision process and frontline management functions. In our supervisor education programmes we have found that new supervisors struggle with this dual focus and have often been hindered by supervision literature which privileges function over process. Seeking certainty, many supervisors have found the safety in a prescriptive model. We know from the countless conversations that we have had with supervisors and practitioners that too often supervision, in times of stress and risk-consciousness, reverts to checklist approaches that smother reflective practice. In a risk-averse professional environment practice may become reactive and mechanistic rather than reflective and creative. 'Checklist' supervision may indeed ameliorate against the anxiety practitioners and supervisors feel but it does not necessarily improve the practice (Gillingham 2006; Gillingham and

Bromfield 2008). Smythe, MacCulloch and Charmley (2009) also caution against over-reliance on technical approaches and suggest that 'the real mark of excellence can only come when we allow ourselves to become lost in the unfolding of each unique moment of a supervision relationship... Some of our most precious moments have come when that process has in some magical way taken flight and given wings to all involved' (Smythe *et al.* 2009, p.19).

Task 4: The management of authority and power

A major issue in the development of new supervisors, and our fourth key task, is the management of the authority that comes with the role and power in its various forms. Richmond suggests that traditional approaches to individual supervision have embedded a 'formally structured process of individual development', in which power relations are embedded through both managerial power and professional authority (2009, p.544). Richmond cites McNamara, Lawley and Towler (2007, pp.79–84) who suggest that power can be asserted through empowerment, 'power with', or disempowerment, 'power over'. They also describe 'power within', in which peer and group models enable supervisors to relinquish power to develop mutual supervision processes (Richmond 2009, p.545).

Key to the effective and non-oppressive use of power and authority in supervision is the clear understanding of the differences between the role of supervisor and the process of supervision. The supervisory role, whether or not it is embedded within line responsibility functions of an organisation, is imbued with authority and power. Both supervisor and supervisee bring into the relationship their ideas and beliefs about authority along with the 'baggage' of previous experiences, good and bad. There may be ambivalence about the extent to which the participants want to see power exerted within this complex relationship, in which knowledge itself is a major source of power. Both may fear being 'found out' as having less knowledge than they should. Both need to be able to create a place where it is all right not to know. Supervisors often fear that they will be expected to be 'all knowing' and the authors have seen hundreds of videos of supervision sessions and witnessed the struggle many supervisors have to resist 'telling' rather than facilitating, and the anxiety felt by new supervisors when a challenging situation is presented in supervision.

Pack describes a personal experience of supervision in which she felt the underlying subtext in the relationship was 'do as I say' and:

> remember I'm in charge. Here was the supervisor who defined my role as being one of unerring compliance for the common good of

all. I was reminded in supervision constantly that she was sharing her years of experience with me to save me from what she considered to be my own incompetence. This experience reinforced my negative introjects (which were already well-developed). My identification with her judgment that was highly critical of my not being 'good enough', led to cycles of demoralization, shame, retroflection and withdrawal. (Pack 2009b, p.66)

Later, writes Pack, 'I [could] empathize with the supervisor who was struggling to find her voice within the team and was anxious about her professional identity and authority as a new manager.' She notes that in this situation there was no process in place to support 'the kind of dialogical engagement that would have allowed both of us to explore the process of what was occurring between us, or so it seemed from my perspective' (Pack 2009b, p.67). The adoption of a collaborative approach and a conceptualisation of supervision as a learning activity, rather than a managerial process, enables supervisors to 'acknowledge that learning is a shared adventure' (Hair and O'Donoghue 2009, p.76).

Hughes and Pengelly distinguish three sources of authority which are useful to consider in the supervisory relationship. These are 'role authority' conferred by the organisation, 'professional authority' earned through credible practice of knowledge and skill and, last, 'personal authority'. This latter form of authority comes from the individual's demeanour and ability within professional relationships to exercise the other two without challenge (Hughes and Pengelly 1997, pp.168–169). Too much reliance on any of these sources of authority leads to distortions in supervision relationships. Too little exercise of legitimate authority can undermine accountability and lead to the collapse of safe practice (Morrison 2001). Supervisees need to know that their supervisor has the confidence to exercise authority if needed in order to challenge unsafe practice.

Coming to terms with the manifestations of authority incumbent in the supervisory role is a significant developmental issue for new supervisors. There are some key tensions to be resolved in the transition to becoming a supervisor. First, new supervisors need to explore their thoughts and feelings about the change in status from full-time direct client work to supervision or to a 'management' role if this applies. Second, there may be some concern over the abandonment of clients for personal promotion. There are new relationships to be forged with colleagues, managers and supervisees. New supervisors often feel that they are exposed to a critical gaze around 360 degrees. It is helpful if educational opportunities for new supervisors explore these tensions within the social and cultural contexts in which they work.

Task 5: Facilitating safe expression of emotions

The fifth key task is to facilitate the safe expression of emotions in supervision. This topic will be discussed in more detail in Chapter 8. As we have noted above, supervisors support practitioners to manage the anxiety and uncertainty generated by the work. The emphasis on risk management and increasing regulation and proceduralism in health and social care creates tension and uncertainty and thus the political context of practice ensures that anxiety levels remain high. In response to this, recent approaches to supervision emphasise the use of self, and explore concepts such as 'mindfulness' in practice, which are seemingly miles apart from evidence-based practice. On the one hand, practitioners can feel pressure to be 'scientific' and objective and turn to empirical models of practice; on the other hand practitioners are urged to trust their feelings and listen to hunches. Supervision provides a space in which these competing voices can be heard and attended to. And this means making room and creating safety for feelings to be exposed. If supervision provides opportunities for the safe expression and exploration of these feelings they may be a source of potential evidence about the degree of risk present. It is important in supervision to value the emotional responses of practitioners as contributing to reflection and therefore safe practice. Ruch describes how the 'linking of feelings and thoughts generates emotional development and cognitive development – thoughtfulness – and contributes to the construction of structures for thinking' (Ruch 2007a, p.662).

Facilitating the expression of feelings in supervision requires careful listening and observation to assess supervisee emotion, what they might be holding back, and the ability of the supervisor to understand his or her own feelings and to manage these in the supervisory relationship. Morrison (2007, p.255) notes that emotions are 'deep level signals about information that demands attention, as to whether a situation is to be approached or avoided. The rapid appraisal of such signals conveys the meaning of the situation and is often a trigger for action.' Emotional intelligence, which includes the ability to recognise and manage one's own feelings, assists supervisors to recognise the feelings of supervisees and influences the way supervision relationships are managed (Dolgoff 2005).

Referring to the work of Goleman (1995), Dolgoff identifies five domains where the 'emotionally intelligent' supervisor will display 'mastery' (2005, p.8). These domains include knowing one's emotion: knowing one's own feelings brings insight and understanding. A lack of such awareness puts supervisors at risk of 'the unacknowledged impacts of those feelings'. Manage one's emotions: an awareness of one's own emotion leads to an ability to deal with those emotions and thus 'recover more quickly from life's stresses and problems'. Motivate oneself: this domain includes the ability to 'organise one's emotions' in order that goals can be achieved. Recognise emotions in others: this domain includes the ability to read and empathise with the feelings of others and so accurately respond to these emotions. Handling relationships: the ability to 'competently handle one's own emotions in relation to those of others, and to be interpersonally effective' (p.8).

As described above, emotional competence on the part of the supervisor facilitates the expression and management of feelings in supervision. It is interesting to note how often 'support' is included as a function of supervision with little attention to the nature of the support offered. Most practitioners seem fairly clear that what is required of their supervisors is more than empathetic 'hand-patting'. As Carroll and Gilbert (2005, p.76) state, 'emotions are not just internal reactions but connect us – in ways we sometimes cannot even imagine – to life and others. Far from being simply a distraction to tolerate or accept passively, feelings become the "inner rudder" of our lives, personally and professionally.'

The highly charged crisis mode of operating in many health and social care environments, however, frequently mitigates against healthy expression of uncomfortable feelings. As Ruch states 'Paradoxically, the ability to admit to one's subjective position, uncertainties and ability to 'not know' is a crucial ingredient in the reflective process' (Ruch 2007, p.644) and yet is often undervalued or seen as unprofessional in the workplace. Approaches to dealing with the emotional content of supervision can include one in which feelings are subject to a technical *focus*. A contrasting, and more collaborative *reflective* approach focuses *on* feelings and can foster more reflective and effective practice. The features of these contrasting approaches are outlined in Table 6.2.

In an exploratory process, feelings can be both accepted and valued as a rich source of information and ideas. If only the accommodation of feelings is required, then the supervisor will rely on prescriptive approaches in which reflection is minimised to avoid close attention to the use of self in practice. For many supervisees, learning about the self in practice is the greatest challenge. Heath and Freshwater (2000, p.1303) note that 'when processes to encourage learning about self are used, the necessary high challenge must be accompanied by high support, and it should be noted that the creation of a therapeutic environment and the therapeutic use of self are not synonymous with therapy and should not be approached as such'. What may often be ignored is the extent to which supervisors feel under-skilled to cope with supervisee emotion, and their struggles with their own feelings. It is in this regard that training in some process-focused supervision mode, such as the 'Seven-eyed supervision: process' model described by Hawkins and Shohet (2006), can assist supervisors of all professions. The building of greater facilitation skills will develop confidence in supervisors who may not have been exposed to the development of interpersonal skills in their previous training. In a safe environment, especially learning with other beginning supervisors, it is possible to experiment widely with a range of strategies which can be constructed, challenged and rehearsed (Davys and Beddoe 2008).

Table 6.2 Feelings in supervision

Technical focus	Reflective focus
• Managing uncertainty through seeking and applying rules • Low tolerance of feelings • Feelings to be tidied away • Prescriptive interventions • Task-oriented practice • Blueprints to determine action • Focus on limited outcomes • Overemphasis on risk • Supervisor retains authoritative stance • Relationship is more hierarchical	• Greeting uncertainty as opportunity • Open exploration of feelings • High emotional support • Nurturing self-awareness • Valuing feelings as information in practice • Facilitative and challenging interventions • Critical reflection on other voices • Experimentation and creativity • Exploring reasoning about risk • Supervisor's feelings can be expressed • Relationship is more collaborative

Heath and Freshwater (2000, p.1303) note that both authors have seen 'practitioners develop an open unknowing stance in relation to their practice via clinical supervision that is process orientated and supervisee defined...such supervision may encourage former closed technically competent nurses to learn questioning practice and to develop primarily client orientated concerns'.

Task 6: The management of risk

As noted in Chapter 4, the identification and reduction of risk has become a significant feature of professional practice in contemporary health and social care. Risk focuses our attention on danger and in current conversations there is much emphasis on dangerous situations, reducing 'professional dangerousness' and dangerous workplaces. Our sixth key task for beginning supervisors is to achieve balance in this environment of risk awareness. Parton (1996) has argued that in this climate both services and professions are judged in terms of how they assess and respond to risk. There are a number of background themes to this. First, in the last few decades there has developed a heightened community intolerance of professional 'misadventure' and greater awareness of social problems. Knowledge of the phenomenon of abuse of service users, fear of harassment, fears of being harmed, privacy concerns, failure in duty of care, violence in the workplace, the effect of overexposure to awful situations are among the many highly charged issues faced by practitioners. All of these issues create a sense of health and social care work being like a 'minefield'.

Second, the removal of the 'paternalistic, benevolent cloak' worn by previous generations leaves practitioners less secure in their identity (Parton 1996, p.103–104). In services subject to high levels of media scrutiny such as local authority/statutory social work and mental health services, one of the consequences has been a narrowing of roles. Practice emphasis has shifted from preventive and development-focused practice to 'management' of those most vulnerable client groups deemed to be 'high risk'. Risk has in itself become a criterion for targeting scarce resources. Alaszewski and Coxon suggest that large bureaucracies (such as health and social care institutions) adopt formal risk approaches which involve collecting and analysing information. This reflects 'the aspiration to control the world and its uncertainties… The required investment of time and resources means that the formal rational approach tends to be restricted to contexts in which such investments are worthwhile, i.e. the threats and potential benefits are high' (Alaszewski and Coxon 2009, p.204). Demonstrations of trustworthiness are seen in the practices developed to make assessments and in this environment supervision has become one of those mechanisms.

For supervisors the management of risk can become a constant source of stress. The feared outcomes may range from simple 'botch-ups', which threaten the team's reputation, to serious harm to service users, staff or the public. Carried to extremes this can stifle practice. Innovation may feel too risky. In one sense risk is about the probability of 'winning' and the estimated costs of 'losing' and it is vital for supervisors and their supervisees to retain a strong sense of hopefulness to balance the sense of imminent danger that pervades their practice world.

EXPLORING CRITICAL REFLECTION

Contemporary education for the professions has been greatly influenced by reflective learning approaches to practitioner development (Bond and

Holland 1998; Gould and Taylor 1996; Johns and Freshwater 2005; Redmond 2004). In this shift good practice is promoted by teaching a framework for continual self-evaluation and improvement rather than a traditional master/student relationship. Much pre-service education for nursing, social work and the allied health professions encourages the development of reflection skills during preparatory education. Chapter 5 has outlined the Reflective Learning Model of supervision which provides a process-oriented framework to foster reflective learning in supervision sessions by making reflection central, rather than peripheral.

A reflective practice process fosters the development of an 'internal supervisor'. 'Reflection on practice' occurs with a professional supervisor and reflects on action which has already occurred. On-the-job reflection is 'reflection in practice' and applies to learning in the field of professional practice. Fook and Gardner see a reflective approach as affirming other ways of knowing, such as personal experience and its interpretation in supporting a holistic understanding of the complexity of experience that practitioners encounter in their day-to-day work. A reflective approach 'tends to focus on the whole experience and the many dimensions involved: cognitive elements; feeling elements; meanings and interpretations from different perspectives' (Fook and Gardner 2007, p.25). Such an approach facilitates the discovery of the kinds of knowledge relevant to the unpredictability of modern day practice. Bond and Holland (1998, pp.107–115) offer some intuitive methods of reflection as a starting point for reflective practice, as they have found nurses can struggle to make the shift from activity to reflection. They also stress the importance of supervisees 'using an experiential learning cycle while you work, rather than only waiting for your clinical supervision sessions [as an] ultimate aim in building these reflective skills' (p.17).

The *Critical Reflection* approach (Fook and Gardner 2007, p.27) is 'a model for improving practice' which involves a bottom-up understanding of theory and practice, the intent being to close the gap between espoused theory and enacted theory in practice. Fook and Askeland acknowledge the contribution of Brookfield (1995) when they state that what 'makes *critical* reflection critical is the focus on power...which allows the reflective process to be transformative... In this latter sense, critical reflection must incorporate an understanding of personal experiences within social, cultural and structural contexts' (2007, p.522). The vignette that follows illustrates Johns' point that reflection is:

> being mindful of self, either within or after experience, as if a
> window through which the practitioner can view and focus self

within the context of a particular experience, in order to confront, understand and move toward resolving the contradiction between one's vision and actual practice. (Johns 2005, p.2.)

Vignette – Lisa

Lisa, a counsellor in her fourth year of practice, starts a new job in an infertility treatment clinic. She works mainly with couples considering specialised IVF treatment who are obliged to have counselling prior to making decisions about treatment. It is hard to get on to the programme. Couples find it very stressful, and face financial, emotional and social challenges. The 'rollercoaster of emotions' for couples in infertility is well reported. Treatment regimes intensify this.

Lisa comes to supervision following a very busy first few weeks and seems stressed and quite agitated. She tells her supervisor she often finds that the male partners, in the couples she sees, are very hard to engage with in counselling. She calls them 'resistant', 'angry', 'defended', 'rigid'. She says their behaviour makes her suspicious and the more she notices that they 'resist' counselling the more she thinks they are probably 'control freaks' or abusive.

Lisa is not a novice and her supervisor decides to unsettle her implicit assumptions using probing and challenging reflective questions. The dialogue below is a summary of key questions and responses:

Supervisor	Supervisee
What sits behind these assumptions?	Men are difficult. Men don't want to deal with emotions. Men aren't supportive. Men have too much power in these situations.
What values and beliefs might sit behind these ideas?	My feminist beliefs. My awareness of women being oppressed.
Do these feelings and concerns seem similar to other experiences?	On my placement I worked with couples who were struggling with difficult pre-school children and the men were always really angry.

Supervisor	Supervisee
How do these emotions affect your use of knowledge in your practice?	I forget why I'm doing the counselling and just want to fight them.
Can you name these feelings? (deeper level reflection)	I feel angry when men argue with me. I feel less powerful than them when I should feel more powerful because I am the professional here.
How do you conceptualise your use of power in this practice?	Clients come to counselling because that's the policy but they should just accept it and support their wives. Just get on with it if they want the treatment. I have some deep attitudes about middle class people who are thwarted in their desire to have children.
Having discovered these beliefs and thoughts what are your feelings?	I feel shocked that I have such a long list of negative thoughts about clients.
What is that feeling of shock about?	I feel that I shouldn't be negative about clients. But then I'm a feminist and I see women so often disempowered by controlling men around fertility issues.

Next steps

There is a disjuncture here between Lisa's idea of professional neutrality and feminist advocacy.

At this point what does she want to change?

What does she see as the appropriate way to manage this disjuncture?

Supervisor	Supervisee
How would you want to act/ feel differently?	I want to be able to understand where those feelings come from and put them in a place that is mine, not my work with clients.
Can you reconcile these two parts of who you are as a practitioner?	I need to stay mindful of my potential to make precipitate judgements. I can look out for my female clients without assuming their male partners aren't vulnerable too.

Supervisor	Supervisee
What might be happening for the men in these couples?	Lack of power for men who feel vulnerable and exposed. People who are dealing with infertility face many intrusive discussions and tests. Counseling may feel like another invasion of privacy.
What's your learning here?	I need to remember that people have multiple and complex reasons for behaving in particular ways. I need to acknowledge that power in professional encounters is not always clear cut.

Next steps

Lisa has started to resolve the disjuncture. Her supervisor guides her to consider alternative ways of engaging the men in the couples she works with. She rehearses some possible interventions. She decides that her 'homework' is to locate some research about men and infertility and to make a time to consult a male counsellor in a similar service.

Through the conflict of contradiction, the commitment to realize one's vision, and understanding why things are as they are, the practitioner can gain new insights into self and be empowered to respond more congruently in future situations within a reflexive spiral towards developing practical wisdom and realizing one's vision as a lived reality. The practitioner may require guidance to overcome resistance or to be empowered to act on understanding. (Johns 2005, p.2)

Exploring culture and diversity in supervision

In countries with a colonial past, such as Australia, Canada, Aotearoa /New Zealand, professional practices came pre-packaged with inherent cultural frameworks of models of learning and supervision. Given the understanding of the importance of isomorphism in supervision practice that has been explored in Chapter 2 (Edwards and Chen 1999), the developments of new approaches to professional practice have required new thinking about whether traditional models of supervision work. Webber-Dreadon writes: 'supervision primarily reflects the cultural values and aspirations of the typically monocultural dominant Pakeha [NZ European origins] group' and the development of alternative indigenous models has 'suffered the impact of subtle continued colonization through the process of avoidance and non-encouragement' (Webber-Dreadon 1999, pp.7–8). Social service agencies are keen to employ indigenous workers to ensure cultural values and perspectives are present but then do not always 'have a process for inviting them in and ensuring they are part of the practice process' (Bradley, Jacob and Bradley 1999, p.6).

New supervisors (of all professions) need to recognise the limiting nature of one world view and how extraordinarily hard it is to ensure another view is able to be freely expressed and incorporated into thinking about the professional practice work we do in health and social care. Being bi-cultural or having experienced and reflected on other 'differences' may assist the supervisor to be more sensitive to different cultural frameworks for practice.

Supervisors from dominant cultures are particularly vulnerable to unconsciously perpetuating institutional racism through assuming models of supervision that are grounded in the dominant culture. In cross cultural relationships in supervision there is often a great deal of unspoken 'talk' happening that impacts on the formation of an open relationship with a high degree of trust. Participants often talk about feeling that there are unstated challenges around competence and that there is the potential for collusion around issues of poor practice. It is simply too scary for either party to ask for or give uncensored, thoughtful and constructive feedback. Supervisors and supervisees who ignore or minimise the differences between them risk mirroring the tensions inherent in oppressive worlds in which their clients struggle.

Ultimately, reflection on cultural assumptions leads practitioners towards an empowering openness which challenges and renews vision. Within reflective supervision a space is created where questions can be asked and cultural differences are valued. Down (2000) writing about supervision of family therapy, values the process of looking for consonance and dissonance between the family, the worker and the supervisor's cultural maps. Unpacking the nature of cultural identity suggests that supervisors unpack their own cultural narratives in considering both their relationship with their supervisees and the professional work that all are engaged in (Hair and O'Donoghue 2009, p.78). This means recognising the journeys by which we all arrived in our current circumstances: our heritage, our migration stories, our different social, cultural and political lens and the ecology of how and where we live and work.

CRITICAL INQUIRY IN SUPERVISION

Noble and Irwin argue that applying a critical lens in supervision will require supervisors to 'explore and reflect on the way the supervisors, the supervisees and the agencies work with the service users/clients' thus ensuring that 'practitioners' actions and those of the organization are more explicit and conscious' (Noble and Irwin 2009, p.354). As noted in Chapter 2, Hair and O'Donoghue (2009) have addressed how power, culture and gender influence relationships and yet are not explicitly addressed in most supervision models. These authors, from Canada and New Zealand respectively, argue that social constructionist supervision differs from traditional approaches to supervision in several important ways. First, following the principles of the strengths-based approaches to supervision described in Chapter 2, it is important for supervisors to develop a collaborative approach and ensure that supervisees manifest agency in a co-constructive process in 'supervision conversations' (p.77). Recognition of plurality and diversity of knowledge requires supervisors educated in the dominant Western models of supervision to practice 'continual critical self-reflection'.

Hair and O'Donoghue's approach brings to the foreground issues of social justice in practice and how supervision sessions can address 'structural barriers such as poverty, legislative policies, and suitable housing alongside clients' relational conflicts and distresses' (p.78). Social constructionist supervisors 'ask "curious" questions about idiosyncratic descriptions of local community knowledge of the supervisees and clients, including the influence of dominant sociopolitical and economic contexts such as national laws, tribal expectations, and spiritual understandings' (p.78). Similar questions to those used in the Reflective Learning Model of supervision are used here, for example: "I wonder..." or "I am curious about..." can help to create a transparent stance and stimulate collaborative knowledge production' (p.79).

Schön (1987) suggests that professionals are critically aware of ethical and moral choices and the implications of decisions when faced with problems in situ. Supervision is always best located in the realm of continuing development during professional careers. Schön's work challenged the notion that professional competence was largely linked to the application of specific technical and/or theoretical knowledge which was gained primarily through preparatory education. Rather he suggested that competent professionals think, reflect, experiment and act within practice situations, thus constructing a more fluid notion of competence. Competence includes the ability to enter into dialogue about difficult situations, to apply thoughtfulness, open-mindedness and moral reasoning to those problems.

Supervision is often seen as the site for this continuing development of practitioners' ethical competence. Supervisors would ensure ethical competence, a major part of the actual 'oversight' component of the role, through questioning actions, seeking the other point of view, considering alternative responses or interpretations and most importantly encouraging and challenging practitioners to think critically. This would be fine if ethics was a simple thing. An important outcome of effective supervision is the creation of a good 'home' for ethical decision making in an era of competing agendas. Banks (2008, p.1239) explains that the 'post modern' turn in sociological and philosophical thinking has contributed to a questioning of universal values, all-embracing foundational theories (including ethical theories) and the legitimacy and roles of 'expert' professional practitioners. This complicates ethical thinking in professional practice. Bagnall (1998) argues that professions are less confident and sure of their legitimate authority in the full gaze of a critical media and public and that the 'rulebook' of ethical codes is no longer absolute. He suggests that enhanced tolerance and understanding of difference and diversity in our society means greater contradiction in the moral dimensions of our professional and personal lives. Situational ethics tend to be grounded in a particular cultural context in contrast to the past 'universal claims' for moral rightness (Bagnall 1998). Paradoxically the professionalisation of those professions more recently regulated has seen a proliferation of codes. New supervisors may feel a very deep sense of insecurity about how to guide ethical decision making. Scaife (2001, p.125) suggests that traditional ethical principles offer a framework for thinking through the challenges of practice. She suggests that explicit consideration of these principles 'gives a degree of assurance that, whatever the actual outcomes, decisions have been taken from an ethical standpoint' and in this era of risk management, 'documenting the thought processes that underpin a decision can also protect the professional in the event of subsequent litigation' (p.125).

What is required of supervisors is the development of an essentially reflective practice incorporating the following qualities: an empathetic responsiveness to the subjective experience of others; sensitivity to the diversity of knowledge and world views, and the recognition that each professional encounter is unique. In complex multiprofessional, multi-agency contexts a supervisor may also need to negotiate contested realities. Awareness of one's own limits of knowledge and competence also underpins a willingness to accept that you cannot meet all the professional needs of each supervisee, and to seek further consultation when indicated.

INTERPROFESSIONAL LEARNING FOR SUPERVISORS

In the first edition of their excellent text for supervision 'in the helping professions', Hawkins and Shohet (1989) identified the way in which interprofessional and indeed inter-agency dynamics could hinder effective services to clients of health and social care services. Since then there has been considerable emphasis on the importance of interprofessional relationships. It is our experience that multidisciplinary exploration of practice challenges can lead to the enrichment of supervision (Beddoe and Davys 2008; Davys and Beddoe 2008). New supervisors benefit from being able to share ideas, experiences and values in relation to practice scenarios from health and social care which in turn allows similarities and differences to emerge and to be considered. We recommend that supervision training is interprofessional in order for new supervisors to be freed from disciplinary constraints; notwithstanding that there will be professional practice guidelines, ethics and agency requirements (Beddoe and Davys 2008). We noted previously that 'when supervision is freed from the minutiae of clinical content and procedure, the generic nature of professional supervision practice comes to the fore...regardless of profession, practitioners often bring the same things to supervision: stress, anxiety, conflict, ethical and moral dilemmas, "stuckness" and so forth' (Beddoe and Davys 2008, p.37).

The provision of an interactive learning environment for multiprofessional groups which enables a realisation of the common purpose, and often shared values about supervision, creates a medium for deeper learning. This can be undertaken through an external programme or within an organisation. Rains (2007) found that new supervisors in a community health service, regardless of profession, struggled with similar issues and needed ongoing support and development. The common issues reported by Rains were:

- difficulty in setting contracts with supervisees

- a struggle to stay focused during sessions and a lack of structure around sessions

- difficulty with exploring emotional aspects of the work

- lack of confidence which meant supervisors 'were frequently letting sessions fall into a chat' (p.60)

- supervisee issues related to their colleagues that left supervisors feeling 'drawn into collusion around workplace dynamics' (p.60)

- an overwhelming feeling that supervisees should be allowed/need to 'vent all their feelings'

- the temptation to fall into problem-solving mode

- lack of confidence in engaging reluctant supervisees.

(Rains 2007, p.60)

Interprofessional learning programmes can provide rich opportunities for small group work using scenarios. Common thematic materials can assist new supervisors to 'reflect upon and interrogate their own beliefs and practices with minimum threat to their personal integrity' (Santoro and Allard 2008, p.174). Santoro and Allard also suggest that learning groups do not have to 'focus on finding solutions to problems'. Stories of success can provide rich opportunities for discussion and debate through the presentation of both confirming and alternative views (2008, p.174). Dirkx and colleagues (2004, p.38–39) suggest that because professionals approach professional development wanting 'something I can use on Monday morning' there must be opportunity to balance content or technical knowledge with 'stories' that enable people to make sense of new ideas: 'as one seeks to make sense of new information or technical skills within the concreteness of practice, the meaning of both is reconstructed' (p.39).

A LEARNING VIGNETTE

The following example is provided in order to illustrate the potential of interprofessional supervision learning contexts (This example and the discussion is adapted from Beddoe and Davys 2008, pp.38–39, and used with the kind permission of the editors of *Social Work Now*, the practice journal of the New Zealand Child, Youth and Family Service.) A group of learners in a supervision training course (including nurses, a general practitioner, a naturopath, a mental health social worker, and several child protection social workers) is presented with a scenario. It is a problem-based scenario which is useful because it has highly emotional content, contains the seeds of interprofessional difference and conflict, and is highly realistic as the kind of 'worry' a clinical practitioner might bring to supervision, where clinical (in this case medical) knowledge is not the main dimension of the problem. This case example is fictional and it has been used in teaching settings on many occasions. The discussion which follows and the views expressed by the 'professionals' are fictionalised and a composite of many different discussions.

Vignette – Timothy

Your supervisee, Timothy, who works in a community health setting, comes to supervision with the following situation on the top of his agenda. He is providing post-operative wound care for Melissa (9) who has multiple, chronic health problems. The treatment plan was provided by the surgical registrar at the hospital and Melissa is due to go back in for a check-up next week. The parents of the child are also engaging the services of an alternative healer. The alternative healer does not support the medical treatment and the parents are following the healer's regime. The alternative treatment is very expensive and Timothy knows that the family is on a very limited budget and is already in huge debt. He has had conversations with the parents and the healer to no avail. Timothy has talked to the family's GP who advised seeking an earlier check-up appointment if the family won't bring Melissa in to her surgery. The alternative treatment is not working and the wound is now infected and at today's home visit Melissa complained of considerable pain. The community health social worker angrily told Timothy in the staff room that this is bordering on a child protection issue and he has to do something soon. Timothy is feeling torn between his concern for Melissa and his desire to maintain a relationship with the parents.

The task for the group was to identify the main issues for Timothy's next supervision session. Inevitably, supervision issues were left to one side while this group of confident and expressive professionals responded to the content. We'll let the reader decide who might have said what in this list of comments that reflect the kinds of statements and questions heard in many group discussions:

'Bordering on child protection – it is abuse!'

'There's a clear duty of care here.'

'What about family rights and empowering people?'

'The paramount rights of the child…'

'What about the views of the rest of the family?'

'Has anyone talked to Melissa?'

'It's a simple thing – they have to be told they'll lose her if they don't comply with treatment.'

'He's got to refer her to the child protection agency.'

'No, he's right; he has to maintain the relationship – she's a long-term client!'

'Yes, but she could die if she gets blood poisoning.'

'The family loves her; they're trying to do the right thing...'

What the case study shows is that all the participants bring their own assumptions, reactions, disciplinary and theoretical orientation, emotional responses and political perspectives to this one situation. It demonstrates how much is going on beneath the surface when people encounter a situation.

In the discussion there was a lot of playful point scoring but this may not be fun in a real situation where power and authority are real. The critical question is whose views will prevail when all these differences are present in a real organisational context? Where is the power? Who has the mandate to decide action? What is the role of supervisors when dealing with complex situations where there are multiple perspectives and stakeholders' views to hold in balance?

After some animated discussion the group was able to focus on the supervision issues. They came up with a very sensible plan to support the supervisee. Their exploration of the issues in the scenario enabled them to debate their various perspectives on this case. This debate, freed from the usual power dynamics, was robust and passionate. The learners enjoyed the opportunity to have this discussion but were quickly able to return their focus on the supervision issues while realising that they had things to learn from the differences in their approaches to the same situation.

Professional practitioners develop a cognitive map where personal characteristics and experience, values and beliefs determine some key aspect of their practice (Hall 2005, p.190). Professional values also emphasise aspects of working with service users differently; for some professions, science rules decision making and interaction with service users, for others listening to client stories is what is valued. Language is often an important means of differentiation, and discussions like that above, which, in focusing on a specific aspect of supervision, often highlight the different ways of describing what we do. There is considerable support for improved collaboration amongst profession, and sectors in health and social care, especially in primary care to ensure safety of children and vulnerable adults (Marsh 2006). Marsh suggests key elements may include knowing about the other professionals' practice, being able to communicate well across disciplines and directly working together. In these and other situations where conflict, role and boundary issues may put client and worker outcomes at risk, supervisors have a key role to play (Beddoe and Davys 2008, p.35). While only a small component of work in health and social care, an interprofessional approach to learning for supervision, leadership and management may provide rich opportunities for changing the culture. Learning to focus on relationships and mutuality rather than knowledge from and for specific clinical domains is potentially transformative.

Chapter 7

Skills for Supervision

The key task of the supervisor is to provide the space within which a supervisee reviews, develops and refines his or her practice within the boundaries mandated by professional and organisational standards, knowledge and policy. The Reflective Learning Model of supervision describes a path to this development and refinement through reflective learning. Reflective learning is learning which emerges through exploration of a supervisee's experience. It is a process of discovery rather than instruction.

A supervisor who works from this model of supervision must have certain attributes if he or she wishes to develop and maintain this context for learning. To ensure that the supervisee is free to explore, the supervisor must encourage exploration. In order that the supervisee makes new connections the supervisor must be open to, and be able to recognise and validate these connections. To this end the supervisor must value exploration, tolerate uncertainty, accommodate difference and remain open and curious about possibility. When a supervisor exhibits these attributes, the supervisee is encouraged and able to express ideas, to explore values and beliefs, to examine assumptions and judgements and to acknowledge and express feelings. 'Interest prompts a person to explore new things, and to be open to new ideas, experiences and actions. These broaden a person's options' (Gazzola and Theriault 2007, p.191). The supervisor must also approach the work of the supervisee with good faith. By good faith we mean the belief that, until indicated otherwise, the supervisee is behaving to the best of his or her ability and has the capacity to learn and develop.

A good supervisor, however, brings more than attributes to the supervision forum. Bernard and Goodyear identify two erroneous assumptions which historically have supported supervisors' claims of competence. The first is that 'having been a supervisee is itself sufficient preparation to be a supervisor' and the second 'that to be an effective therapist is sufficient prerequisite to being a good supervisor' (Bernard and Goodyear 2009, p.5). We agree with Bernard and Goodyear's observation that in recent years increasing attention and training has been given to practitioners to prepare for the role of supervisor. We also note that whilst this preparation and training is encouraging it is not universally required by professional bodies or social service organisations. In Chapter 6 we have addressed the process of supervisor development. In this chapter we focus on the interventions and skills of supervision.

Supervision is a skills based activity where conscious and intentional use of 'interventions' is necessary in order that purposeful and quality reflection and learning occurs. Heron (2001, p.3) defines an intervention 'as an identifiable piece of verbal and/or non-verbal behaviour that is part of the practitioner's service to the client'. Within supervision, an intervention can therefore be described as 'an identifiable piece of verbal and/or non-verbal behaviour that is part of the supervisor's service to the supervisee'.

In supervision, as in most if not all human service work, interventions are exercised in the context of a relationship. The qualities brought to the relationship by both parties will influence the success of the interventions.

Several useful frameworks of interventions, identified in counselling literature, have been adapted for supervision. The framework which we find the most useful describes five categories of intervention: facilitative, catalytic, conceptual, confrontative and prescriptive, and is based on that of Loganbill *et al.* (1982, pp.31–36). Each of the interventions comprises a subset of 'skills' and these are set out in Table 7.1.

Table 7.1 Overview of interventions and skills for supervision

Facilitative interventions	Facilitative interventions provide the conditions of supervision – the base on which the supervision process can rest (Loganbill *et al.* 1982). Facilitative interventions convey positive regard and include attention to comfort and privacy.
	Skills of facilitative interventions:
	• core listening and attending skills
	• paraphrasing
	• silence
	• self-disclosure
	• closed questions
	• feedback (confirmatory and reflective)

continued

Table 7.1 Overview of interventions
and skills for supervision *cont.*

Catalytic interventions	Catalytic interventions are aimed to promote growth, development and learning. Catalytic interventions are intended to promote change through assisted self-examination and self-discovery. Skills of catalytic interventions: • open question enquiry • logical consequences • feedback (confirmatory, reflective and corrective) • reframing
Conceptual interventions	Conceptual interventions provide the supervisee with information and knowledge. This knowledge can range from empirical research findings to procedural information and to shared practice wisdom from the supervisor. The aim of conceptual interventions is to provide information which will assist the supervisee in his or her understanding and problem solving. Skills of conceptual interventions: • information giving • prompts for procedural and formal knowledge
Confrontative interventions	Confrontative interventions are designed to confront the supervisee with aspects of themselves of which they may not be aware or which they have not considered to be important but which are limiting their practice or understanding. Confrontative interventions are also intended to promote change and often involve 'home truths'. Skills of confrontative interventions: • challenge • corrective feedback
Prescriptive interventions	Prescriptive interventions are used when it is imperative that a supervisee behaves or acts in a certain way. This may be at a time of crisis, where there is potential risk or because of prescribed policy or protocol. Skills of prescriptive interventions: • directives

SUPERVISION INTERVENTIONS AND SKILLS

Facilitative interventions

Facilitative interventions are the baseline skills which underpin all supervision. They are the foundation from which the other interventions can be made and help to create an open and accepting environment for supervision where reflection and introspection can occur.

LISTENING, ATTENDING, PARAPHRASING

This cluster of 'basic' skills provides the underlying conditions of supervision and supports the supervision relationship. The skills demonstrate positive regard, interest and the importance of the supervisee as the central player in the supervision process. Smythe and colleagues describe listening as 'the how of supervision that perhaps also tends to be taken for granted, yet sets the play in motion' (Smythe *et al.* 2009, p.18).

SILENCE

Silence provides a space for the supervisee to internalise and consider what has happened in the session to date. Exchanges between the supervisee and the supervisor, insights which have occurred, the supervisee's internal response to issues raised and general private reflection on the issue under discussion are all examples of what can be considered in moments of silence. Silence also provides a space in which the supervisee can determine his or her response. Moments of silence are particularly important for supervisees who have an 'introvert' learning profile and who require time for internal processing of information. Farmer, for example, found that when supervisors paused for approximately 3–5 seconds after a supervisee spoke, a number of changes were observed. These included increases in: 'supervisee confidence, shown in fewer inflected responses'; the 'incidence of supervisee speculative thinking'; supervisee questions; the 'variety of supervisee utterances 'and perhaps most importantly an increase in the 'contributions by 'quiet' supervisees' (Farmer 1988, pp.34–35).

SELF-DISCLOSURE

When using the skill of self-disclosure the supervisor draws from his or her own experience and practice to share thoughts, feelings and learning with the supervisee. These may be thoughts and feelings which have occurred during the supervision session or may be experiences from the past. Importantly, this sharing of information, when it includes doubts, uncertainty and mistakes, has been shown to increase the value of the supervisor in the eyes of supervisees (Krause and Allen 1988 reported in Lizzio *et al.* 2009, p.130). Lizzio *et al.* suggest that 'supervisor openness may initiate a virtuous cycle: supervisor openness leading to increased trust, promoting, in turn, supervisee openness, providing the basis for authentic learning' (Lizzio *et al.* 2009, p.130).

CLOSED QUESTIONS

Closed questions are those which can be answered by 'yes' or 'no'. They are used to verify or confirm situations and to gather and clarify information. Closed questions can be used to provoke quick answers and to shape, define or identify details of situations.

POSITIVE FEEDBACK

Feedback is a central and important skill which is woven throughout supervision. Because of its importance we discuss this in a separate section later in this chapter.

Catalytic interventions

Catalytic interventions are aimed to promote growth, development and learning through self-discovery and exploration. The skills of catalytic interventions include: open question enquiry, logical consequences, feedback and reframing.

OPEN QUESTION ENQUIRY

Open question enquiry is central to the Reflective Learning Model of supervision. Open questions allow exploration of all aspects of practice and lead to new and revitalised work through insight and understanding. The art of open question enquiry requires the supervisor to have the capacity for meaningful engagement in the supervision relationship, the humility to put self-preoccupation aside and listen, curiosity and a versatile framework of questions.

LOGICAL CONSEQUENCES

Logical consequences are aimed to alert the supervisee to the probable results of their actions and to assist him or her in decision making.

FEEDBACK

See section on feedback later in this chapter.

REFRAMING

Reframing is a skill where the supervisor employs a combination of practice wisdom and professional perspective to present the supervisee with an alternative framework through which to view his or her supervision issue.

Vignette – Damien

Damien, a team leader, was distressed that two of his best team members had, with very little warning, resigned. He discussed this with his supervisor and shared his concern that, although he had done his best to support and extend their work experience, he had obviously not done enough to keep them interested in their roles. His supervisor suggested that, rather than not doing a good job, Damien had done an excellent job and had provided the two team members with confidence and skills which enabled them to expand their professional horizons into new areas.

This reframe encouraged Damien to consider the team members from a different frame of reference and allowed him to consider how he could offer more opportunity for development in his team and so move forward rather than remain 'stuck' in his preoccupation with his own 'incompetence'.

Conceptual interventions

Conceptual interventions provide the supervisee with information and knowledge in order to assist the supervisee in his or her understanding and problem solving. This knowledge may be empirical research findings, procedural information or it may be shared practice wisdom from the supervisor. A clear distinction needs to be made between information giving and education. Supervision is educative but it is not formal teaching. When a supervisor finds that he or she is spending large amounts of supervision time 'providing information' it is important to consider whether the supervisee has professional development needs to be addressed which are beyond the learning that can occur in supervision. Has the supervisee become 'dependent' on receiving information rather than seeking it themselves and has supervision 'blurred 'into an education session?

Bond and Holland offer a useful suggestion to assist supervisors to identify when it is appropriate to give information or advice: 'a general rule of thumb is that the more technical a problem is, the more relevant it is to offer information or advice' (Bond and Holland 1998, p.153). Lizzio and Wilson (2002, p.29) state that the purpose of developmental approaches to supervision is to support 'the supervisee's progression towards autonomous mastery' but note that practitioners may vary in their motivation and capacity for increasing self-management. Lizzio and Wilson recommend a focus on the skills of self-regulation: 'self-organisation, self-evaluation, information seeking, goal setting and planning and self-monitoring of actions' (p.29). To avoid supervision becoming dominated by didactic interventions, supervisors might set 'takeaway' tasks that foster self-directed learning and active problem solving.

Confrontative interventions

Confrontative interventions are designed to present to supervisees aspects of themselves of which they may not be aware, or which they have not considered to be important, and which are limiting their practice or understanding. 'A confronting intervention unequivocally tells an uncomfortable truth' (Heron 2001, p.59). Despite the name, confrontative interventions are not adversarial but rather aimed to promote change and movement. When faced with aspects of themselves of which they have not been previously aware, supervisees typically will become unsettled and feel a degree of discomfort. It is through the process of resolving the unsettled state or discomfort that the supervisee discovers learning and change occurs.

When handled well confrontative interventions can be exciting (if at times uncomfortable) moments when a supervisee sees new possibilities and gains new understanding about him or herself. The two key skills of confrontative interventions are challenge and feedback.

CHALLENGE

In supervision moments for challenge can arise when a supervisor hears or sees the supervisee limiting his or her understanding and effectiveness in practice through beliefs, attitudes or actions. Most often these behaviours will be outside, or on the edge, of the supervisee's awareness. The process of challenge is to draw to the supervisee's attention these aspects in order that the supervisee becomes aware of the behaviour and can consider change. Lizzio et al. identify four ways in which a supervisor may challenge a supervisee: 'Inviting critical reflection of their assumptions and ideas…, identifying their inconsistencies or 'blind spots', or by providing critical feedback or raising uncomfortable issues that have emerged in supervision' (Lizzio et al. 2009, p.129).

Vignette – Honoria

Honoria was considering options for an elderly service user who was in the terminal stages of her illness. Her supervisor noticed that all Honoria's options included some form of residential care. When the supervisor pointed this out to her Honoria argued passionately against the proposition that the service user might want to die at home.

With the supervisor's help Honoria recognised that she had a belief set about the needs of the elderly who she regarded as having little voice to assert their rights and who, as a consequence, seldom received the care they needed and deserved. Dying at home without 24-hour nursing care was, in Honoria's view, an example of this type of neglect. She had never considered that there was an alternative view.

The behaviour 'challenged' by the supervisor may include discrepancies between different aspects of the supervisee's behaviour or discrepancies between the supervisee's assessment of a situation and the assessment of others. These discrepancies can be between:

- what a supervisee says and what he/she does

- what a supervisee says and his/her non-verbal behaviour

- how the supervisee assesses a situation/client and how the supervisor assesses or experiences that client or situation.

Vignette – Richard

Richard was describing a practice situation which he found very frustrating when his supervisor asked him how he would describe his approach to working with this particular service user. Richard was quick to reply that he was taking a very supportive and accepting role encouraging the service user to plan and initiate her own course of action. Given the preceding supervision conversation the supervisor challenged Richard on this.

'I am very puzzled about what you have just said. On the one hand you tell me that your approach has been supportive and allowed the service user to act in her own time – on the other hand you have just spent ten minutes expressing your frustration that she has not followed your plan for her.'

By juxtaposing the two contradictory aspects of a supervisee's story or presentation the supervisor provides the supervisee with the opportunity to consider and explore these incongruities.

Challenge is possibly one of the most potent and useful of the confrontative intervention skills: 'confronting is about consciousness-raising, about waking people up to what it is they are not aware of in themselves that is critical for their own well being and the well being of others' (Heron 2001, p.60). Challenge, however, is a skill which is not independent of support. Lizzio *et al.* describe an orthogonal relationship between challenge and support and caution that whilst a 'supervisor's goal is to provide sufficient challenge to stimulate growth and development' this challenge needs to be balanced by sufficient support so that the supervisee will not 'retreat' from the learning forum (Lizzio *et al.* 2009, p.130).

CORRECTIVE FEEDBACK
See section on giving and receiving feedback later in this chapter.

Prescriptive Interventions

Prescriptive interventions provide the supervisee with a specific plan of action for a particular situation. These are generally situations where there are no options. Prescriptive interventions are commonly used in a crisis situation or where client or supervisee safety is at risk. Apart from crisis situations, which apply to practitioners at all stages of experience, prescriptive interventions will most often be used with new practitioners, or practitioners who are new to a particular practice setting. The main prescriptive skill is a directive.

A directive may be used in three ways. It may be informative, in that it provides the supervisee with precise instructions about how a certain procedure must be carried out: 'When this situation occurs you *must* ensure that form 362a is completed and given immediately to the lead practitioner.'

It may be instructive about how the supervisee must act now (usually in a crisis or where safety is an issue): 'You must immediately phone the crisis team and alert the emergency services' or 'I want you to immediately report what you have just relayed to me to your manager.'

Finally, it may be corrective and require a supervisee to address a particular situation: 'It is not appropriate to receive gifts of that nature. You must return it immediately.' Situations where directives are corrective may lead to performance issues and a supervisor will need to consider his or her position vis-à-vis the supervisee, the service user, the profession and the organisation.

In most supervision relationships prescriptive interventions will rarely be used and when they are it will be in situations similar to those above. If prescriptive interventions are the norm it is probable that supervision has slid into performance management.

GIVING AND RECEIVING FEEDBACK

Availability and the way that feedback is given by supervisors in CS (clinical supervision) are considered important variables in the effectiveness of CS from a supervisee's perspective. (Pack 1994a, p.664)

Definitions of feedback vary but there is general consensus that it is 'the process of telling another individual how they are experienced' (Hawkins and Shohet 2006, p.133). Carroll and Gilbert (2005, p.53) note that feedback provides information on behaviour (observable behaviours are the focus) and the effects that that behaviour has on others. Freeman (1985, p.5) meanwhile suggests that feedback may address some or all of the following: 'a particular aspect of behavior, to a total behavioral sequence or performance, or to the nature of a message itself; e.g. the message may convey information about the individual's emotional state, attitude, or relationship to another person'. Usefully Carroll and Gilbert (2005) identify three types of feedback: corrective, confirmatory and reflective. The latter we call 'wondering' feedback.

Feedback is a central skill of supervision and carries an expectation that the supervisee will hear, acknowledge, consider and review his or her understanding, behaviour or attitude in response to the feedback. Reports from practitioners, however, suggest that feedback is frequently poorly handled in supervision by supervisor and supervisee alike. Critical (or corrective) feedback can be heavy-handed and destructive. Termed 'killer' feedback by Carroll and Gilbert this feedback 'hurts, wounds, shames and humiliates and does little to contribute to learning' (Carroll and Gilbert 2005, p.52). On the other hand, positive or affirmative feedback can be limp, generalised, at times patronising or, worse, rarely given. In the absence of positive feedback Gazzola and Theriault found that supervisees 'felt overly criticised and did not feel appreciation for what they may have done well' (Gazzola and Theriault 2007, p.197).

To be effective feedback needs to be present at all stages of a supervision session. The giving and receiving of feedback both enhances and tests the supervision relationship and is a skill which can be employed by both the supervisor and the supervisee. To build relationships requires work from all parties concerned. To maintain a relationship also requires work and includes the opportunity for needs and feelings to be expressed and for feedback to be given and received. When, within a supervision relationship, giving and receiving feedback is a regular and accepted practice there is opportunity for honesty and integrity to be 'known to occur'. Giving and receiving honest feedback requires courage which in turn contributes to a robust and trusting relationship.

Corrective feedback is possibly one of the hardest skills to master. It is often accompanied by associations of reprimand and powerlessness from past experiences, particularly from childhood when powerlessness was more often the reality and reprimand frequently the case. Within supervision, feedback is intended to assist learning. Corrective feedback, as a confrontative intervention, may not be a comfortable experience but when handled well is a catalyst for learning.

Confirmatory feedback may also be problematic if it becomes distorted by cultural or familial messages about praise and self-glorification. In these situations positive feedback may be dismissed, minimised or critiqued to find ulterior messages. The art of giving feedback includes preparation, appropriate timing, thoughtfulness about context and clarity of purpose. When feedback is given with respect, honesty and with an opportunity for discussion, learning can occur.

Preparation for feedback in supervision

There are two key opportunities to plan how feedback will occur in a supervision relationship. The first is during the negotiation of the contract when the importance of regular feedback is explored and expectations clarified in general terms. The second is before giving feedback on a particular planned event, for example following live observation of work with service users or where the supervisor makes a contribution to appraisal or personal professional development plans.

Giving corrective feedback can be as difficult as receiving it. Preparation will therefore assist both parties in this task. Feedback is best received when it has been requested, though this may not always be possible in supervision. If, however, feedback has been identified as an important component of supervision and has been discussed during the establishment of the supervision contract, there is an opportunity for both the supervisor and supervisee to negotiate how feedback can best be given and received during supervision.

Vignette – Russell

When they were negotiating the supervision contract Russell and his supervisor discussed how Russell would like to receive feedback in supervision. Russell was pleased to be asked this question. He was excited about the idea of receiving feedback from his supervisor but he knew that in reality it may not be so comfortable. Russell was able to identify his ambivalence and his concern that he might become defensive and not hear what his supervisor had to say. Together Russell and his supervisor discussed ways to minimise Russell's possible defensive reaction. Russell knew that he appreciated the opportunity to be his own critic in the first instance. They agreed therefore that the supervisor would ask Russell to give his own assessment of any situation before the supervisor gave her feedback. They also agreed that, if it were not possible or appropriate for Russell to provide his own critique, the supervisor would announce that she was going to give feedback before launching into it. 'I want to give you some feedback...' would be a cue to Russell and allow him to hold himself open to hear what the supervisor had to say. Russell also realised he would value opportunities for specific feedback on aspects of his practice which he identified himself. His supervisor was very happy to give him this feedback and suggested they could also arrange for her to directly observe his practice and give feedback if he wished. They agreed to review this particular aspect of supervision after six months.

This exchange during the negotiation of the supervision contract not only prepared the relationship for moments of feedback it also placed the supervisee in a position where he was responsible for his behaviour and took shared responsibility for the feedback process.

Regardless of the focus there are some helpful guidelines for the effective feedback process. Hawkins and Shohet (2006, p.134) describe a very useful framework for giving feedback; this has the acronym 'CORBS' and is summarised in Table 7.2. Brief guidelines follow.

Table 7.2 The CORBS feedback framework

Clear	Be clear about what feedback you want to give and why you want to give it.
Owned	Use 'I' statements – you are describing your own perception of the behaviour.
Regular	Feedback needs to be threaded through all, or most, supervision sessions not something that happens once or twice a year.
Balanced	A range of feedback needs to be given – corrective, confirmatory and reflective (wondering).
Specific	The feedback needs to be concrete and relate to specific behaviour or events.

Source: Hawkins and Shohet 2005

Feedback must be clear

The first important step before giving feedback is to be clear about what feedback is to be given and why. If the feedback is very confronting, when in the session will it need to be given to ensure that the supervisee has sufficient time to reflect and to respond? If a particular supervisee is grappling with a range of issues it may be helpful to prioritise feedback in order that he or she is not overwhelmed. Even the most robust practitioner has only so much capacity to hear and integrate corrective feedback. Similarly, when the feedback is confirmatory, care needs to be taken to ensure that the supervisee has space to 'hear' the feedback.

The relationship between feedback and change

When giving feedback it is important to be clear about the intended outcome. Feedback, according to the earlier definitions, does not include a request for change. Rather, there is an invitation, an 'implied' request for change. Feedback is thus the process of 'telling' a supervisee, or 'informing' a supervisee, about how his or her behaviour is experienced or perceived in order to bring it to the supervisee's awareness for consideration.

Before giving feedback to a supervisee, it is therefore important for the supervisor to consider whether the supervisee has the option not to change. If the intent is clearly for the supervisee to change his or her behaviour, then the supervisor needs to make an explicit request to that effect. If change is required what are the parameters around that change?

When change is the required response the feedback needs to be followed by a prescriptive intervention. The DESC Script (Table 7.3) which had its origins in assertiveness training and literature (Bolton 1979, p.153) of the

1970s and has later been developed by Bower and Bower (1991, pp.87–96), continues to be a most useful formula for moving from feedback to a request for change.

Table 7.3 The DESC Script

Describe the behaviour you want changed:

When you speak to family members I hear you giving out a lot of very detailed information with no checks to see if the family understands what they are agreeing to.

Express your concern (feelings):

I am really concerned that this important information is not being absorbed by the families.

Specify the change in behaviour you want:

In future I want you to spend more time and to check that the family understands what you are saying. I also want you to give the family a written summary of the discussion.

Consequences – explain the reason you want the change:

In that way we will know what information has been given and that the family has a record of the discussion.

Feedback must be owned

The use of 'I' statements is a basic tenet of good communication. When the person giving the feedback uses the first person pronoun 'I', the feedback is firmly located as the perception, or assessment, of that person and allows the recipient a space in which to consider the information. 'I think that your behaviour is disrespectful when you talk over your colleagues.' This statement avoids labelling and generalisations. Whereas 'everyone thinks you are rude and disrespectful' is generalised, non-specific and may provoke defensiveness and denial.

Feedback must be regular

Feedback needs to be a regular and normal part of the supervision process. In Chapter 5 we talked about feedback as being a routine process in the supervision cycle of the Reflective Learning Model of supervision. If feedback is not integrated as a regular part of the supervision process, then when it does occur the 'moment' of feedback may be overwhelming. Feedback is most effective when it is given as close to the event as possible. This allows both supervisor and supervisee to explore 'fresh' moments which are readily retrieved from memory, and unhelpful behaviours should not have been reinforced by repetition and will be more easily addressed.

Feedback must be balanced

Feedback needs to be a balance of the corrective, confirmative and reflective types. Different thoughts have been expressed as to how this balance should occur. The 'sandwich approach' recommends that corrective feedback is sandwiched between two confirmative pieces of feedback, whilst the 'trade off' approach suggests that every piece of corrective feedback needs to be balanced by one piece of confirmative feedback. A variation of the 'trade off' approach, in recognition of the power of corrective feedback, recommends that two pieces of confirmative feedback are needed to balance the effects of every one piece of corrective feedback. We do not subscribe to either of these approaches.

When confirmatory feedback is coupled to corrective feedback it loses its potency, is often dismissed, not heard or treated with suspicion. It is important that supervisees know and can trust what their supervisors think of their practice and can trust that positive feedback does not come with a proviso. Supervision is a professional practice and as such there is an expectation that professionals will accept and use corrective feedback without the need for sugar coating. That being said, it is important that there is a balance of all types of feedback and particular generosity with regard to confirmative feedback. Many practitioners work in extremely stressful situations where feedback from either the community or service users may seldom be positive. Supervision is the place where work, effort and commitment can and should be recognised, validated and celebrated without being tied to conditions.

Feedback must be specific

Finally, feedback must be specific. It must be factual, concrete and behavioural. The supervisee needs to know what it is that he or she is doing well or could do differently.

When giving feedback to another person it is a useful exercise to reflect on what we have said and wonder how we would have felt if we had received that feedback delivered in that particular way. Would we understand what behaviour was being commented on? Would we have felt free to comment and discuss the feedback without defensiveness?

Reflective or 'wondering' feedback

Carroll and Gilbert's (2005) inclusion of a category called reflective feedback is a most helpful addition to the feedback skill group. They define reflective feedback as moments where behaviour is held 'up to the light to review it' (Carroll and Gilbert 2005, p.53). We call this 'wondering' feedback, which is often the moment in supervision when the supervisor shares his or her thoughts about, or responses to, the supervisee's practice with a 'wonder', or a tentative interpretation, that can hang in the air for consideration: 'I wonder what [the patient] was thinking when you made that comment, I noticed she drew a big breath and looked frustrated?'

During supervision the supervisor will encounter situations where the supervisee has behaved in a manner which is 'interesting'. This may mean that he or she has behaved in a manner which is different from the way the supervisor would have behaved or the supervisor may be unsure about what is the best way to act. The reflective feedback provides the opportunity for supervisees and supervisors to consider situations with 'wondering'. It is important to distinguish this from giving information, sharing practice wisdom or self-disclosure. It includes the opportunity for the supervisor to share his or her own processes or thoughts with the supervisee as a resource which may add to the information and data being considered in supervision. In this regard it includes elements of Hawkins and Shohet's (1989, 2001, 2006) 'Seven-eyed supervision: process' model of supervision where, in mode 6, the supervisor is 'tentatively bringing this material into consciousness for the supervisee to explore' (Hawkins and Shohet 2006, p.95).

Vignette – Henry

Henry was describing his exchange with a service user. One aspect of this exchange caught the supervisor's attention. She was uncertain what she thought about this exchange and in particular Henry's approach, so brought it forward to be 'wondered' about. 'When I heard your response I was initially concerned that it was too sharp and abrupt – but I am wondering now if it might be the best way forward...'

These moments allow the supervisor to be a co-explorer with the supervisee, sharing and debating possibilities and options.

Receiving feedback

Giving feedback in a constructive manner requires care, preparation and thought. Receiving feedback likewise requires thought and preparation. It is easy to hear feedback as an attack and, despite an understanding of the value of feedback, it is easy to take it personally.

The experience of receiving feedback is often shaped by how individuals are feeling about themselves and their practice at any particular time. When practitioners are feeling confident and competent in their professional roles, feedback can be exciting and stimulating. They may be looking for challenge and to be extended in their work. At other times, for instance when practitioners are new to positions or roles, confidence can be low and they look for support and reassurance rather than challenge. Acknowledgement of this, either privately or in the supervision session, is useful preparation for receiving feedback. The following are some guidelines to assist with receiving feedback:

- Take the initiative and ask for feedback.

- Negotiate with the other person how you want to receive feedback.

- Evaluate yourself first – how do you think you performed/behaved in a given situation? What would you like to do differently next time? What aspects are you pleased about?

- Remind yourself that feedback is another person's perception of you and not the 'truth'.

- Request clarity if feedback is non-specific or unclear.

- Separate positive and negative feedback so that you hear each clearly.

We include here two useful guidelines for receiving feedback from Hawkins and Shohet:

- Listen to the feedback all the way through without judging it or jumping to a defensive response...

- Try not to explain compulsively why you did something or even explain away positive feedback.

(Hawkins and Shohet 2006, p.134)

USE OF INTERVENTIONS IN SUPERVISION

During the course of supervision, supervisors will employ interventions and skills in a manner which reflects the supervisee's developmental level and experience of the practice context.

As discussed earlier facilitative interventions, particularly the skills of attending and listening, are fundamental to all supervision. They are the medium through which the other interventions are woven and will be used consistently throughout all sessions, regardless of the experience of the supervisee. The frequency of the use of other interventions will, however, be influenced by the experience or developmental level of the practitioner.

New practitioners, and those new to a particular field of practice, will generally require more structure and active intervention in supervision than experienced practitioners. Le Maistre, Boudreau and Pare (2006) studied the school-to-work transition of teachers, social workers, occupational therapists and physiotherapists. Drawing on situated learning (Lave and Wenger 1991), Le Maistre *et al.* describe a journey that addresses the needs of beginning practitioners thus:

> By engaging newcomers in authentic but not critical or central tasks, by gradually increasing both the difficulty of the work and the autonomy of the learners, and by the subtle application of just-in-time teaching and assessment, oldtimers create a centripetal force that pulls these newcomers toward capable, central participation in the community's activity. (LeMaistre *et al.* 2006, p.345)

New practitioners will need information, they may need assistance to identify consequences of actions and often require a high level of reassurance and support. Supervisors may also find that new practitioners ask for, and need, regular feedback and require challenge as they develop their own practice competence and wisdom.

Conversely, experienced and competent practitioners generally have developed practice wisdom and require little procedural information. These practitioners will use supervision to target, develop and hone their practice. Of interest to this group is the opportunity to critique and develop new practice options. Challenge, particularly feedback, is welcomed and seen as stimulating and providing interesting new perspectives. The supervision of experienced practitioners is usually rewarding, though it can at times be challenging, for supervisors. Reflective feedback offers a chance for in-depth discussion and debate and supervisors' own practice can develop through these ponderings.

It is useful to note the distinction between experience and competence. In their seminal developmental model of supervision, Loganbill *et al.* (1982) identify a category of practitioners who are 'stuck' in their practice. This group may be experienced in service but their practice has become limited. These practitioners will need confrontative (feedback and challenge) and catalytic interventions (open question enquiry) to create the insight and understanding to change.

The section above provides a brief overview of the interventions and skills of supervision. We refer readers to other texts (Bond and Holland 1998; Hawkins and Shohet 2006) for more detailed information. The focus for the remainder of this chapter is how the interventions and skills relate to the Reflective Learning Model of supervision.

THE REFLECTIVE LEARNING MODEL OF SUPERVISION
Open question enquiry in supervision

> *Great supervision is about asking the right questions. Through careful facilitation of a reflective process, utilising the learning cycle, each supervision session can build the practitioner's skills in self-supervision. For it is this ability to 'do' and 'know' and 'be with' clients while simultaneously reflecting on process and future intervention that is at the heart of professional excellence. (Davys and Beddoe 2000, p.449)*

The Reflective Learning Model of supervision presented in Chapter 5 describes a model of supervision which positions the supervisee as the central figure in supervision and the supervisor as the facilitator or guide. This model relies on the supervisor having both the skills to create an accepting environment for supervision and the skills to invite and facilitate an exploration of practice by the supervisee which leads to discovery, insight and understanding. As we have emphasised in Chapter 3 the key to creating the environment or context for supervision is the establishment of the supervision relationship. The effective facilitation of a supervisee's exploration of his or her practice, however, requires the supervisor to have command of open question enquiry.

Open question enquiry, Socratic questioning, which prompts a supervisee to explore his or her practice, encourages him or her to open sensitive areas for consideration and to unpack feelings and motivation, will only be useful if the discussions are candid and truthful. The importance of establishing a trusting relationship is thus once again evident. A supervisor who is genuinely engaged in the supervision process and who is interested in the opinions and experiences of his or her supervisees will be an instinctive 'good' listener. A good listener attends, clarifies and asks open and expansive questions and so provides the encouragement and safety for his or her supervisees to take risks and explore their practice. Questions allow supervisees to find their own answers or solutions to their own problems and places them in the position of responsibility for their work. 'Questioning thus follows attentive listening that looks for understanding rather than claims to know' (Smythe *et al.* 2009, p.22).

The questions which assist supervisees to consider their work in depth are open questions. Open questions most commonly begin with who, what, where, when and how, and invite supervisees to review situations and to deepen the 'telling' of the supervision story. Questions which begin with 'why' are also open questions but can easily become interrogatory and, rather than encouraging reflection, can provoke defensiveness and justification from the supervisee. 'Why' questions therefore need to be used judiciously.

It can be useful for the supervisor to have a framework around which he or she can consider which questions to pose. Most practice can be defined by three parameters: action or doing, knowledge and thinking, and awareness of self and feelings. These three parameters also represent the reflective learning cycle. The work which a supervisee presents in supervision can be reviewed in terms of what did the practitioner do (or not do), what was he or she thinking (what knowledge, assumptions or judgements informed the action) and how or what was the practitioner feeling. This level of review, however, is not sufficient to transform practice. In order to uncover meaning and understanding, and so promote change, a higher order critique is required. Thus it is not sufficient to 'know'. Understanding and change comes from the critical examination and questioning of what lies behind this knowing, the implications 'knowing'.

The art of asking 'good questions' is inexorably linked with facilitative interventions and in particular the skills of good listening. Questions will follow the narrative of the supervisee rather than the internal meanderings of the supervisor. In this way each supervision session will be unique and particular to time and place. 'Such an approach must release both parties to a process of "play" where a question finds response and response provokes a more searching question' (Smythe *et al.* 2009, p.20). To promote critical reflection the supervisor is attentive to the supervisee's story and actively curious. The supervisor listens for moments of choice in the narrative and notices inconsistencies, assumptions and incongruities. He or she listens for balance in the supervision 'story'. Does the supervisee speak of actions and knowledge but avoid feelings or does the supervisee become absorbed by his or her own processes and so overlook the connections between knowing and theory?

Supervision stories are also located in time and place. Consideration of the past in relation to the present assists supervisees to notice movement and change both in themselves and in their clients. Similarly anticipation of, or hopes for, the future provides opportunity for planning new strategies and developing resources and skills. Once again, however, simple review is not sufficient and past, present and future need to be examined for meaning and an understanding of the patterns and threads which connect them.

Drawing together all these elements, Figure 7.1 shows a matrix for the questions of supervision. It shows two overlapping triangles, one of action, thinking and feeling, the other indicating past present and future, held in tension by the central imperative of critical reflection.

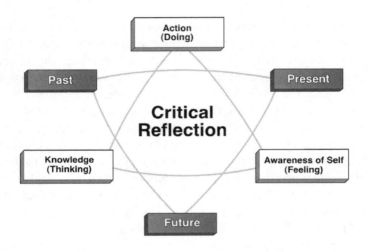

Figure 7.1 Reflection matrix

At the end of this chapter we provide a list of questions for supervisors. These questions have been arranged according to the four stages of the Reflective Learning Model of supervision. This ordering is not hard and fast and many questions can be asked in more than one stage of the model. We see the list as a 'starter pack' and encourage readers to create their own list of questions to reflect the uniqueness of their own practice style and that of their supervisees. But for a start we offer our list. The questions however come with a warning. Supervision is more than the posing of questions. The questions need to be relevant to the dialogue and the context. This is not supervision by numbers!

Whilst questions may be central to the Reflective Learning Model the interventions listed earlier in this chapter are also relevant and in the dance of supervision are essential to good footwork. Open question enquiry when used as critical reflection is a skill of catalytic intervention. Questions, however, are not always appropriate or necessary in every supervision exchange. Bond and Holland offer a useful warning in this regard. Questions, they say, can be overused: 'Compulsive counselling may occur when the clinical supervisor continues to use support and catalytic interventions when some information or advice may be more appropriate' (Bond and Holland 1998, p.158).

INTERVENTIONS AND THE REFLECTIVE LEARNING MODEL OF SUPERVISION

The above discussion of open question enquiry describes in some detail the use of questions within the Reflective Learning Model of supervision. Whilst open question enquiry and facilitative interventions comprise the core skill structure, other skills and interventions are important to this approach to supervision. Again there are no hard and fast rules, and Table 7.4 provides a summary to identify where these skills might typically be used to assist the supervisee to progress through the process of reflection and learning.

Table 7.4 Interventions and skills in supervision

Interventions	Skills typically employed
Event	Listening and attending Open question enquiry Information giving (minimal)
Exploration: Impact	Listening and attending Open question enquiry Feedback: confirmatory and reflective Reframing Challenge
Exploration: Implications	Listening and attending Open question enquiry Feedback – confirmatory, corrective and reflective Reframing Challenge Information giving Directives
Experimentation	Listening and attending Open question enquiry Feedback – confirmatory, corrective and reflective Challenge Directives
Evaluation	Listening and attending Open question enquiry Feedback – confirmatory and reflective

One hundred and more questions
EVENT

- What have you brought to supervision today?
    - Why have you brought this particular situation?
    - What would a successful outcome look like?
    - Where do you want to start?
    - What is your top priority for today?
- What do you want from me?
- What don't you want from me?
- What is the goal for the issue?
- What is it that you wish to take away from the session regarding this issue?
- How will you know you have got what you want?
- Tell me about it.
- How much do I need to know in order to understand the situation?

EXPLORATION
Impact

- What have you done so far?
- How are you feeling right now about this situation?
- How were you feeling at the time?
- What, if anything, has changed since this happened?
- Have you been in a situation like this before?
- What has helped you on previous occasions?
- How is this situation different from others in the past?
- What stops you from…?
- If there were no consequences what would you like to do/say now?

- If you were to give yourself wise counsel what would it be?
- How do you see your relationship with this person/client?
- Who do they remind you of?
- How much of yourself do you see in the client?
- Have you discussed this with the person/client?
- What do you like about this client/family?
- What do you think the client/family likes about you?
- What do you not like about this client/family?
- How do you think the client sees you?
- What is your greatest concern?
- How important is it for you that the client...?
- How does this situation affect you?
- Who have you been able to talk to about this?
- What is your greatest fear?
- When this happens what are you thinking?
- When this happens what are you feeling?
- What do you do with your feeling of...?
- What do you think might be going on for the client?
- How might the client be feeling?
- What prevents you/makes you hesitate/ignore, etc...?
- Whose problem is this?
- What is your gut feeling about this situation?
- What assumptions have you made?
- What is the basis of your assumptions?
- What is the most challenging aspect of this situation for you?

EXPLORATION

Implication

- What have you thought of so far?
- What were you thinking at the time?
- What do you think now?
- What have you done on previous occasions?
- How is this situation different?
- How has your presence/intervention changed the situation?
- Who else could have done what you have done?
- What did you see?
- What did you say?
- When did this...start?
- How do you determine your priorities?
- How did you come to that conclusion/decision?
- What is the advantage of what you do now?
- What are the disadvantages of what you do now?
- What would happen if you stopped...?
- What is your role?
- Who is your client?
- Who are you accountable to?
- When you do..., what is the client learning?
- What are the tasks associated with your role?
- What is your goal?
- What do you need to remember to say, do or look out for?
- What other approaches could you take?
- How do you acknowledge difference in this situation?
- Who holds the power here?
- What are the sociopolitical implications of this?
- Have you considered...?

- What do you know about...?
- What is your area of strength?
- What are your limitations?
- Why might the client be behaving as they are?
- What are the implications for you/the client/the agency, etc?
- What is the purpose of your thinking on this matter?
- From what perspective are you thinking?
- What assumptions are you making?
- What information are you using?
- How are you interpreting that information?
- What conclusions do you come to?
- What is the theoretical base of your interventions?
- Why have you taken this approach?
- If you were the client what would you have noticed?
- If you were to give yourself some wise counsel what would it be?
- What do you think you have done well?
- What strengths does this family/client have?
- What changes have you observed in this client/family?
- What goals does this family/client have?
- How might you ascertain what the client/family thinks/wants?
- What expectations does the client/family have of you/agency?
- Are the client's goals realistic?
- What are the limitations of your role?
- What would you have liked to change about this situation?
- If this situation was resolved what would it look like?
- What do you wish you had done differently?
- What are the policies and procedures which direct your work?

EXPERIMENTATION

- Where are you going to start?
- When are you going to…?
- What are you going to do first?
- How might you approach this person?
- What might you do?
- How are you going to say that?
- What words will you use?
- What is the most likely response from the client/family?
- How will you respond to the client's/family's response?
- What response are you most concerned about?
- How would you deal with resistance/refusal/aggression/denial, etc?
- What are the possible consequences of your plan?
- Who needs to be there?
- What resources might you need?
- What would happen on a future occasion if this occurred?
- How could the decision be sabotaged – by whom?
- What if there is no change in this situation?
- What contingency plan do you have in mind?
- Who else needs to know?
- How will results be measured?
- What will you notice about your/your client's behaviour?
- What have you learned?
- What areas do you need to work on here – skills, knowledge, attitude?
- What do you need to record about this session/client/family?
- Are there issues of safety involved?

EVALUATION

- Given where you started where are you now?
- How has the issue been addressed?
- At the beginning how would you rate...?
- How would you rate...now?
- What other issues have arisen?
- How will we follow up, review, evaluate, debrief?
- What is the time frame?
- How has this process been?
- How could it have been different?
- What have you discovered/learned?
- How are you feeling?
- Any issues remaining about the issue or with me?

Chapter 8

Communication and Emotion in Supervision

CHAPTER OBJECTIVES

In Chapter 2 we indicated that support was a core condition of effective supervision. In Chapter 6 managing the emotional content of supervision was described as a key focus for learning for beginning supervisors. In this chapter we will explore the place of strong emotion in professional practice and supervision and the relevance of this to the understanding of and responding to challenging moments in practice.

> To become wiser is to stay tuned to the insights bred of challenge, tension, joy and breakthrough 'felt' within the experience of being there. Such glimmers of insight are brought to understanding by reflection and somehow embodied into discerning judgement. (Smythe *et al.* 2009, p.20)

INTRODUCTION

Working in health and social care is stressful regardless of the context. At every interface, and often on a daily basis, practitioners are engaged with other human beings who are at various stages of critical decision making, distress or crisis. Many practitioners will be required to assess client situations, make decisions and intervene in ways which can have far reaching effects on their clients' lives. These engagements will, on occasion, create a level of stress, doubt, anxiety and, sometimes, despair for practitioners, regardless of that practitioner's level of experience or training. All too often there is no clear way forward and situations are characterised by changing circumstances, new and contradictory information and uncertainty. In order to deal with these recurring practice situations practitioners need to be strong and confident in themselves. 'To feel good about others we need to feel good about ourselves. Our own feelings of inadequacy, anger or distress get in the way of how we relate to others, or get projected onto colleagues or clients' (Hawkins and Shohet 2006, p.21).

The importance, and indeed the necessity, of acknowledging and exploring feelings in supervision is clearly stated by Hughes and Pengelly (1997) who argue that practitioners cannot avoid being emotionally affected by their work with clients and that these feelings will, in some form or another, be present in supervision. These feelings hold important information about clients and about the practitioner–client relationship. If these feelings can be expressed and examined in supervision this information will become available to help inform the current and ongoing work with that client. Finally Hughes and Pengelly assert that such examination and expression is essential, indeed a prerequisite to safe practice (1997, p.82).

Nordentoft (2008) found that group clinical supervision with a focus on 'emotion work' seemed to both 'introduce and legitimize a different emotional vocabulary and a different organization of talk' at case conferences in a palliative care team (p.924). In addition she found that treatment beliefs and practices within the team were questioned in group supervision by including the views of those who didn't usually contribute in the case conferences. Nordentoft observed that the supervisors became role models and less participative practitioners became more willing and confident in leading challenging discussion (Nordentoft 2008, p.919).

Nordentoft's findings highlight the dual nature of care in the emotionally demanding work of palliative care where the needs of both the patients and the palliative care staff need to be addressed. In support of previous research, it also appeared that the promotion of an exploration of feelings in supervision for these health professionals increased 'moral thinking and ethical reflections on care and treatment' (Nordentoft 2008, p.924). Nordentoft further suggests that the new way in which staff considered treatment and care also led to changes in the ways in which they related to one another and shared resources which in turn helps to prevent stress and burnout (p.924).

Whilst the important role of supervision is to 'hold and support the supervisee in times of crisis and doubt' (Hawkins and Shohet 2006, p.220), not all supervision arrangements offer the required safety for such expression and exploration. A number of factors are identified as contributing to the creation of barriers to this emotional work and include the personal views and personalities of both practitioners and supervisors, the culture of the organisation and of the profession, and the degree to which it is safe to expose one's vulnerability (Hawkins and Shohet 2006; Morrison 2001). In addition, the current focus on evidence-based practice which urges practitioners to seek rational answers to practice situations does not encourage an examination of the uncertainties and hunches of emotional responses. Where such professional objectivity and detachment are valued, subjectivity is regarded as a weakness rather than applauded as awareness (Bond and Holland 1998). In this type of professional climate practitioners require considerable self-confidence and assertion (and sense of safety) if they are to expose the more uncertain aspects of their practice.

The barriers which prevent an exploration of feeling in supervision by a supervisee can be regarded as stemming from three fears: fear of being overwhelmed by feelings, fear of the judgements of others and fear of distortion in the professional encounter. These fears are detailed in Table 8.1.

In the same way that supervisees may repress expression of feelings in supervision, so can supervisors deter exploration of the emotional content of the work. Like supervisees, many supervisors are caught up in the expectations and limitations of professional and organisational culture and feel exposed and vulnerable to public criticism. Supervision at the interface of risk (see also Chapter 11) may prioritise risk management over attention to the practitioner's own process and affect: quite simply the supervision session runs out of time to deal with this aspect of practice.

Table 8.2 summarises the barriers for supervisors to encourage and promote the expression of feelings in supervision.

The challenge for supervisors and supervisees is to create a supervision space where there is sufficient mutual trust and respect to withstand an examination of the multilayered emotional work of human service practice. This space will also need to be secure enough to hold at bay the criticisms which can arise from particular organisational and social contexts. In order for this to happen both participants require a clear understanding of the boundaries of supervision, the courage to face the fears of exposing feelings and the willingness to value moments of uncertainty. When the opportunity to explore the emotional impact of practice is not available to practitioners the feelings surrounding practice do not cease to exist and practitioners are left to manage the emotional impact of their work alone (Dwyer 2007, p.53).

EMOTIONAL INTELLIGENCE

The ability for either the practitioner or the supervisor to attend to the 'emotional' business of supervision will depend on a number of factors, the most critical of which is their emotional capability or level of emotional intelligence.

Table 8.1 Barriers to the expression of feelings in supervision by the supervisee

Fear	Contributing factors
Fear of being overwhelmed by feelings	• Feelings may be too painful and distressing to be acknowledged • The act of reflection may open a deep well of unexplored scenarios from the past which threaten to overwhelm • Practitioners under stress often feel very vulnerable and any acknowledgement or expression of feelings could be 'out of control' • Accessing feelings may risk experiencing shame and failure • Feelings may be suppressed when practitioners are too busy and task focused to take time to listen and reflect
Fear of the judgements of others	• Feelings may be perceived as a sign of weakness and evidence of 'over involvement' • In work contexts where public opinion is critical any exposure of a practitioner's own vulnerability and feelings may be too risky • Practitioners may feel uncomfortable about strong negative feelings about service users when unconditional respect is the professional norm • Practitioners may feel uncomfortable about strong positive feelings, particularly of sexual attraction, towards clients • In organisations where supervision is viewed as 'hand holding', 'soft' or emotional babble
Fear of distortion in the professional encounter	• Practitioners may wish to be perceived as scientific and objective • Practitioners may believe that the expression of strong emotion belongs to the counselling realm and has no place in supervision • Practitioners may not trust the ability of the supervisor to 'hold' the emotional content • Practitioners may believe that an expression of feeling may prejudice a client's rights

It is not personal intellectual intelligence alone that enables us to successfully navigate life's various situations, either as direct workers or as supervisors our emotions also play a part. The skill of self-awareness helps us to counter our biases and reach for greater objectivity. (Dolgoff 2005, p.7)

Table 8.2 Barriers to the expression of feelings in supervision by the supervisor

Fear	Contributing factors
Fear of being overwhelmed by the supervisee's feelings	• Fear of becoming overwhelmed by the supervisee's pain • Old unresolved practice issues of the supervisor which threaten to resurface • Supervisor's own burnout and vulnerability • Fear of sharing supervisee's sense of shame and failure
Fear of exposing inadequacies as a supervisor	• Lack of skills and confidence to 'hold' the supervisee and deal with the feelings • Fear that the supervisor will not be able to 'make it better' • Feelings may be perceived as a sign that the supervisee is not coping and reflect badly on the supervisor • Conflict of demonstrating 'best practice ' when traditional practice norms have held feelings at a distance • Need to balance priorities of risk with expression of feelings
Fear of criticism	• In organisations where supervision is viewed as 'hand holding', 'soft' or emotional babble • In work contexts where public opinion is critical the focus of supervision becomes task and compliance centred • Where the practice ethos is evidence based • Where performance issues are evident and require urgent attention

The relevance of emotional intelligence to practitioners, Morrison (2007) notes, is well captured by Shulman (1999) who states that 'the capacity to be in touch with the client's feelings is related to the worker's ability to acknowledge his/her own. Before a worker can understand the power of emotion in the life of the client, it is necessary to discover its importance in the worker's own experience' (Shulman 1999, quoted in Morrison 2007, p.251). Emotional intelligence is thus recognised as an attribute which is as important to competent practice as the acquisition of skills and knowledge. Emotional intelligence influences how interpersonal relationships are managed and was originally thought to be a relatively stable trait. Recent research now indicates that it can be developed and improved, but opinions differ as to what activities will effect this change. Where Schutte *et al.* (2001, p.535) suggest that it is possible that training could influence an improvement in emotional intelligence, Clarke offers an alternative view. Clarke's study of hospice workers suggests that rather than training, 'team-based learning activities and supervision in particular figured most prominently as the major sources where this learning (emotional ability) took place' (Clarke 2006, p.459). In this study Clarke found that the process of reflection and discussion, both elements of supervision, enabled emotional abilities and experience to become visible and thus to be accessed. In this manner tacit learning becomes more 'explicit'. Clarke (2006) also emphasises the importance of the specific work context, and the surrounding cultural, social and organisational norms on the learning and demonstration of emotional abilities. Emotional intelligence is regarded by some as an essential attribute of practice and is considered by Morrison (2007, p.247) to set apart those practitioners who demonstrate that they possess it. According to Morrison the presence of emotional intelligence can be identified in a number of ways. He sees it, for example, in masters-level students who are distinguishable by a 'congruence of professional, academic and personal mindfulness' and 'an ability to make a positive impact above and beyond their competent colleagues'. Lack of emotional intelligence is seen in staff who 'lack accurate empathy, self-awareness and self management skills'. Finally, Morrison sees emotional intelligence as operating in competent practitioners whose understanding of, and facility to address, both the emotional and practical/technical components of practice is 'inextricably connected' (p.247).

Emotional intelligence is generally considered to comprise four interrelated domains. Two of these domains, 'self-awareness' and 'self-management', can be considered as intrapersonal domains whilst 'other awareness' and 'relationship management' are interpersonal (Morrison 2007, p.25). The interrelatedness is circular. Thus the awareness of one's own emotions leads to the understanding of and ability to monitor and manage those emotions. Awareness of one's own emotions also facilitates an awareness and understanding of the emotions of others. The management of one's own emotions, and an awareness of the emotions of others in turn assists the management of relationships. Howe suggests that emotionally intelligent people use their 'emotions to improve their reasoning' and typically 'cooperate and collaborate with others in mutually rewarding relationships' (Howe 2008, p.14).

As a necessary attribute for effective practice, Morrison argues that emotional intelligence contributes to practice through five core activities. These include engagement, assessment and observation, decision making, collaboration and cooperation and dealing with stress, building resilience and coping strategies (Morrison 2007, pp.253–258). In a similar manner emotional intelligence contributes to effective supervision.

Emotional intelligence is the ability that enables the supervisor to understand his or her own feelings and to manage these in the supervisory relationship. It is the ability to accurately read how his or her supervisees are feeling and to manage these feelings in relation to him or herself within the supervision relationship. Emotional intelligence will enhance the supervisor's ability to maintain the tensions and balance between support and challenge within supervision and to manage the complexities of power, authority and any dualities of role. A person who has high emotional intelligence is someone who conveys warmth and respect and elicits those response from others, communicates clearly and does not play power games, achieves a balance between personal acknowledgement of others and the formal aspects of professional relationships, has broad networks of relationships, is optimistic, examines mistakes for opportunities to learn and looks for solutions with mutual benefits (Dolgoff 2005, p.9). The capacity for meaningful interpersonal connectedness is thus seen to have a direct relationship to emotional intelligence.

It is clear that the high emotional demands of work within health and human services exacts a toll on the emotional resources of practitioners which can lead to stress and burnout (Morrison 2007, p.258). The role of supervision, and in particular the task of the supervisor, to attend to this interface between the practitioner and the practitioner's experience of and response to the emotional demands of practice is therefore critical to both the ongoing emotional well-being and resilience of the practitioner (Dwyer 2007) and to safe practice (Hughes and Pengelly 1997). At its best supervision is 'the forum in which the emotional resonance of practice on the practitioner is recognised and deliberated upon' (Dwyer 2007, p.52).

In Chapter 3 we discussed the development of the supervision relationship, in Chapter 6 we identified the facilitation of safe expression of emotion as a key task for a new supervisor and in Chapter 7 we identified some of the skills for conducting a supervision session. Here we recall this earlier information and, specifically, its application to the moments in supervision where emotion and emotional needs are central to the agenda. The first and most basic requirement of a supervisor is to be capable of listening and being present. In this manner the supervisor can be witness to, can validate, and 'hold' the emotional energy, pain, distress or possible despair of a supervisee. 'How one listens and feels listened to underpins what is said. If a person does not feel safe to speak, what is 'unhearable' becomes 'unheard of'. 'All is well' may rather mean 'all has not yet been spoken' (Smythe *et al.* 2009, p.22).

In his study of the experience of and handling of fear in supervision Smith concludes that 'participants did not want clever or 'helpful' interpretations of what they were feeling and why. They wanted to be allowed to rediscover their sense of self in the company of another' (Smith 2000, p.24). Smith describes the need for the listener to listen at a level which matches the intensity of the experience being recounted. Action, so often the panacea of discomfort, is not always required. In Smith's study the participants welcomed 'acceptable attempts to 'hold' and think about experiences rather than act as a result of them. 'Don't just do something – sit there!' seems to be the message' (p.23). The appreciation and importance of a supervisor's ability to 'meet' the supervisee's varied emotions is noted in other studies (Davys 2005b) and Toasland (2007, p.200) describes the role for the supervisor to 'receive, experience and make bearable' the emotions generated in the course of a practitioner's work.

The emotional work of supervision, however, extends beyond validation and support. If professional practitioners (and their supervisors) 'can tolerate experiencing and thinking about' their emotional responses to client work 'they will find in them a rich source of information about the core issues in the lives of their service users' (Hughes and Pengelly 1997, p.82).

In reflective supervision, taking the lid off is essential, not to expose or make a counselling client of the supervisee, but in order to explore the impact and the implications of strong feelings on practice (see also Chapter 6).

In this exploratory process, feelings are accepted, valued and examined for the information they hold and understanding they offer. With new information comes the possibility of choosing from a wider range of theories from which new strategies of intervention can be devised and reviewed. Possibilities for future action can be considered and rehearsed within a safe space where ongoing concerns and anxieties can be also be addressed. A consideration of the emotional threads of practice can lead to an identification of alternative motivations of both clients and practitioners and contingency plans can be made to address the possible implications of these.

WORKING WITH EMOTION IN SUPERVISION

The emotional work of supervision is the dual responsibility of both supervisor and supervisee. Bond and Holland (1998) describe the two primary emotional skills as awareness and acceptance. Awareness involves the ability of the practitioner to notice, value and evaluate his or her feelings.

Awareness thus promotes choice. When a practitioner knows how he or she feels he or she can decide how to respond to and behave in the moment. When situations are complex this choice may be to 'hold' or contain the feelings in order that they are taken to supervision where they can be expressed and more closely and extensively explored for meaning and understanding. Emotions can be identified by physical effects. Changes in body sensations, warmth and energy provide clues to underlying emotions both pleasant and unpleasant. Awareness, however, does not guarantee that practitioners will bring feelings to supervision for discussion. Practitioners must also be accepting and non-judgemental about whatever feelings arise in the course of their work: 'awareness and acceptance go hand in hand. The more you can come to accept your feelings non-judgementally, the easier it will become to be increasingly aware of your emotions and the energy that goes with them' (Bond and Holland 1998, p.125).

Containment

Containment of the feelings which arise from the content and context of practice is an important task for supervision. As discussed above, however, a clear distinction must be made between containment and accommodation. Hughes and Pengelly (1997, p.176) note that containment in supervision is often used as a form of 'collusive support' or as if it were a means of control . This latter approach to feelings is a valid strategy of practice but not of supervision. Containment in practice is employed 'in the moment' to 'contain' feelings until an appropriate time and safe place is available for expression and exploration. In this way Bond and Holland describe containment as an emotional skill. In situations in practice where, for valid professional reasons, it is not appropriate to express emotions 'containment is about expanding your sense of your own personal strength so that you can contain the feelings, gently "holding" that part of you which is feeling emotional and postponing expressing the feelings until a more appropriate time' (Bond and Holland 1998, p.125). Containment in this sense is a postponement, not suppression, of expressing and exploring feelings.

Containment, however, goes beyond the 'holding' of emotional material. Again, as described above, it requires the supervisor and the supervisee to examine and understand the information brought to supervision. Hughes and Pengelly (1997, p.176) define containment as 'the process in which authority becomes translated into effective interaction'. In this manner containment 'provides a concept for the capacity both to be truly (rather than collusively) supportive and to challenge effectively' (p.178). In a similar vein Gazzola and Theriault describe the need for supervisors to both create 'an atmosphere of safety and challenge the supervisee to go beyond his/her comfort level' (Gazzola and Theriault 2007, p.200). The process of containment supports the practitioner beyond the supervision session and provides an inner strength which the supervisee can carry into practice situations. 'If a worker is effectively contained through the supervisory process, they would introject a containing manager to support them through their work, and strengthen their abilities to contain their client's projections' (Toasland 2007, p.199). In this manner the supervisee is resourced and supported to withstand the emotional content of their work on a day-to-day basis. Of particular importance is the ability of the practitioner to manage the transferential processes which occur in all relationships, but in particular those between practitioners and their clients.

Importantly Hughes and Pengelly (1997) distinguish between the container and the contained. Effective containment includes the capacity of the supervisor to know him or herself as 'different' from the supervisee and thus to avoid becoming overwhelmed or wrung out by the emotional material which is brought by the supervisee to supervision. In this regard it is important for supervisors to access their own containment through their own process of supervision.

Transference, counter transference and parallel process

The feelings which supervisees bring to the supervision room emanate from a variety of sources and are not always immediately identifiable or palatable. The situations and accompanying feelings are often a product of the distortions of transferential and parallel processes. As Hughes and Pengelly so aptly observe 'the significance of supervision lies... in the search for meaning in the "grime" of difficult work-related feelings' (Hughes and Pengelly 1997, p.87). Transferential material provides useful information about and understanding of client situations. Examination of this material is also necessary in order that it does not interfere with or distort the supervision process. In order to explore these processes they first need to be identified and named (Page and Worsket 1994).

Definitions of transference describe a process whereby the feelings, attitudes and responses which belong to an earlier relationship are transferred or projected onto a person in the present (Bernard 2009; Hawkins and Shohet 2006; Hughes and Pengelly 1997). In social service settings transference may include the unwanted or painful feelings of the client which are projected onto the practitioner/supervisee. The transference, originating from the client's history, will thus intrude onto the client–practitioner relationship. Counter transference is the response of the person onto whom the feelings or attitudes have been transferred. Supervisees in turn may transfer feelings and attitudes onto their supervisors. It is possible that the supervisor may also have a counter response (counter transference) to the supervisee. The process can thus be multilayered and complex.

Transference can be identified in a number of ways. Careful attention to a supervisee's language and the images and metaphors which accompany a supervisee's description and experience of practice can provide useful clues (Hawkins and Shohet 2006). 'I feel like I am banging my head against a brick wall' or 'It is just like taming a wild animal.' These, often exasperated, comments by supervisees are metaphors which can reveal the hidden dynamics of relationship between the practitioner and the client. They provide a starting place for questions. 'In what way is this client like a wild animal?' 'How does this suggest the client views the relationship with you?' These are the sorts of useful exploratory questions which can begin to open discussion. In some cases a supervisee may first become aware of a client's transference when he or she recognises his or her own counter transference.

Counter transference is also an unconscious response, in this case by the practitioner in response to the client's situation. The importance of exploring counter transference is twofold. First, as it is outside of a practitioner's awareness, it brings this aspect of the relationship into consciousness in order that it can be 'known' and explored. Second, this exploration increases knowledge about, and understanding of, the client situation which will thus inform and assist in the 'work' with this client. Hawkins and Shohet (2006) name five types of counter transference:

- feelings/attitudes of the supervisee which have been stirred up by the client

- feelings/attitudes which have arisen as a result of the attributes assigned to the practitioner by the client

- the supervisee's (oppositional or counter) response to the role assigned by the client

- feelings, sensations, physical symptoms which have been projected by the client and which the supervisee has taken on

- the supervisee's desire for the client to change for his or her (the supervisee's) sake and not the client's own sake.

Transferential material is thus a rich source of information which can provide useful understanding of relationship dynamics. It is important, however, to delineate the boundary between supervision and therapy. Supervisee counter transference (or transference) may extend beyond the brief of supervision and require more than identification and naming for resolution. Page and Wosket refer to this when they advise supervisees to take any unresolved issues to his or her 'own therapeutic arena for further exploration and resolution' (Page and Wosket 1994, p.102).

Parallel process, sometimes called mirroring or reflection process, is a phenomenon considered to be unique to supervision (Bernard and Goodyear 2009, p.10). Parallel process is where the dynamics of the here and now or current relationship are unconsciously acted out in a second relationship. Thus, the dynamics of the client–practitioner relationship are repeated in the supervision relationship. A supervisor may discover that when discussing an equivocal 'yes but' client in supervision, a normally receptive supervisee presents as defensive and dismissive of any possible solution to his supervision issue. Parallel process is reversed when the supervisee behaves in client work in parallel to the relationship with his supervisor. In this manner supervision can have a direct effect on the work and dynamics of therapeutic relationships. The following vignette demonstrates how the dynamics of a client situation become mirrored in the supervision relationship.

Vignette – Sasha

A practitioner and her supervisor are discussing the case of Sasha, a 10-year-old boy who had been admitted to a foster care home because he was withdrawn, not communicating and was assessed as very depressed. Sasha had lived with his elderly grandmother since the age of six after his mother, a drug user, had overdosed and died. The grandmother lived in a small rural community where unemployment was endemic and educational aspiration low. The grandmother, however, still grieving the untimely death of her daughter (Sasha's mother), was determined that Sasha would break free from the limitations of the town. She had high expectations of his behaviour and scholastic achievement and did not encourage him to play with local children.

In the foster home Sasha flourished, participating in the activities with the other children, learning to play and responding to overtures of friendship. His grandmother was concerned with these changes which she interpreted as the first signs of the carefree lifestyle adopted by her daughter. She began making complaints against the foster home caregivers. The practitioner was working very hard with the grandmother and Sasha. She was concerned by this turn of events and was sensitive to the importance of their ongoing relationship.

During the supervision session, the supervisor made a number of critical observations about the practitioner's work with Sasha and questioned whether the foster care was really the best option. The practitioner, normally articulate and confident about her practice and ready to discuss and provide a rationale for her actions, accepted these observations from the supervisor without comment and left the session feeling hopeless and inadequate. Afterwards the supervisor was concerned by the critical attitude she had taken with regard to the practitioner's work. The practitioner was very capable and always thorough in her work.

After some reflection the supervisor realised that she and the practitioner might be behaving in parallel with the dynamics of the relationship between Sasha and his grandmother. The supervisor had become anxious and highly critical of the practitioner's work and the practitioner, in response (and out of character), had become withdrawn and defeated. When she raised this with the practitioner both recognised the parallel process and were able to explore this new insight and discuss future plans for Sasha with optimism and a fresh perspective.

As demonstrated in the vignette, parallel process is seldom conscious and generally enters into supervision as a form of 'discharge' by the supervisee or as an 'attempt to solve the problem through re-enacting within the here and now relationship' (Hawkins and Shohet 2006, p.94). The task of the supervisor is to first 'notice' the process. In order to do this the supervisor must be aware of, and value, his or her own responses in supervision and in particular notice when his or her response to a particular supervisee is 'different'. In this manner a supervisor can make conscious, or bring to the fore for consideration, dynamics which have originated in the client–practitioner relationship and which have been transported into supervision. As in the example above it may not be until after a supervision session that the supervision participants become aware of the 'altered' dynamics in the relationship. Unless the process is named it is not available for examination and the supervision process is at risk of highjack by the very dynamics it seeks to resolve.

RELATIONSHIP DYNAMICS IN SUPERVISION

Thus far in this chapter we have considered the emotional work of practice and the impact of this within the supervision relationship. We have emphasised the importance of reflection and the difference between accommodation and expression of feeling. We have also identified that containment is not 'suppression' and is more than support. Containment includes the ability to move beyond support to challenge and explore feelings for meaning and understanding.

We wish to conclude this chapter with discussion of the 'drama triangle' (Figure 8.1) which, in our experience, is one of the most frequently played out relationship dynamics in both social service practice and supervision. Karpman's triangle, or the drama triangle (Karpman 1968), comprises three roles: persecutor, rescuer and victim. This relationship dynamic or 'unhealthy process' (Morrison 1996) is frequently played out in situations where there are issues of inequality or power and is often transferred to supervision through parallel process (Hughes and Pengelly 1997).

The power of the drama triangle is in the switches or changes in role: each role has its own payoff. As such the drama triangle constitutes a game. 'Games are sets of ulterior transactions, repetitive in nature, with a well-defined psychological payoff' (Berne 1978). Morrison (1996) provides a very useful checklist of the common features of psychological 'games'. In summary this includes:

- non-specific, generalised and incomplete information is shared

- abrupt and inconsistent mood swings

- an avoidance of discussions about feelings or needs

- discussions become person rather than issue based

- incongruity between verbal and non-verbal communication

- feedback is unclear and indirect

- lack of resolution of issues

- pervasive sense of blame of self or the other(s)

- no acceptance of responsibility.

Morrison concludes that 'problems cannot be resolved when games are in action' (1996, p.93).

The very nature of the health and social service professions, particularly at the critical interface of care and protection, leaves practitioners susceptible to an enactment of the drama triangle. Organisational arrangements and relationships can also trip practitioners into roles which generate their own momentum and race around the three points of the triangle as participants struggle to gain clarity. As represented in Figure 8.1, the drama triangle comprises three roles: victim, persecutor and rescuer.

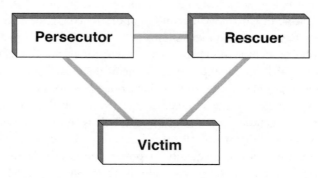

Figure 8.1 Drama triangle
Source: Reproduced from Karpman 1968 with kind permission from the author

A key to the drama triangle is to understand that it does not represent a whole person but rather particular roles which one person may assume in relation to another. The other key feature of the triangle is the absence of responsibility taken by any of the players.

Thus the victim eschews responsibility for events or actions and attributes blame onto the persecutor. The victim seeks a rescuer to save him or her from this unfair and untenable position.

The persecutor likewise does not consider themselves responsible for his or her actions and locates a victim or scapegoat to blame for shortcomings and failure. The rescuer meanwhile finds in the victim a 'worthy cause' and, in order to 'save' the oppressed and attribute responsibility, identifies the persecutor as the cause of all this distress. Of particular significance to the 'helping' professions, where there can be a wish to assist the oppressed, is the role of rescuer. It is the role of rescuer which completes the triangle. The victim requires a persecutor and the persecutor requires a victim. But it is the rescuer who requires both a victim and a persecutor and thus ensures that all roles are filled. The very nature of the triangle, however, is that the roles switch and change, thus ensuring that the drama continues and no resolution is reached. The victim, having gladly welcomed the rescuer, is ultimately disappointed with his or her efforts and 'blames' (persecutes) him or her for failure. The roles are thus switched and the rescuer becomes the victim and the victim the persecutor. The new victim may look to the original persecutor for 'help' or rescue or may draw in a new player to fill that role and so on. In the following vignette Nelly is readily hooked into the role of rescuer of the client only to find herself the victim of his criticism when things go wrong.

Vignette – Nelly

Nelly, a community mental health worker, was approached by a long-term patient of her service. The client had a long history of supervised care in a local hostel. The client (victim) approached Nelly with claims that he was very unhappy in the hostel where he said his money was being withheld and he was not being given the same freedom as other residents. On behalf of the client Nelly (rescuer) wrote a letter to the manager of the hostel. When the manager (persecutor) replied that he was unwilling to alter the care arrangements Nelly (rescuer/persecutor) organised alternative care for the client in a facility which had more flexible supervision. Within a week the client was picked up by the police as drunk and disorderly and admitted to the public hospital. The client (persecutor) was very upset and blamed Nelly (victim) for not having sent him to an appropriate new care facility. He missed his friends and this is why he had got drunk. He now wanted to return to his original hostel. The original hostel was now unable to accommodate the client as all beds were full. In supervision Nelly (persecutor) complained about the inflexibility of the original hostel manger and (victim) expressed her hurt that the client had not appreciated her help. The supervisor heard Nelly out and then asked her about her process of moving the client in the first instance. Nelly (victim) saw this as an attack on her professional decision making and accused the supervisor (persecutor) of being unhelpful and not open to allowing mental health clients any choice.

The victim, persecutor, rescuer role dynamic is one of the most common problematic interactions which is brought to supervision. Whilst recognition of the process and identification of the interactions can be sufficient to break the cycle and open the way for creative resolution there are other helpful models which can also be used here. In supervision, and all transactions for that matter, games can be initiated by any member of the interaction. It is important to remember that if a 'game' is in action then everyone is playing. In order to stop a game one need only stop playing. In supervision either a supervisor or a supervisee can be the initiator of a game. It is also important to note that many interactions during one's daily activities have elements of game playing and family interactions in particular can often include 'gamey' interactions. What is important is to recognise, acknowledge and stop those interactions which we do not want and which lead to unhealthy relationships and prevent the resolution of problems.

Morrison (1996, p.98) identifies a list of strategies which can be employed to stop a game. Amongst these he notes the importance of identifying how the 'game' starts, who starts it and how one gets 'hooked' into the exchange. Most significantly Morrison recommends that participants identify what 'payoff' keeps them playing and the corollary 'What would be the cost of stopping'?

Over the years a number of variations have been applied to Karpman's triangle (Karpman 2007). One variation which we have found to be a most useful tool is the 'empowerment circle' (Cornelius and Faire 2006). The 'empowerment circle' identifies alternative roles which can be employed to break the repetitive cycle of the drama triangle. Essentially the 'empowerment circle' pairs each of the three psychological roles identified by Karpman with an alternative constructive role. The shift of roles brings with it an accompanying shift in behaviour and elicits a different response. Cornelius and Faire describe their model as a circle but for consistency of structure here we have represented it as an empowerment triangle (Figure 8.2). The roles are paired as follows: persecutor–educator/consultant, victim–learner, rescuer–mediator/facilitator (Cornelius and Faire 2006, p.106).

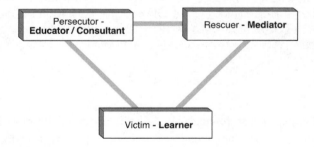

Figure 8.2 Empowerment triangle
Source: Adapted with permission from diagrams in Cornelius, H. and Faire, S. (2006) *Everyone can win: Responding to Conflict Constructively.* Sydney: Simon and Schuster, p.106.

Thus, if one finds oneself assuming a persecutor role the challenge is to become an educator or consultant. As an educator the task is to educate and provide information. An educator asks the question 'What information would be helpful for others to know in this situation?' An educator or consultant is interested in the ideas of others and listens to and acknowledges their needs and considers differing views. When decisions are made the process is open and, where possible, collaborative and includes the views and needs of others.

If one finds oneself invited into, or if one assumes, the role of rescuer the challenge is to become a mediator or facilitator. Implicit in the rescuer role is an assumption that the 'victim' is not capable of helping him or herself and therefore needs rescuing. Questions which ask 'victims' to identify how they might themselves resolve the issue convey the belief that they are indeed capable. Similarly, assisting someone to take action rather than 'doing' it for them conveys respect. A discussion of the broader context of situations and the possible reasons for behaviour (which have appeared persecutory) can help a 'victim' to understand other perspectives and possible motivation for behaviour.

Finally, in situations when one feels like a victim it is useful to become a learner. 'What can I learn from this situation? What action can I take here? Can I approach this situation myself? What support might I need to do this? Why do I need to complain to others? How do I benefit from this position am I in? How willing am I to resolve this situation? What responsibility am I avoiding here?' These questions generate responsibility and promote a sense of ownership for both action and inaction and create choice rather than passive acceptance and powerlessness.

Vignette – Nelly: the alternative script

Nelly, a community mental health worker, was approached by a long-term patient of her service. The client had a long history of supervised care in a local hostel. The client (potential victim) approached Nelly with claims that he was very unhappy in the hostel where he said his money was being withheld and he was not being given the same freedom as other residents. On behalf of the client Nelly (mediator) organised a meeting between the manager and the client to discuss this situation. At the meeting the manager (potential persecutor) replied that he was unwilling to alter the arrangements. He (educator) explained that over the years the client had consistently refused to abide by the rules of the hostel. Nelly (mediator) encouraged the manager (educator) to explain what the client would need to do in order to hold the same privileges as other residents. The client (victim) was very upset and blamed Nelly (potential persecutor) for not standing up to the manager. Nelly (educator) reiterated the reasons put forward by the manager. She (mediator) encouraged the client to list the things he did like about the hostel and what specifically he (potential learner) would be prepared to change. The client (victim) left in an angry huff. In supervision Nelly (victim) complained about the client's lack of appreciation for her efforts and how she was fed up with working in this area where there were no resources and loads of frustrations. The supervisor heard Nelly out and then asked her what she had learned from this episode. Nelly (persecutor) said she resented this approach from the supervisor and was not going to fall for that game and that she had nothing to learn. What had happened was not her fault and she had done her best. The supervisor (educator) summarised her view of the case and praised the work that Nelly had done, acknowledging the care she had taken to get both the client and the manager talking and agreeing that this was a hard and sometimes thankless job. Nelly, feeling heard and appreciated began to plan for her next encounter with the client.

Challenging moments in supervision arrive in various forms and will often be a combination of the situations and dynamics described in this chapter. At these moments supervisors may feel overwhelmed, anxious, inadequate or just plain tired. What is most important is that supervisors take note and value their own responses in the same way that we have adjured practitioners to notice their responses from practice. It is through noticing and valuing these responses that the first clues about relationship dynamics and disturbances can be found.

The following checklist can be a helpful start for supervisors in these situations:

- What am I noticing in this situation?

- How does this differ from my usual feelings with this supervisee or in supervision?

- What are we not talking about here?

- What information is implicit, not defined or not available?

- Who is carrying responsibility for this situation and do I think that is reasonable?

- What am I feeling right now about this situation?

- How am I contributing to this situation?

- What can I do differently right now?

Chapter 9

Promoting
Professional Resilience

The role of personal support in supervision is often contested due to concerns about slippage across professional boundaries (Yegdich 1999b). The functions of supervision have long included the 'supportive' (Kadushin 1976) and the 'restorative' (Proctor 2001) functions, which essentially address those aspects of supervision where the personal and professional spheres intertwine. Generally it is accepted that professional boundaries impose limits to the depth of 'personal work' that is undertaken in supervision. While there are tensions at the boundary of the personal and the professional, we agree that 'support' is retained as a core condition of effective supervision, underlining the significance of the self in professional work (Hughes and Pengelly 1997). However, it is by no means straightforward to try to define the boundaries, and the nuanced accounts of much supervision practice demonstrate that the personal and professional do collide. In their 1998 review article, Yegdich and Cushing asserted that confusion was created by Butterworth (1994) when it was suggested that clinical supervision would:

> promote both personal and professional development. That these areas are intimately connected is not in dispute...what is lost for refinement are the nuances of how professional development may feed into personal development and vice versa, while the notion that one will automatically bolster the other is naively accepted. (Yegdich and Cushing 1998, p.15)

Recent research clearly indicates that supervision can provide some protection against the corrosive effects of exposure to demanding, stressful work and the impact of working closely with service users who have traumatic stories and are distressed by emotional, psychological and physical experiences (Mor Barak et al. 2009). Increasingly governments, professional bodies and employers have developed responses to reduce the risk that professionals working in health, social care and justice settings will be harmed by their work. Western governments have acknowledged the obligation to ensure workplaces and practices are safe and that workers have access to a range of mechanisms to prevent harm. Employee assistance programmes, monitoring workload and leave and supervision are amongst these services.

For supervision practice new insights from supervision research (Mor Barak *et al.* 2009) and from studies in other fields such as resilience, emotional intelligence (Goleman 2005) and positive psychology bring increased awareness of the potential for supervisors to make a difference. This chapter will review the research on problematic stress in health and social care and consider a range of useful strategies for both strengthening protective factors for professionals and methods for assistance when stress becomes a problem.

STRESS IN THE HELPING PROFESSIONS

Much of our work demands that we draw extensively upon our own personal resources, and these are likely to be worn down through constant use... The accumulation of stress may be gradual and insidious, and sometimes it arrives suddenly and overwhelmingly. (Brown and Bourne 1996, p.107)

In social services the aim of reducing harm from stress and the detrimental effects of work on staff is visible in fields such as child protection, mental health and the oversight of criminal offenders where 'high-stakes' risk assessment imposes greater accountability on practitioners, and public expectations may often be experienced as overwhelming and unrealistic. As we have seen in Chapter 4 the attempts to reduce workplace harm is often undermined by workloads and the impact of frequent organisational change.

Maslach delineates three major components to the experience of severe work-related distress, or burnout, as it is commonly known in the helping professions. These are emotional exhaustion, depersonalisation and diminished personal accomplishment (Maslach 1978, p.58). Kalliath and Beck (2001, p.72) note that each of these components need to be considered when examining the impacts of caring work. Stress is corrosive of practitioners' engagement in their organisation and work with service users, as well as their overall well-being.

In the previous few decades the demands of high pressure environments have required practitioners to be highly skilled at rapid and accurate assessment of patient and service user problems and the application of evidence-informed interventions in an efficient and accurate manner. Workers feel pressure to be 'scientific' and objective and employ empirical models of practice but, somewhat paradoxically, practitioners are urged to be mindful of their own feelings and interpret and reflect on these. There is increased understanding of the significance of emotion at work and supervision is intended to create a reflective space in which these competing voices can be heard and attended to. The helping professions employ both science and emotion in everyday practice. Good practice requires the updating of knowledge for practice and the support of practitioners' emotional strengths.

THE STRESS SYSTEM

Collins describes stress 'as the product of complex interactions between environmental and organizational demands and the individual's ability to cope with these demands'. Problematic stress or 'distress' arises 'from a disparity between the perceived demands made on an individual and their perceived ability to cope' (Collins 2008, p.1176). Thompson also reminds us that many factors in practitioners' personal lives also impact on work and vice versa (Thompson 2009, p.8). Most practitioners may experience role strain, where stressful working conditions and caring roles within families compete with time for rest and recreation. In health and social care, stress factors can be generated at numerous sites (Brown and Bourne 1996): in the practice itself, in teams and organisations and the other bodies encountered by professionals in their work. Relationships in these sites contain myriad problems compounded by deficits experienced by practitioners in their agencies – lack of resources, inadequate supervision, inadequate debriefing after critical incidents and the acceptance of a high level of personal abuse from service users (Beddoe 2003) and colleagues (van Heugten 2009). Workplace exposure to verbal and physical abuse is an ever-present part of the job despite the 'zero tolerance' rhetoric (Elston et al. 2002; Gabe and Elston 2008). Supervision is a key component in the ongoing management of the impact of this traumatic exposure, although it must be seen as one part of an ecological approach to worker well-being in high stress organisations and not the panacea for all problems (Adamson 2001). Figure 9.1 illustrates the practitioner's position in the centre of a complex set of systems.

Figure 9.1 The stress system

Table 9.1 maps how stress factors can emerge from all aspects of the stress system, starting with the personal life of the practitioner, including their health, personal and family relationships and obligation, social and cultural dimensions, practice strengths and challenges. All these factors collide with the demands of practice in professional life. Brown and Bourne took a systems approach to stress in social work that has utility across professions. Their model identified stressors at the following points: the practitioner's personal life, their current and past practice and the intersection of this with previous stressful or traumatic events, the team and agency context (1996, pp.108–109). Examining this 13 years later, we note the need to add stress factors that have intensified in their impact on practitioners and supervisors in all fields. Accordingly, we have added to Brown and Bourne's model the dynamics of community expectations and relationships; the pressures of inter-agency and interprofessional work and the impact of rapid policy change and political agendas. For professionals working in services for children and vulnerable adults, general community and societal understandings and attitudes towards service also impact on practitioner stress. We note also the associated stresses of working with groups who may be stigmatised.

Table 9.1 A systemic perspective on stressors in health and social care

Systems	Stressors
1. *Personal*	Stress factors in the practitioner's personal life, for example: • relationship difficulties • health • addictions • loss or bereavement • financial difficulties • familial responsibilities • personal history of abuse or difficulties
2. *Practice*	Stress factors arising from the practice: • overly high proportion of high complexity 'cases' • abuse and/or violence in the field or clinical setting • racism, sexism, homophobia, religious intolerance, cultural stereotyping • being the subject of threats and vexatious complaints • large caseloads, high proportion of difficulty • high-profile cases where risk assessment is a major factor
3. *Workplace*	Stress factors emanating from the practitioner's team situation: • status and power issues and dysfunctional teams • personal conflicts • bullying and/or harassment • frontline staff feel undervalued • involvement with other colleagues' work stress
4. *Agency*	Stress factors arising in employment: • restructuring and redundancies • competitive environment, contracting and funding uncertainties • interprofessional conflict • poor physical working conditions
5. *Community*	Stressors emanating from the social environment: • attitudes towards illness (physical and mental) and social distress • attitudes towards service users • public ambivalence about intervention • care and control contradictions • unrealistic expectations
6. *Sociopolitical environment*	Stressors emanating from the sociopolitical environment: • low tolerance of mistakes and the crisis of trust • the political nature of public services • audit culture • media interest in exposing professional fallibility • for some professions, low status and poor public understanding of the professional role

Source: Adapted from Brown and Bourne 1996

Vignette – Jenny: part 1

Jenny is a 45-year-old nurse in a community health setting working in a child development team. She is the principal earner in her household, her partner is a part-time student and 'house husband'. Jenny's mother has struggled all her life with alcohol and Jenny is frequently called to her care home because her mother is drunk and aggressive. Her father has not been seen for 16 years. She has always identified heavily with service users with addiction problems and has been challenged before about her boundaries.

Jenny's service is much stretched, major budget cuts have led to recent staff reductions and restructuring. Jenny plans to apply for a promotion to team leader. Her partner needs more money for his university fees and they really need the additional salary the promotion will bring. She is suspicious that she won't get the job because she feels strongly the service manager doesn't like her.

Jenny is currently working very long hours and is under a great deal of stress with one particular case. She has been working with the Grimm family; James (six), a child with fragile health, is currently very unwell. His mother, Tamsin has a serious gambling problem and her ability to cope with the care of James is deteriorating. Jenny is in conflict with the family's child protection social worker who is insistent that James is better off with Mum. Jenny sees the household becoming dirtier and more chaotic and worries about the poor nutrition and personal care James is getting. Jenny has been visiting James's home virtually every day and another worker in her team was shocked to find that Jenny had taken James out to medical appointments and even to the park on the weekend because she knew that Tamsin was regularly leaving James and his sister (nine) at home alone to go to the casino. Jenny has not reported this to the child protection social worker.

Back at the office things are very difficult – Jenny is now the source of gossip and doesn't get on with several people in the team and she is seen as shirking her share of caseload and focusing on her favourite clients.

Table 9.2 illustrates how Jenny's situation can be mapped out against the systemic stressors illustrated in Table 9.1. There is no expectation that a supervisor can or will address all of these but they are inevitably going to feature in the 'business' of supervision and the personal may intrude more, as Jenny's distress increases.

Table 9.2 A systems approach to assisting stressed supervisees

Stressor systems	Jenny's story	Systems interventions
Personal	Financial Gambling Mother's addiction	Refer to employee assistance programme
Practice	Difficulties with service users with whom she over-identifies Previous performance feedback Professional boundaries	Refer to employee assistance programme or personal counselling or treatment Supervision and links to appraisal
Team	Personal relationships Workload and equitable allocation	Team meetings Negotiation and transparent mechanisms to allocate work
Agency	Promotion Interprofessional relationships Restructuring Budget cuts	Supervision and support for personal professional development Team and agency meeting – open communication
Community	Inter-agency relationships and protocols	Regular focused meetings Clear expectations of staff relationships with other practitioners and developing partnerships
Sociopolitical climate	Gambling Addictions Resourcing for health and social services	Communication from 'the bottom up' to organisational hierarchy, professional action through membership of professional and community advocacy groups

THE SUPERVISOR'S APPROACH TO STRESS

In Table 9.2 we suggested supervisory interventions that could assist Jenny in her situation. A map of systemic sources of stress is useful and we suggest that supervisors follow Brown and Bourne's suggestion that mapping their own situation can be helpful to practitioners in understanding the complexity of their work environment (Brown and Bourne 1996, pp.109–110). Starting a new supervision relationship is a good time to explore with supervisees their personal experience of any workplace stress that has become distressing. Questions might include:

'Tell me about a time that you were distressed and what strategies you employed to manage this?'

'What do you think are the major triggers of distress for you in your job?'

'How will I know when you're stressed?'

'What's helpful for you when you're stressed?'

'What is unhelpful for you when you're stressed?'

'What can we put in place to assist you to avoid distress and strengthen your own good strategies?'

'Can we talk about how you want me to approach support for you if I notice that you are becoming distressed by work pressures?'

Asking specific questions and focusing on the behaviours rather than the problems assists supervisors to develop an understanding with their supervisees about their coping styles and takes a collaborative rather than a problematising approach to stress.

Supervisors can employ many skills and resources to aid them to work with supervisees: referral to employee assistance programmes for personal problems; referral to personal counselling or treatment; using transparent processes to discuss workload in individual and team meetings (where applicable); developing clear expectations of staff relationships with other practitioners and developing partnerships. At the organisational level supervisors can develop and model communication from 'the bottom up' to the organisational hierarchy, and support supervisees to find constructive ways to contribute to improving the workplace and processes. A constant source of stress in organisations is practitioner frustration with 'red tape' – compliance activities or procedures that pose barriers to good practice and their ability to meet the needs of service users. Finally, practitioners can develop their active participation in and leadership of advocacy for change through membership of professional organisations and community advocacy groups.

There is evidence that supervisor support can make a difference to practitioner well-being at work. Kalliath and Beck tested the idea that low levels of supervisory support would impact on job burnout and the turnover intentions of nurses. This study hypothesised that low supervisory support would have a direct effect on emotional exhaustion, depersonalisation and turnover intentions. The study tested a model against data from 250 nurses and found that 'low supervisory support results in higher levels of exhaustion, depersonalization and intention to quit' (Kalliath and Beck 2001, p.76). Kalliath and Beck's research strongly supports consideration of supervision as a support mechanism available to nurses to combat the negative impact of emotional exhaustion and depersonalization (p.76).

Mor Barak *et al.* recently reported a meta-analysis in which they found that 'effective supervision, therefore, can delay or mitigate the effects of detrimental factors and can contribute to positive outcomes for workers in social service organizations' (Mor Barak *et al.* 2009, p.25). Citing Kadushin and Harkness (2002) they assert that 'accumulating research on supervision indicates that the various dimensions of supervision may have protective, proactive, or preventive roles in ensuring a positive work environment that can contribute to worker effectiveness and potentially to quality service delivery' (p.25). With a focus on broad welfare and service organisations Mor Barak *et al.* encourage organisations to provide supervisors with training that covers three key supervisory dimensions emerging from the study: task assistance, social and emotional support, and strong supervisory interpersonal interaction (p.27). Andrea's story illustrates how supervision can support practitioners to develop an approach to their work that takes account of feelings.

Vignette – Andrea: part 1

Andrea works in a child health service as a community-based nurse with specialist skills in child development. The service is extremely over stretched, workloads are high and a series of restructurings have meant that many practitioners have not had supervision for months.

In working with a four-year-old boy and his mother, Andrea has been monitoring Timmy's progress with a medication regime in which medication dosages are increased if improvements are not reaching a certain level at prescribed intervals. Timmy is not making progress and Andrea discusses the results of testing with the team consultant and they agree to raise the dosage.

As Andrea drives away from Timmy's house the following day she is struck by an uncomfortable feeling that she is missing something. She feels nauseated and a little shaky. Timmy's mother Angela is very anxious and has been very reluctant to take on the medication regime as she feels that a 'good mother' should be able to make her child well with diet and loving care.

Andrea wonders if Angela is not giving Timmy all his tablets but dismisses this thought as silly. She fleetingly considers mentioning this to her team leader but he's more stressed out than she is so she moves on to their next task. As she gets out of the car at the next house she mutters to herself that this is not what she was taught in her nursing degree... As she knocks on the door the feelings of nausea return.

In this situation Andrea is suppressing her feelings about this potentially explosive case. The recognition that use of self is a key component in effective practice leads to a consideration of the usefulness of techniques such as mindfulness. The construct of mindfulness offers a composite of skills that can provide workers with a deeper understanding of the process of reflection. Mindfulness involves a focus on the present moment and sustained attention, concentration, limiting reactions and suspending judgement. Birnbaum used relaxation, mindfulness meditation and guided meditation to focus on students' capacity to become 'observers of self' and to develop their inner voice in order to facilitate self-awareness and the use of 'self' as a tool in helping relationships. Birnbaum notes: 'The ability to observe ourselves is acquired and entails listening and tuning in to ourselves and the world around us. The observing self is better able to listen and identify the different voices that exist within and around it' (Birnbaum 2005, unpaginated).

It is assumed that the more conscious practitioners are about the way they perceive, interpret and interact with phenomenon in their environment the greater the likelihood that they will be able to select responses that are effective in practice. Skills cultivated by mindfulness practice comprise: self-awareness, self-observation, self-care, emotion regulation, a deepened sense of empathy and a predisposition for personal responsibility (Baer 2006; Birnbaum 2005; Claxton 2005; Kondrat 1999; Lau *et al.* 2006; Morrison 2007). Each of these skills is pertinent to the development of an emotionally competent practitioner (Morrison 2007). In learning to be mindful, practitioners create the opportunity to consciously use themselves to best effect in the complex and challenging situations encountered in professional practice.

Vignette – Andrea: part 2

We return to Andrea, who notices her symptoms and decides to stop for a few minutes and practise her mindfulness techniques, rather than rushing off to her next activity. Andrea noticeably calms and feels better as she focuses on her breathing and relaxing her muscles. The nausea lessens. She returns to her busy role but has noted that she should trust her own feelings and follow up on her concerns about Timmy and Angela. She makes a mental note, too, that she must take this experience to supervision. She wants to urgently plan the next steps in ensuring that Timmy is safe.

TRAUMATIC INCIDENTS AND THE ROLE OF SUPERVISORS

It is not just the everyday experience of stress that challenges practitioners. All practitioners in the helping professions are in line to experience either directly or indirectly a critical incident or traumatic event in their workplace or in a work-related context. Stressed practitioners are particularly vulnerable to traumatic or critical incidents. Adamson reminds us that 'our assumptive worldview relies on an ontological security that we are safe, that the sky is not going to fall in on us today' (1999, p.30). Both serious incidents and the juxtaposition of stressful everyday events can propel practitioners into a situation where they may feel deeply distressed and unable to cope. It is not uncommon for people in such situations to use expressions such as 'I didn't see that coming' or 'it was like a bolt from the blue'. Their equilibrium is disturbed by the unexpected event or even the unexpected strong emotional reaction to an event.

There are numerous ways in which professionals can experience harmful exposure. Apart from the longer term impact of stressful workplaces there are times when the boundaries of service user and work experience become blurred. Adams, Figley and Boscarino (2008, pp.239–240) note that 'empathic engagement with traumatized clients often requires the professional to discuss details of the traumatic experience'. As a consequence health and social care workers may report symptoms connected to 're-experiencing the client's traumatic event, wishing to avoid both the client and reminders of the client's trauma, and persistent arousal' (p.240).

As noted earlier in this chapter health workers also face the daily risk of verbal and physical abuse (Elston, Gabe and O'Beirne 2006), and to illustrate this we will return to Jenny's experience.

Fear in practice: promoting practitioner safety

Jenny's story continues in order to consider the impact of critical incidents and to explore the supervisor's role.

Vignette – Jenny: part 2

As a result of feedback from James's school, Jenny and the child protection social worker decide to do a joint visit to address James's care and protection needs with Tamsin. They find her aggressively drunk and hard to engage. Tamsin's temper quickly flares up when James's well-being is questioned. She lashes out at Jenny, giving her bruises and an abrasion on the arm, before falling awkwardly and cutting her head open on the fireplace. There is a lot of blood: Tamsin is initially moaning and incoherent. At this point, the care and protection social worker freezes, and Jenny has to take charge and call an ambulance.

James returns from school and as no family members can be located he is taken into care. Tamsin threatens to 'get' Jenny as soon as she is out of hospital. 'I know where you live,' she says. Jenny returns to the office at 6.15pm. Everyone else has gone home except her supervisor.

The supervision literature tends to be somewhat silent on workplace violence, with a notable exception being Brown and Bourne (1996) who emphasise that the skills for dealing with stress and traumatic events are essential components of a contemporary supervisor's repertoire. There may be some acculturation in supervisors' experience that has blunted their awareness of what might be happening for supervisees. Just as frontline workers may have reduced empathy in the face of constant human suffering, supervisors may become less responsive to supervisee concerns. In child protection and adult services, the stigmatisation of service users adds to the critical attitudes of the public generated by practice failures. Supervisors may unwittingly be modelling unhelpful strategies (Beddoe 2003), unaware of the impact of hostile public attitudes on their own approach to practice.

BEING FEARLESS – 'IT'S A WAR ZONE!'

This kind of practice involves defensive practice. There is a danger of internalising negative expectations and being prescriptive and authoritarian. The message is 'this is how to survive!' (Beddoe 2003, p.22). Unfortunately these practitioners are likely to be blamed if they are assaulted. This approach may place supervisees at grave risk through exposing them to unnecessarily dangerous situations (Smith 2006).

BEING PASSIVE AND AVOIDING CONFLICT – 'IT'S A MATTER OF SURVIVAL – LIVE TO FIGHT ANOTHER DAY!'

This approach can signal a serious threat to competent decision making. The dangers are well documented, especially in the child protection literature (Goddard and Tucci 1991; Morrison 1997). Practitioners who strive to use verbal engagement skills to enable a positive relationship with service users may avoid conflict to the detriment of children and vulnerable adults, their own safety and that of colleagues. In addition they may 'miss' vital information generated by their personal experience of the hostile and angry person (Beddoe 2003, p.22).

Smith studied the responses of practitioners to the question 'What responses would you like from an ideal supervisor to whom you took an experience of fear?' What participants wanted was their supervisor to make time to 'listen to them without criticism… A capacity to understand, acknowledge and recognise' the experience, followed by 'reflection, non-critical exploration, validation, affirmation and confirmation of the supervisee' and support and action as needed (Smith 2000, p.18).

What then are Jenny's needs after the event described above, where as an already stressed nurse she has now experienced a frightening incident and has been injured herself? There are some essential differences between regular scheduled supervision and a supervisory response to a critical incident response (Adamson 2001). Supervision is planned – incidents are not. Intervention post incident may be directive, practical and time limited while supervision involves a longer term engagement. There are multiple agendas in supervision (support, education, administration), there are also multiple agendas within critical incident management (e.g. practical assistance, 'normalisation', debriefing and reintegration) and 'the demands of an incident make these tasks less parallel and more sequential' (Adamson 2001, p.41). Immediately after a critical event the needs of the incident predominate. Where 'normal' supervision is essentially reflective, this is a crisis and premature reflection may be inappropriate (p.38).

Where a supervisor also has organisational responsibilities he or she may have to balance 'damage control' strategies in terms of service user safety issues with the needs of the practitioner in front of them. Adamson notes that the 'enabling' aspects of supervision may need to be balanced with any 'ensuring' components (p.40). In Jenny's situation there may be compelling management responsibilities which need to be addressed, follow up with the hospital, alerting others who need to know.

Critical incidents will clearly affect more people than those immediately involved and some effort may be needed to address this at both individual and team level. There is a level of additional stress generated in teams and workplaces after an incident such as Jenny's where post incident reactions on the part of the survivor may include intense irritability and an apparent inability to acknowledge the impact of the event.

An additional issue to consider is that supervisors, especially if they work in the same service as an affected supervisee, may also face strong feelings (Adamson 2001). These may include feelings of inadequacy and incompetence, worry about the impact on the wider team, the supervisor's own fears and anxieties, concerns about 'victim's' competence and fears about consequences and organisational vulnerabilities (Bourne and Brown 1996).

COPING AND RESILIENCE

Collins identifies two styles of coping strategy: problem-solving coping and emotion-focused coping (Collins 2008, p.1177). The former strategy involves active efforts to change the current negative circumstances: planning, seeking the involvement of others, communication and seeking practical advice, assistance or information. Goal-oriented strategies encourage a sense of control (Collins 2007, p.262). Emotion-focused coping includes seeking support for emotional reasons, seeking sympathy or understanding (Collins 2008, p.1180). Opportunities to talk about stressful situations and distressing thoughts and feelings can help practitioners make meaning out of negative events and situations which in turn aids integration and resolution of stressful experiences (Brown and Bourne 1996; Collins 2007, 2008). Supervision provides the space for the ventilation of emotion. Ventilation is important but there is some evidence that overemphasis on venting emotion in supervision can be negative. Collins draws on Carver et al. (1989), suggesting that 'over-use of ventilation and sympathy seeking for long periods may not always be adaptive and can impede "adjustment", as it is believed too much focus on distress can distract people from active coping and movement beyond distress' (Collins 2008, p.1180). An active engagement of positive emotions is important to avoid disengagement, depersonalisation and anger or disillusionment with service users (Satymurti 1981).

Extensive venting of emotion in supervision can also be corrosive of supervisors, and this is perhaps exacerbated when supervisors and supervisees share stressful circumstances. At the lower end of intensity, this may mean supervisors can be overexposed to the complaints and stress narratives of others and become desensitised and irritated. Under these circumstances reflection is difficult and venting is easier. This passage by Busse about becoming a supervisor illustrates this clearly:

At the beginning of supervision I was faced with dissatisfaction and a stream of abuse. Apart from spontaneous flight tendencies as a result of this scenario, I also felt a desire to reflect. The combination of issues...offered everything a supervisor needs to feel challenged. Initially it was difficult for me not to give in to the urge to offload, which time and again manifested itself in complaining and moaning by the supervised. (Busse 2009, p.166)

Busse noted over time that he himself started 'to complain about these difficult and unprofessional people... The situation that the supervised experienced in their everyday life threatened to reproduce itself in supervision' (Busse 2009, p.166).

At a level of greater intensity of stress, in circumstances that are more emphatically traumatic, Dekel and Baum developed the term 'shared traumatic reality' to describe where practitioners 'live and work in the same community as the people they serve' and are exposed to the same 'traumatising circumstances as their clients' (Dekel and Baum 2009, p.8). In crisis intervention, especially after major disasters, terrorism or violence, professionals are not only helping survivors to navigate through a stressful event and cope with the emotional consequences, but are also having to cope with their own circumstances and emotions, and if in leadership roles having a duty of care to look out for the needs of their teams (p.8).

PROMOTING RESILIENT PRACTITIONERS: HOPE, OPTIMISM AND BALANCE

It is important to maintain a balanced view of the experiences of professional practitioners in the helping professions. A study of Canadian child welfare workers (Stalker *et al.* 2007) unexpectedly found participants scoring high on a measure of emotional exhaustion and, at the same time, 'high on overall job satisfaction' (pp.182–183). Individual characteristics, for example finding support in relationships with supervisors and colleagues, strong personal reward in helping others, 'having a commitment to the mandate of child welfare and believing that one's labour is "making a difference", contribute to satisfaction with child welfare work in spite of work overload and emotional exhaustion' (p.182). Reviewing this research confirms that there are preventive strategies to promote continuing optimistic engagement with the work, although Stalker *et al.* sound a note of caution that the incidence of emotional exhaustion should not be ignored because of its potential to contribute to depersonalisation (p.189).

Collins (2007, p.256) asks: 'What might enable some workers to persist, endure and thrive in their careers, compared to others who may become ill and sometimes eventually leave individuals the profession?' Collins notes three kinds of coping strategies which relate to positive affect: 'positive appraisal, goal-directed/problem focused work and the infusion of ordinary events with meaning' (p.255). Recent research has indicated that resilient qualities are important for workers in the helping professions. 'Psychological resilience refers to effective coping and adaptation although faced with loss, hardship, or adversity' (Tugade and Frederickson 2004, p.320). Resilient individuals experience the frustration and anxiety brought to the surface in adverse times but even at the centre of these experiences they are able to call upon positive emotions and use humour, creativity and problem solving. Luthans, Yousef and Avolio (2007a, p.3) have used the phrase 'psychological capital', which is 'an individual's positive psychological state of development and is characterized by: (1) having confidence (self-efficacy) to take on and put in the necessary effort to succeed at challenging tasks; (2) making a positive attribution (optimism) about succeeding now and in the future; (3) persevering toward goals and, when necessary, redirecting paths to goals (hope) in order to succeed; and (4) when beset by problems and adversity, sustaining and bouncing back and even beyond (resilience) to attain success'. Research on the linked constructs of 'hope, resilience, optimism, and efficacy supports that they are developable' (Luthans et al. 2007b, p.545). A study of nursing care assistants confirmed that 'supportive relationships, adequate resources, encouragement by others, and improving perceptions of self-efficacy (ability to achieve goals in their workplace) may foster their hope' (Duggleby, Cooper and Penz 2009, p.2376). As a general rule coping skills, access to personal and social support and the fostering of individual characteristics such as hopefulness and self-efficacy are cited as beneficial in protecting practitioners from the potentially debilitating effects of their work.

Feudtner et al. (2007, p.187) draw on Snyder (2000) in delineating three main components of hope: 'first, individuals who are able to anchor their thinking about the future to specific desired goals are more likely to be hopeful. Second, people who can imagine or plan ways to achieve these goals (step by step...) have greater hope. Third, individuals who think that they themselves as capable of pursuing goals successfully, who believe in their own capacity to get what they want, are more hopeful'. Feudtner et al. found that 'nurses' level of hope is associated with their self-reported comfort and competence regarding palliative care' (p.187). The vignette which follows illustrates Feudtner *et al.*'s view that 'hopeful thinking enhances personal performance and is pivotal in confronting the challenges that life-threatening illness and end-of-life care present' (p.191).

Vignette – Moana

Moana, an experienced nurse, was working on the paediatric oncology ward in a large public hospital. There had been a recent increase in the number of admissions of severely ill children and associated deaths. Of particular concern to Moana was a child who had died very unexpectedly. To Moana it 'felt like the straw that broke the camel's back'. Normally robust and resilient, Moana felt overwhelmed by this latest loss. She felt vulnerable, unable to cope with her own emotions and had begun to doubt her ability to work any longer in this area. In supervision Moana's supervisor asked Moana to talk about this child, why was he in particular causing her so much distress? What was different about this child? Moana was able to identify that the unexpectedness of the death meant that she felt she had not been able to do all she could for this child. The supervisor asked Moana to describe what her aims were when working with these children. She then asked her to identify how this applied to the child in question. Moana was surprised to realise that she had in fact been working within these aims with the child but had not had the time to formally detail her plans. It had been short and intense but Moana had offered this child all the very best of care at every step of his journey. 'What,' the supervisor asked, 'was Moana's learning from this?' Moana realised that she had an internalised framework which she readily applied to all her work and that she could trust herself to adapt to different circumstances. Moana left supervision feeling sad but knowing that she had the knowledge and the skills to offer appropriate and competent care and in particular that she was able to adapt her work to accommodate different circumstances.

Thus, resilient practitioners 'use positive emotions to bounce back' from emotionally challenging experiences (Tugade and Frederickson 2004, p.320). The ability to find personal resources including positive emotions during periods of high stress or in the face of critical incidents is a key attribute. Each practitioner has a unique personal history, and many social workers, counsellors and other health professionals may have been attracted to their career because of their exposure to challenging personal, familial events. Supervision can foster a secure place where fears and anxieties can be named (Ruch 2007a) and explored but also where positive emotions can be called upon (Howard 2008). This is of considerable importance in relation to stress 'where the dominant discourse has the potential to pathologise the individual' (Howard 2008, p.110).

A sociological understanding of stress, risk and resilience is also useful when thinking about the protective factors to be nurtured in order to promote safe, optimistic and effective work environments. Furedi argues that the experience of resilience cannot be:

> reduced to a factor isolated from the rest of social experience. It is inextricably intertwined with the everyday life of a community. Underpinned by a sense of individual coherence gained through being embedded in a wider system of social interaction, it is not an individual attribute but part of a wider legacy of community life. (Furedi 2008, p.658)

Furedi suggests that technocratic approaches towards the issue of resilience are unlikely to succeed in solving problems (2008, p.658) and that resilience can be 'encouraged, cultivated or disrupted, but certainly not taught or imparted by well-intentioned professionals' (Furedi 2009, p.99). Rather, resilience emerges from the actions people take when faced with challenging and unexpected circumstances and 'through improvisation and adaptation' to changeable and challenging circumstances (2008, p.658).

We have explored the nature of stress and the impact on individuals but professional practitioners rarely work entirely alone, and increasingly work in teams, often multidisciplinary in nature. Ruch notes the important 'potential of teams in general and co-working in particular' especially given the observation that 'increasingly individualistic' approaches to professional practice dominate and these 'emphasize the role and responsibilities of individual practitioners at the expense of collaborative interventions' (Ruch 2007a, p.666). Teams that can provide strong support, underpinned by coherent, shared values, beliefs and hopes can be seen as similar to Furedi's depiction of 'communities that are bound together by a robust system of meaning' (2008, p.659). Group supervision and team consultation approaches may provide opportunities for a greater experience of professional practice as a community and in Chapter 11 we will explore how group approaches can support good decision making within child welfare teams.

CONCLUSIONS: SUPERVISORS AS ADVOCATES

To what extent should supervisors be advocates for practitioners in health and social care? Morrison (1996, p.19) cites Richards and Payne (1991) as including the 'mediation' function to supervision and identifies the role of supervisors as both a buffer and a conduit between professional practitioners and managers. Supervisors can actively lead the charge to foster safe and supportive workplaces, however Bogo and Dill found that:

> supervisors do not view themselves as leaders or generators of change. Rather, they feel like conduits, like messengers, and like they are in the middle between senior administrators and frontline workers. Whereas staff might perceive them as having power, they experience an illusion of power. (Bogo and Dill 2008, p.151)

This middle position ('piggy in the middle' as Hughes and Pengelly put it) is often an extremely difficult place to be. For the external supervisor, who holds an ambiguous position in relation to their supervisee's organisation, there can be a sense of powerlessness and concern about the degree of responsibility to report on serious stress factors. Where does the 'duty of care' begin and end? External supervisors require good supervision so they can explore the complex ethical dimensions of supervisory responsibility in relation to supervisee distress.

Brown and Bourne note that supervision is a very stressful activity. They note that supervisors need their own supervision 'in managing…to strive to disentangle their own needs from those of supervisors' (Brown and Bourne 1996, p.181).

> The future fascinates us. With our insatiable desire to know the future comes an alternation between seeing the future as a fatalistic or deterministic given (que sera, sera – what will be will be), to viewing it as a series of possibilities over which we have some power. (Carroll 2007, p.237)

Michael Carroll provides a potent message in the passage above; being future oriented and having a belief in possibilities and a commitment to the search are key dispositions in the resilient practitioner. Supervision that models these dispositions and highlights successes and achievements can make a major contribution to better outcomes in health and social care.

Chapter 10

Supervising Students in Clinical Placements

The clinical placement brings the student into the world of professional practitioners. The beginning practitioner 'learns their conventions, their constraints, languages and appreciative systems, their repertoire of exemplars, systemic knowledge and patterns of knowing in action' through interaction with experienced practitioners (Schön 1987, pp.36–37). A student entering this world brings his or her own knowledge, understandings and beliefs. Teaching within the clinical placement can provide the basis for their enduring professional dispositions by exploring new meanings for behaviour, enhanced interpersonal communication skills and a reflective and inquiring stance in professional practice. Placements also provide students with an understanding of the social, cultural and structural differences amongst health and social care organisations. In the health and social care professions student placements also provide the opportunity to test out the capacity to demonstrate critical thinking and anti-oppressive practice (Nzira and Williams 2009). As we noted in Chapter 4, the organisational context of professional practice hugely shapes the everyday work processes and relationships, for example a medical intern will find the working relationships in a busy rural GP practice quite different from the complex hierarchical arrangements in a major teaching hospital. A child protection social worker might struggle with practice in a women's refuge.

Why supervise students? There are benefits for both placement educator and supervisee in this process. As we noted in Chapter 6, Urdang (1999) found benefits for supervisors through mastery of new skills, enhanced self-esteem, increased self-awareness and the capacity to analyse their own work. Thomas *et al.* (2007, pp.S4–S5) found that responses from 132 field educators of occupational therapy students rated the following benefits highest: future recruitment; developing staff supervision skills; developing clinical reasoning; organisation and time management; promoting exposure of the service to the university; updating clinicians' skills and promoting diversity in the workplace. Additional benefits associated with student supervision included: 'students conducting evidence-based practice, quality improvement and in-service activities, an improved ability to 'stay connected' with tertiary institutions, the tendency for students to indirectly promote the occupational therapy role within supervisors' work settings, and improved opportunities for running larger client group programs' (p.S5).

The central aim of clinical education is to provide opportunities for workplace learning to enrich students' understanding of their profession and to foster beginning competence. Field education is valued as a major site for the integration of theory and practice, the development of professional identity and deepening of disciplinary socialisation. Placement educators play an important role in shaping dispositions, including those about other professions by modelling attitudes, behaviours and expectations (Arndt *et al.* 2009, p.19). Arndt *et al.*'s study found that students understood the specific roles of other professions in the classroom but did not appreciate how to communicate and complete tasks which required cooperation with other disciplines (pp.21–22). Given the current emphasis on interprofessional working in health and social care, field education may need to play a greater role in preparation for work in complex environments.

This chapter addresses three main topics: the role of supervision in clinical placements in the health and social care professions and the potential for interprofessional learning; the tension between didactic instruction and the facilitation of reflective practice in placements, and the utility of a reflective learning process for supervision for students. Space does not permit exploration of teaching processes or the major issue of assessment.

A note on terms: There are numerous terms used in relation to the student placement and the participant roles in professional education for the health and social care professions. In this chapter we will denominate the learner as the student, the teacher/supervisor as the placement educator and the context as the clinical placement.

SUPERVISING IN CLINICAL PLACEMENTS

Supervision within the clinical placement is a structured, interactive and collaborative process which takes place within a purposeful professional relationship. The supervision relationship may involve some or all of these components: observation, monitoring, teaching, coaching and supporting and providing reflective supervision for students during their placement. The placement educator has a dual role within this relationship (Beddoe 2000) to simultaneously motivate the student's professional development while often managing a busy clinical practice load. An effective working relationship must be established between the student and the fieldwork educator to provide a vehicle for learning, with a strong focus on the tasks of building professional identity, learning to work in teams and managing the demands of the workplace in professional practice. The field educator also makes a significant contribution to the student's learning about supervision itself and more broadly about self-management within the complex web of professional relationships at work.

The student–field educator relationship is the major vehicle for learning in field education (Beddoe 2000). Both parties will bring into this the sum of previous experiences. Where students have had previous negative experience of supervision and placements, they may be reluctant to participate. It will take time and positive experience to enable trust in the relationship to grow. Frequently, negative experiences have been related to conflicts over power and student difficulty with critique. The dimensions of power and authority in the field placement situation are complicated by the potential for serious role conflict for the practice educator who 'must be guardian of standards and safe practice, friend, mentor and counsellor to the student, but also educational assessor and in part, gatekeeper to the profession' (King *et al.* 2009, p.142).

One of the key differences between student supervision and supervision of qualified practitioners is that the work of relationship building needs to happen very quickly because of the short time frame of the fieldwork placement. There are several other key elements that differ and all contribute to the need to consolidate a positive relationship to support student learning. Figure 10.1 demonstrates the key differences between student and practitioner supervision.

The agenda for interprofessional learning

Interprofessional education (IPE) is part of a substantial international movement to improve health and social care by reducing interdisciplinary barriers and encouraging collaborative work. Leonard and Weinstein (2009) acknowledge the many barriers to effective IPE at pre-registration level citing structural barriers, cultural differences, logistical problems with programmes, timetables and the requirements of regulatory bodies (see also Low and Weinstein 2000); added to this is an ongoing scepticism, lack of robust evidence for effectiveness and teaching challenges (Freeth *et al.* 2006). In spite of all these challenges, Leonard and Weinstein (2009, pp.215–216) feel that clinical placements, valued very highly by all stakeholders, provide an excellent pre-service experience of working

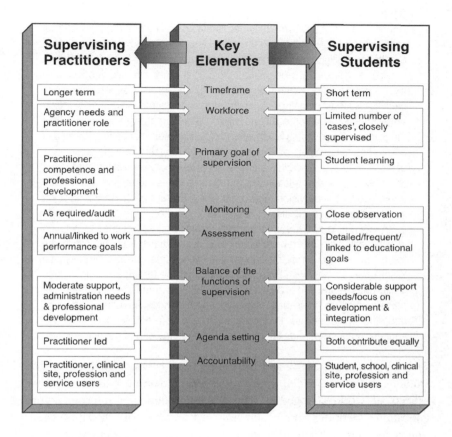

Figure 10.1 Student and practitioner supervision
Source: Adapted from Davys and Beddoe 2000

together. Developing a programme of shared activities with other health and social care field educators can provide additional learning opportunities for both fieldwork educator and student. Fieldwork educators can encourage students to work alongside other disciplines and learn how each has a role, perspective, professional culture and expectations about how they will relate to service users and others (Beddoe 2010a, p.261). This provides rich opportunities for learning both from other bodies of knowledge but also from the experience of teamwork (Smith and Anderson 2008). Field educators from other disciplines can contribute to success with your students both by providing peer support (for both students and educators) and by sharing learning activities.

Scenario

Robert and Wenli are two nursing students on placement in a busy special care baby unit with Rachel and this coincides with the fieldwork placement of Sunita and Philippa, who are social work students in the child development service. Both Rachel and Maria, the social work practice teacher, are experienced field educators who meet regularly for peer support and have often talked about planning to bring the students together. Before the students arrive they planned some joint activities. When comparing notes about how the placements are going Maria talks about difficulties in engaging Philippa in one-to-one supervision, as she is very reluctant to talk about the challenges of cross cultural practice in the diverse local communities. Rachel and Maria use peer supervision relationship to rehearse some ideas, and agree to try a joint student supervision session to see if this is helpful. In this session some discussion of families of newborns known to all the students results in an interesting and lively debate about roles and approaches to working with families with different religions. It is noted that the six people in the room represent five religions, four different cultures and two professions! Wenli offers to meet with Philippa to help her to better understand Chinese family roles. At the end of the session the students agree to meet without the placement educators to discuss their research projects. As Rachel and Maria debrief over coffee later they consider this to be a highly successful joint supervision session and plan one more towards the end of the placements.

The experiences of Maria and her colleague illustrate how bringing both students and placement educators together can demonstrate the important aspects of working together. The Leicester model of interprofessional education identifies the following advantages of interprofessional immersion during training: patient and professional experiences, deeper understanding of different professional perspectives, theory and policies and the provision of opportunities for joint work to find solutions to problems identified (Smith and Anderson 2008, p.769).

Attributes of excellent placement educators

Kilminster and Jolly reviewed the literature across the health and social care professions and found a fairly stable and consistent set of characteristics of effective supervisors: direction and constructive feedback and opportunities to carry out procedures and review them (medicine); provision of advice, feedback, opportunity to reflect and being a role model (psychology); teaching skills, interpersonal style and professional competence (radiographers). In summary effective supervisors have empathy, offer support, flexibility, knowledge, interest in supervision, good tracking of supervisees, and are interpretative, respectful, focused and practical (Kilminster and Jolly 2000, pp.832–833). Sloan (1999, p.719) found supervisees wanted a 'supervisor who inspires them, someone they look up to, and who they respect for their knowledge base and clinical skills'. Conversely, Watkins found that ineffective psychotherapy supervisors demonstrated 'rigidity, low empathy, low support, failure to teach...being indirect and intolerant, being closed...lacking in praise and encouragement, being sexist, and emphasising evaluation, weakness and deficiencies (Watkins 1997, p.168). In social work Barretti found that students want placement educators who are 'available, respectful, responsive, supportive, fair, objective, and who are knowledgeable and able to directly communicate their knowledge, encourage autonomy, observation and feedback, and facilitate professional development' (Barretti 2009, pp.50–51).

Cole and Wessel (2008) found that a clinical educator could enrich the learning experience of physiotherapy students in the following ways: good preparation, demonstration and time to obtain confirmation of learning through the provision of feedback and recapping and the provision of 'hands on experiences appropriate to students' knowledge, skills and comfort' (p.163). Students appreciated respect and valuing of individual input, time and being allowed an appropriate level of independence. As in the case of Barretti's review, Cole and Wessel found students valued clinical educators who demonstrated professional behaviour related to communication, evidence-based practice and continuing education (p.163). Summing up these attributes it is apparent that field educators have a challenging set of expectations to meet, all the while demonstrating congruence with professional values through their behaviour and communications (King *et al.* 2009). The greater focus on teaching and learning in student supervision differentiates it from the supervision of experienced practitioners. This role is not without tensions.

TENSIONS BETWEEN TEACHING AND FACILITATION IN FIELD PLACEMENT SUPERVISION

It is our view that students in placement benefit from clear, structured facilitation of their experiences as reflection may not always come easily to every student. Three fundamental tensions (Davys and Beddoe 2009, p.920) are present in student supervision:

- the need to maintain balance between teaching (information giving and instruction) and facilitating review and reflection

- the fostering of reflection in situations where there is limited experience and which are overlaid by high levels of student anxiety. This anxiety may stem from a number of sources which include the nature of the work, interpersonal dynamics and the student assessment process (Ruch 2002, p.205)

- the management of the dependence–autonomy continuum as students test their new knowledge and skills in 'real' work (Beddoe 2000).

A key focus of student supervision is the promotion of a sense of ownership, mastery and understanding in clinical practice. At the same time, the placement educator is charged to both facilitate reflection in beginning practice, and instruct and guide the student in practice activities in which they will be assessed. The balance of these two dimensions of supervision enables the focus on the student's experience rather than the supervisor's expertise (Davys and Beddoe 2009, p.920). The supervision process, undertaken with a clear contract and negotiated expectations of all the parties, provides an excellent vehicle for learning.

Key tasks for the student in placement include the consolidation of learning, managing both critical and complimentary feedback and self-regulation in the workplace. During this phase students may experience conflict between their need for their placement educator to be confidently in charge and their own emerging sense of professional competence and desire for greater autonomy. As King et al. (2009, p.140) have asserted, the 'journey from dependence to independence is both dynamic and contextual' and during this time students can be vulnerable and require assistance. For some, over-confidence may need to be tempered and for others, lack of confidence may mean they require considerable support to undertake even relatively simple tasks. Good preparation for undertaking clinical activities, with clear parameters, opportunities for reflection and regular review are all essential components in building student confidence. Continuous opportunities for feedback and reflection can contribute to a growing sense of accomplishment, confidence and belonging in their chosen profession. Ideally during this phase the student is able to experience some independence while appreciating constructive input and oversight of their work.

Students look to placement educators to assist them to manage the reduction of anxiety (Ruch 2002) and to provide structure and teaching along with facilitative support (Lizzio, Stokes and Wilson 2005). Balance between the features of student supervision is important and we have found that students need to experience a 'mixture of interventions which are equally weighted at both ends of the didactic – facilitative continuum' (Davys and Beddoe 2009, p.921). The duty of care in relation to the safety of all participants requires relatively high levels of instruction and information (the didactic mode). This is necessary in order that students have a context and guidelines to begin to undertake the basic tasks of practice, and high levels of positive feedback and supportive interventions (the facilitative mode) are required in order that they can accept the challenge to reflect upon the action taken and the consequences of that action (Davys and Beddoe 2009, p.921).

We have previously noted that the literature cautions that didactic supervision creates over-dependence on the instructions, experience and expertise of the placement educator and produce surface learning (Davys and Beddoe 2009, p.921). Surface learning focuses on content rather than underlying purpose and meaning and Clare, discussing the work of educationalists Marton and Saljo (1976), describes surface learning as 'extrinsically motivated, passive and reproductive' in contrast with deep learning which is an 'intrinsically motivated process of personalised meaning construction' (Clare 2007, p.434). Lizzio et al. have explored the didactic–facilitative tension in supervision in a study which investigated supervisee perceptions of the learning processes in professional supervision. Their study explored whether 'deep/surface learning, anxiety and self management are salient to supervisee's perceptions of their approach to professional supervision' (Lizzio et al. 2005, p.243). Lizzio et al. did not find a polarised relationship between didactic and facilitative approaches; in fact the use of the one did not exclude the other. Field educators who were perceived by their supervisees as helpful used a wide range of interventions, including didactic interventions to instruct and inform students on best practice. Where supervision includes a clear focus on learning and development then didactic interventions are not an obstacle to deep learning.

The placement educator's challenge to achieve the necessary balance is clearly indicated by Lizzio et al., who outline the need to find 'an appropriate balance between supervisory authority and supervisee autonomy, between evaluation and support and between transmission of required knowledge and the reflective engagement with the supervisees' experience' (Lizzio et al. 2005, p.240). While a perceived lack of supervisor support can negatively impact on supervision, Lizzio et al. (2009) note that 'too much support...can also inhibit the effectiveness of supervision. For example, if a supervisor is overly concerned with 'being supportive' they may become too permissive and not address 'touchy issues' such as supervisee competence or performance' (Lizzio *et al.* 2009, p.129). This can result in superficial engagement in supervision and if an incident arises in which the placement educator is obliged to be directive, or deliver critical feedback, this can elicit hurt and defensive responses. The student, who has interpreted the placement educator's support as unconditional support, may feel that any direction or critique is a retreat from that supportive stance, no matter how carefully the feedback or instruction is given. As in practitioner supervision, the development of a clear contact and mutual expectations about the nature and focus of feedback is vital.

Developmental approaches

As we have noted in Chapters 2 and 5, developmental models usefully incorporate an assessment of a supervisee's level of experience. Most developmental models consist of three to five stages and range from 'novice' to 'expert' (Butler 1996) or describe the steps towards a mature integration of the self and professional competencies and foci (Hawkins and Shohet 2006, pp.70–75). As these models are more educative in focus, their success is often determined by a supervisee's previous experience and level of education for their discipline. Developmental models are characterised by stages and assume that people will move through all stages over time and are thus often subject to the criticism that they are rigid, and blind to cultural and social differences, difference, power and context. Prescriptive approaches to professional development can equate the norm with success and regard divergence as a deficit, minimising factors of diversity and context (Gardiner 1989). Cultural assumptions implicit in developmental models therefore need to be evaluated in light of students' prior experience, especially those impacted on by their race, class, gender, sexual orientation and other factors of influence (Moffatt 1996). In particular, stages of dependency and autonomy can vary widely and Nye suggests that developmental models 'recognize an early, time-limited phase of dependence in supervision as the norm, the ultimate goal...is to move supervisees out of dependence to an independent autonomous stance. These models reflect...U.S. culture and traditional clinical developmental theories' (Nye 2007, p.84).

Despite these notes of caution, developmental models can be useful for beginning placement educators in that they provide an explanation of how skills develop over time and therefore provide a guide by which to assess new practitioners' development and competence. The supervision model developed by Loganbill *et al.* (1982) and Stoltenberg and Delworth (1987) has been highly influential in supervision, particularly because of the assessment framework it provides. Developmental approaches assist placement educators to understand the transitions challenges that occur for students learning as they cycle through stages, always drawing on previous knowledge and skills and making meaning through interpretations of new experiences by reflection on earlier but similar or even contrasting events.

STAGES OF STUDENT LEARNING

Elsewhere (Davys and Beddoe 2009) we have noted the usefulness of Butler's 1996 work on reflective learning for professional practice. Butler rejected explanations of competence that suggested it was merely the acquisition of an increased repertoire of skills and techniques. Rather he described a model of performance development based on reflection asserting that, 'through reflection, performance is transformed. And it is this transformation that brings about improvement in the performance' (1996, p.277).

Novice, the first stage of Butler's model, describes a context where students are new to the work and have little real experience of the situations which might arise in practice. At this level the student seeks rules and certainty. Rules provide safety and help to shape and guide practice. Butler describes the behaviour of novices as 'extremely limited and very inflexible' (1996, p.278).

The second stage of Butler's model, *Advanced Beginner*, is characterised by the student's belief that there will be a correct solution for every problem and frequently expects the placement educator to hold most of the answers. At this point dependence on others will be high. A field educator once commented 'the students are like Lorenz's geese – every time I turn around they are there!' As we noted in Chapter 5, Nye has found Vygotsky's ideas are helpful in revaluing 'dependence' on the other as 'essential to learning and development across the life course. For Vygotsky, this is not a process with an end point...something to be outgrown...[but] inevitable if learning and development are to occur' (Nye 2007, p.84). Cultural difference, age and gender may have an impact on the degree of independence sought and previous educational experience may influence problem-solving approaches. At this stage the student will draw on formal knowledge and previous experience to identify the main facts and issues in any given practice scenario but his or her repertoire of interventions will be limited. In a similar vein, Loganbill *et al.* (1982, p.17) describe a beginning practitioner as exhibiting 'naïve unawareness... narrow and rigid thought patterns' and a having a strong dependence on supervision, however, reflecting the cautions considered above, Lizzio *et al.*

(2005, p.251) remind us that student dependence is appropriate behaviour to ensure safety. Deferral to the expertise of experienced practitioners also indicates the student's self-awareness of their limitations.

At this beginning stage students may be resistant to reflection and seek clear solutions rather than complex answers or facilitation to think through practice issues in supervision (Butler 1996, p.278). Butler concludes that novice and advanced beginners 'can take in little of the complexity of their performance situation, it is too new, too strange, and they have to spend time remembering the rules they have set for them'. Three requirements need to be met to assist students: support to understand the performance setting; help to set priorities, and assistance to learn to reflect on their own performance and become less rigid and more flexible by developing and trusting their own personal practical knowledge (Butler 1996, p.278).

A NOTE ON STUDENT ANXIETY AND STRESS

It is important to remember that students are not all the same; many will be young and still developing their personal skills and belief systems; some will be mature students and some may be training in a new profession and having to adjust to being a novice again. Student anxiety in placement is well documented (Gelman and Baum 2009; Sprengel and Job 2004) and studies have frequently reported specific worries including: lack of skills and experience, practical matters, safety, difficulty in engaging service users, making mistakes. In addition students are concerned about the quality of their placement, their relationship with colleagues and supervisors. Lizzio *et al.* (2005) have demonstrated that supportive empathetic communication between a placement educator and their student reduces this anxiety. Students predict the challenges of field education, especially in direct work and in practice teams and are often very anxious about exposing their lack of experience and skill as they test out their skills in new situations. It can be helpful for fieldwork educators to share his or her own journey from student to seasoned professional. Being open to an exploration of mutual hopes and using empathetic self-disclosure can normalise these concerns and help build a constructive and trusting relationship (Beddoe 2010a, p.261).

Developing critical thinking

Deal suggests that there are specific strategies that clinical supervisors can use to encourage their supervisees to think critically (Deal 2004, p.11). Among these is the modelling by supervisors of a self-critical perspective, being able to share challenges and undertake transparent thinking and decision making (pp. 11–12).

Placement educators can encourage students to continuously test their assumptions against research and good practice guides in order to ensure that in their clinical work they are able 'to differentiate between opinions (e.g. preferences and personal theories of causality or change) and data (e.g. facts about clients, relevant research findings)' (Deal 2004, p. 14). Such practice protects against unchallenged stereotypes, cultural assumptions and poor reasoning and assists in the development of integrating a framework for addressing social justice issues in supervision (Chang, Hays and Milliken 2009; Hair and O'Donoghue 2009). For Deal, 'supervisors can best apply these strategies when their own critical thinking skills are well developed, they are comfortable with ambiguity' (2004, p. 11), and do not attempt to expedite the process by oversimplifying it. Critical thinking essentially requires practitioners to ask questions of their practice and to examine the structural issues associated with any professional intervention. This can be seen as demonstrating a 'critical spirit'.

Why does critical thinking matter? Are service users in health and social services likely to receive better services if practitioners use critical thinking skills? Critical thinking skills are essential for effective practice in complex, ambiguous and uncertain situations. This especially applies to practice contexts where there is an element of risk assessment and the management of ethical dilemmas. Beginning practitioners often struggle in their search for certainty and safety and need to develop the following attributes: curiosity, the motivation to stay well informed, respect for reasoned inquiry, openness to divergent world views, flexibility in considering alternatives, honesty about one's own biases and cultural assumptions, the courage to suspend judgement, and the ability to reconsider decisions in the light of new information (Facione 1998, p. 9). A practitioner deficient in these attributes might be 'close-minded, inflexible, insensitive...unfair when it comes to judging the quality of arguments' and as a consequence 'never is willing to reconsider' (p. 10). Placement educators can play a major role in encouraging critical thinking skills in their students through selecting tasks that draw on different perspectives – for example seeking information about a mental illness by looking at formal codified knowledge, reading narrative accounts of service experience, consumer websites, talking to patient advocates, interviewing relevant health professionals – prior to direct contact or observation in clinical work. Deal and Pittman (2009, p. 98), however, caution that to ensure that these experiences translate into skills, educators need to purposefully engage students in reflecting upon and evaluating their experiences. Furthermore field educators need to be open to their students' ideas and by 'sharing with students how they make decisions and evaluate their own work, and asking questions that require reflection and analysis, field instructors can help students use their new experiences to sharpen their critical thinking' (p.98).

THE REFLECTIVE LEARNING MODEL FOR STUDENTS ON PLACEMENT

The world of contemporary education for the health and social care professions is dominated by two major themes: reflective practice and evidence informed practice. Each approach has at its heart the aspiration to deliver the most competent professional practice to service users. Evidence informed practice utilises positivist approaches to ensure that practitioners deliver services and 'treatments' that have been proved 'to be effective'. At the core is the desire to ensure that scarce resources are well used on 'what works' and the approach addresses the technical–rational paradigm of seeking certainty of outcomes in intervention. Reflective practice addresses the messiness of the processes and relationships in professional work, recognising that practitioners work more often with uncertainty, emotion and contested understandings of what good outcomes are in the 'zone of ambiguity' (Brookfield 2009, p.294). As we noted in Chapter 5, reflective practice is driven by the desire to improve practice through thinking about experiences and teasing out the assumptions and perceptions that underpin practice.

Reflective practice then is a core feature of pre-registration learning for the professions and is inherent in the many requirements within field education. Critical reflection is an extension of reflection to require reflective practitioners to address explicitly issues of power and justice in their work. Brookfield (2009, p.295) argues that pre-service needs to place *critical reflection* at the core of practitioner development and what 'makes reflection critical is its foregrounding of power dynamics and relationships and its determination to uncover hegemonic dimensions to practice'. Critical reflection is a process that seeks to unsettle assumptions in order to change practice and helps us to understand the connections between our public (professional, organisational) and private worlds (Fook and Askeland 2007, pp.522–523). For Brookfield a critically reflective practitioner retains a critical perspective on their profession and 'always asks whose interests are served by particular codes of practice, and stays alert to the way they are embracing ideas and behaviours that are subtly harming them' (2009, p.294).

Butler sees learning the art of reflection as crucial to the progress of the practitioner's competence (Butler 1986), however, students and beginning practitioners may be challenged by reflective processes. Yip cautions that premature encouragement to reflect can overwhelm the student and create resistance and distress (Yip 2006). Supervision is one occasion where reflection is 'guided' in order that learning may occur. The appropriate conditions for reflection include a 'supportive environment', 'readiness to undergo self-reflection, and awareness of one's limits and breaking point' (Yip 2006, p.781). Utilising critical reflection in field education supervision requires preparation, an assessment of the student's readiness to examine assumptions and beliefs and attention to a clear and understood process in which reflection occurs.

The Reflective Learning Model of supervision described in Chapter 5 has proved equally useful in working with students on placement (Davys and Beddoe 2009). It is assumed that the placement educator and student will have spent time developing their placement contract and supervision agreement and have built an effective relationship in the beginning stages of practice learning (Beddoe 2000). This chapter finishes with an illustration of the Reflective Learning Model by a vignette describing in detail a significant supervision session involving social work student Keli and her supervisor Nancy.

Beginnings

Supervision begins with greetings and sharing any significant 'news' before beginning to focus on the agenda for the session (see Chapter 5). Taking time to reconnect also models the maintenance of ongoing professional relationships. The 'beginning' process includes agenda setting, with a major focus on issues generated by the student. In student supervision it is important that the field educator is alert to what might be left out and to comfortably introduce topics which require attention. When the placement educator and student have established and prioritised the agenda the reflective learning process can begin.

The Reflective Learning Model for students (illustrated in Figure 10.2) describes the four stages: *event, exploration, experimentation* and *evaluation* which are addressed sequentially but allow for the student and the supervisor to move back and forth between the various stages if necessary. The model utilises the stages of experiential learning as described by Kolb (1984).

Figure 10.2 Reflective Learning Model for students
Source: Reproduced with permission from Davys, A. and Beddoe, L. (2009) 'The Reflective Learning Model: Supervision of Social Work Students.' *Social Work Education 28*, 8, 919–933, available at www.informaworld.com.

In the vignette below Keli is experiencing the dilemmas of a novice and we specifically locate a reflective process approach to supervision. We focus on the micro-process of supervision rather than the more typical focus on the student's development over time. This approach was developed as a teaching model as the authors found that social work field educators were searching for approaches to supervision that provided a structure for action, rather than just an explanation of theoretical models (Davys and Beddoe 2009).

Vignette – Keli

Beginning

Keli is a social work student on her first field placement in a community parent support service. She is working alongside Nancy, an experienced worker, to provide counselling and supportive services to parents facing crises. Nancy also provides her supervision. Keli arrives late to supervision and seems lacking in her characteristic joie de vivre. Nancy comments on Keli's flatness. Keli says she's really tired. After a few minutes catching up they start to develop an agenda for the session. First up for discussion is the recent work she has undertaken with Mary Anne, a 38-year-old woman whose life has changed dramatically due to a tragic accident in which her husband Owen was killed. Mary Anne and Owen had together run a successful family business that was largely dependent on his technical skills. Complex financial matters mean that for at least six months Mary Anne cannot gain access to any funds from the sale of both properties. Mary Anne is now a widow with three young children, one of whom has learning difficulties and very fragile health. Yesterday Keli had arranged to meet Mary Anne at the benefits office.

Keli launches into an account of her meeting and what went wrong. Nancy listens sympathetically to Keli's experience for few moments and then asks Keli what she wants to talk about in supervision today. Keli says with a shaky laugh that there is only one thing on her mind at the moment. Nancy agrees but comments that this encounter has obviously brought up a lot of feelings and is dominating her attention at the moment. She wonders if there were other things that Keli has noted during the week which she wanted to put on the agenda as well. She asks if Keli has noted anything in her notebook as preparation for supervision as they had agreed when they contracted for supervision. Nancy knows that Keli is usually very well prepared but wants to reinforce the expectation of preparation for supervision. Keli mentions another service user she wants to follow up and a request to attend a workshop. The agenda thus has three items and Keli wants to start with her meeting with Mary Anne.

Keli's task was to meet Mary Anne at the benefits office to support her to apply for a sole parent benefit and housing assistance. When she arrived at the waiting room she was surprised to see Mary Anne wearing dirty jeans, an old t-shirt and scuffed shoes. Mary Anne has always been immaculately dressed. Mary Anne sees Keli's shocked expression and says loudly 'I thought I should look like I'm on the benefit. I was going to give myself a fake black eye as well but I thought that was going too far.' She laughs heartily and asks Keli 'I'm a single parent now, do I look the part?'

Event

Having identified the item of top priority on the agenda, the student and placement educator begin to focus on this item. The task for this stage of the model is for the student and Nancy to identify the core issue or key question which the student wants to address in supervision about this agenda item.

Keli is invited to tell the full story. Ownership of the situation leads to responsibility for the subsequent intervention and assists the student to gain both confidence and competence (Ford and Jones 1987). It is *her* story and the act of retelling the story enables Keli to re-experience the situation. In recounting it she begins her process of making meaning from the encounter and she should be heard without interpretation at this stage. This enables Nancy to hear the story from Keli's perspective and to hear what she emphasises.

The task for Nancy is to encourage Keli to tell enough of the story for both the student and Nancy to understand the context and issues but not, at this stage, to begin to address the issue. Ford and Jones (1987) suggest here that the field educator is framing the problem from two perspectives. The first is to get a clear understanding of the issue presented and the second is to hold the student and the problem in a broader context. What is the significance of this particular problem and what might it suggest about the student's stage of knowledge and competence?

The task for Nancy and the student in the event stage is to explore the issue sufficiently in order to identify what it is that the student wants from supervision. What is Keli's understanding of the problem and what does she wish to take away from the session? Nancy encourages Keli to elaborate her story of the Friday's events but contains it within the context of 'Let us work out how best we can use supervision to help you with this situation. What do you want from supervision about this situation?' Keli said she wanted to know how she should have reacted to Mary Anne's remarks. Nancy knew Keli to be an enthusiastic student who was respectful of others and polite. She suspected her inexperience would not have prepared her for the embarrassing situation created by the service user.

Exploration: impact and implications

The exploration stage of this model is where the work of supervision occurs and where the issue is explored, understood and potential solutions identified. The stage is divided into two phases: impact and implications.

IMPACT

The impact phase of the exploration stage is the time where the student is encouraged to reflect on the issue and how it has impacted on him or her and what meaning this event has in terms of current or previous experience. Learning is often unsettling and the student's world view will be impacting on how she experiences these interactions (Butler 1996, pp.274–275). How is he or she feeling about the issue? How have these feelings been addressed, accommodated, expressed? How have the feelings affected the work in hand? What ideas, thoughts, judgements or opinions has the student had about the situation? Are there any patterns to these ideas, feelings? Have they been experienced anywhere before? (See Chapter 5 for suggestions for supervisory questions.)

The task for Nancy in this phase is to help the student to locate herself in the event. What meaning does it have for her as a beginning social worker?

IMPLICATIONS

The second phase of exploration, implications, moves the student from a focus on themselves to a broader focus on the context of the 'event' or issue. The presenting problem is considered here with reference to policy, legislation, treatment protocols, and professional ethics and understandings of the social worlds of service users.

The stage allows Nancy to assess Keli's knowledge and awareness and is the phase of supervision where Nancy is most active and where she has an opportunity to teach, inform and prescribe. She can ask questions to promote critical reflection on power and authority issues in this situation (Brookfield 2009). She can jog Keli's understanding of critical theory and point out that the 'forces present in the wider society always intrude into our work with clients and colleagues' (Brookfield 2009, p.300). It is also a place for feedback, reassurance and affirmation.

During the exploration stage of the model the student and placement educator may move between impact and implication phases as questions of a more conceptual nature and reflection on feelings and patterns may be identified. The task of the exploration stage is to reach some decision or understanding about the issue being discussed.

Impact and implications

Nancy can see that Keli is still very upset about the incident and encourages her to talk about how she feels. Keli describes a range of feelings: anger, frustration, helplessness and embarrassment. She talks about all her enthusiasm for the visit and how she had looked forward to 'empowering Mary Anne at the benefits office'. She describes her feelings of surprise that Mary Anne could be so insensitive to the other people in the room – 'the worst thing was that I just said "oh you didn't need to do that" and tried to change the subject but she then made a loud speech about people ripping off the taxpayer and that she was at least "only getting back some of my taxes, because at least I paid some, unlike most of these scrubbers", and then it got really nasty. Two women in the waiting room had reacted angrily and made threatening remarks. Keli tells Nancy 'I wimped out, I couldn't get her into the interview room fast enough. And I didn't say anything. I should have said something.' She has spent the weekend feeling conflicted over her lack of courage.

Nancy sympathises with this experience and affirms Keli for her honesty and courage in owning her strong negative feelings. She observes that it is hard when service users treat others badly and wonders if Keli has ever experienced anything like this before. Keli is able to connect her feelings with a similar experience in a youth group she ran as a teenager and is encouraged by Nancy to recall how she handled that.

With support Keli is able to examine her own position in the situation. She realises that she wanted so badly to be helpful and yet Mary Anne had embarrassed her by making her a party, however unwillingly, to stereotypical and judgemental comments about single parents. How can she be a social worker if she's so lacking in courage?

Implications

Nancy asks Keli how she would have liked it to be. What was her goal in going to the benefits office? What was her role? Keli is clear that her goal was to support Mary Anne as she thought she might be vulnerable having to ask for help. Mary Anne's negative and discriminatory attitude to single parents strikes a discordant note in Keli's up until now positive regard for Mary Anne. Keli is unable to imagine what was happening for Mary Anne when she made those comments. Nancy recognises this as an important teaching moment in supervision.

Brookfield (2009, p.295) points out that learning frequently begins with an event that highlights a 'discrepancy between assumptions and perspectives that explain the world satisfactorily and what happens in real life. This is what Mezirow (1991) and other theorists of transformative learning call a disorienting dilemma'. Bennett and Deal (2008, p.106) note that cognitively students tend to 'understand clients…in generalized, somewhat stereotypical terms… High anxiety and an underdeveloped ability to understand complex situations leads beginning students to engage in action oriented, concrete interventions', in this case moving on quickly when faced with a professionally challenging moment. Nancy reviews with Keli the purpose of attending and asks how she might have better prepared Mary Anne?

Is Keli able to hazard a guess at what might have been going through Mary Anne's mind as she dressed to go out that day? Keli is now able to make some thoughtful comments about how Mary Anne may have been responding to her visit and as she explores this she is able to recognise that her criticism of Mary Anne is lessening and her criticism of her lack of preparation is increasing. Nancy applauds her for this shift and encourages her to focus, not on what she has done wrong, but on what she can learn from this situation. Nancy again asks what Keli could have done differently.

From her response Nancy recognises that Keli has not considered how anger and bitterness are emotions related to grief and loss. Before assumptions can be challenged, Brookfield (2009, p.295) asserts, 'they need to be identified clearly. This is the first discrete task of reflection. Assumptions are the understandings we hold about how the world works, or ought to work'. Nancy thus spends some time outlining some features of grief and gives Keli some relevant literature.

Nancy checks out what Keli is thinking and how she is feeling about this situation now. Keli acknowledges her sense of helplessness and incompetence. She remembers the multifaceted nature of individual values and beliefs. Mary Anne's self-image is not congruent with her current financial and emotional vulnerability. Keli understands more clearly the dynamics at play in the visit and how her newness and lack of preparation have compounded an already complex situation.

Nancy asks Keli what she is going to do next. Keli appears a little startled at this and says she doesn't want to see Mary Anne again though she does understand her better. Nancy encourages her to plan a careful visit which will include an exploration of Mary Anne's emotional needs.

Experimentation stage: implementation

It is our experience that the focus on an issue brought to supervision often ends when a solution has been chosen or when insight has been gained. The supervision session will then move on to the next item on the agenda. All too often in these situations the plan or strategy identified by the supervisee is not put into effect or the insight is not integrated into practice or awareness. In the Reflective Learning Model, the experimentation stage explicitly attends to how the student will move forward with the issue. Is this the best plan? What are the limitations? What will happen if the plan fails? What resources are needed? Nancy is thus able to consider what extra support or resources the student may need to promote a successful outcome.

Experimentation
Keli feels good about her plan and the decision to visit Mary Anne. Nancy asks when she is going to do this visit and asks her to imagine the steps. She suggests they role play a possible conversation with Mary Anne. As they explore this conversation Keli finds her own words to express what she wants to say and grows more confident in her delivery. Nancy affirms her development.

Evaluation

The evaluation stage brings Nancy and Keli full circle to consider whether or not the agenda item has been successfully addressed. Does Keli now have the knowledge and confidence to move forward? What has she learned from the supervision session? On reflection Keli says she is very happy with the outcome which is more than she had asked for and 'much better'. She has discovered a way to approach her next contact with Mary Anne and along the way has changed her assessment.

Nancy also enquires what Keli has learned from talking about this experience. After some thought Keli says that she realises that she might have been able to identify in advance the nature of this meeting for Mary Anne. She also ventures, tentatively, that she is learning about the importance of learning from mistakes.

Ending

Bennett and Deal (2009, p.106) note that 'gradual cognitive change is expected to occur in students' development of complex, nuanced, differentiated understanding of clients, their situations, and the helping process itself'. Guided reflection, augmented with some teaching as demonstrated in Keli's supervision supports this development.

When Nancy and Keli have addressed all of the items on the agenda or the supervision time is up, the supervision session ends. The ending of the session is important as it marks the conclusion of this period of learning. It is useful for Keli and Nancy to spend a moment reflecting on the placement challenges and progress. The spectre of assessment is ever-present and regular feedback can be reassuring.

> Keli and Nancy have now addressed all three issues on the agenda and the supervision time is almost up. Nancy asks Keli how the session has been and asks if there are any themes Keli has noted. Keli is warm in her appreciation of the help she received in relation to the first issue. She still feels bad about having not considered all the issues for Mary Anne. Nancy reiterates that it is not the mistakes which are of concern but rather whether or not Keli has learned from them.
>
> She sets Keli two tasks for the next supervision session: to prepare an agenda, and to spend time thinking about her approach to 'preparation' for direct work with service users.
>
> Nancy rounds off the session with an affirming comment on Keli's progress to date and they confirm the time and place of the next meeting.

CONCLUSION

A reflective learning model applied within supervision is flexible enough to enable both teaching and the facilitation of reflection. Students need parameters, guidelines and information, as well as some gentle challenges to their assumptions and expectations of themselves and others, in order to begin to construct their own sense of mastery of the skills and interventions required by practice. This approach and the vignette in illustration support supervisors to find a middle ground between didactic teaching and reflection (Davys and Beddoe 2009). Within this reflective framework the personal, communicative, cognitive, social, emotional and cultural dimensions of learning in professional practice can be addressed: ideas teased out, intellectual challenges separated from raw emotion and reaction and within a supportive environment put together again as meaning is made in the clinical placement.

Chapter 11

Supervision in Child Protection

Work with at-risk children and young people and their families is one of the most challenging fields of practice in health and social care. This chapter will focus mainly on supervision of social workers, as it is the profession of social work on which the challenge of addressing child abuse and neglect largely rests, certainly in the public eye. Green Lister and Crisp (2005) noted that nurses and health visitors may have significant exposure to child protection issues and require supervision; nevertheless the intensification of decision-making responsibility for child welfare in the public discourse is with social work.

This chapter will explore the contribution supervision can make to enhancing accountability, professional development and support of social workers in child protection. Both traditional and contemporary models of supervision have emphasised the importance of balancing the administrative, support-oriented and educative aspects of supervision (Brown and Bourne 1996; Hughes and Pengelly 1997; Kadushin 1976). In the current climate the traditional tripartite approach may be found wanting (Ruch 2007b), not in least part due to the tensions between the quality assurance aspects of supervision, increasingly associated with surveillance, and the supportive and learning-focused aspects of supervision (Beddoe 2010b; Peach and Horner 2007). We maintain our perspective that support is a core condition of supervision and this is very well supported by research on well-being and retention issues for child welfare workers. The development of group consultation approaches (Lietz 2008; Lohrbach 2008; Strand and Badger 2007) linked to effective assessment frameworks (Connolly 2007; Lietz 2009; Munro 2008) will be outlined. The potential for creating communities of practice within and between health and social care organisations that have a common concern for child well-being will be considered. In particular we will explore how collaborative approaches to supervision can assist to promote critical reasoning strategies.

THE CHILD PROTECTION ENVIRONMENT

It is well documented that child protection social work is often practised in a climate characterised by risk-averse social service agencies, stringent regulation, prescribed practice and an ever-present fear of media scapegoating (Green 2007; Littlechild 2008; Parton, Thorpe and Wattam 1997; Scourfield and Welsh 2003; Stanley 2007). A sociological understanding of risk has been extensively applied to the social services for more than a decade (Littlechild 2008; Parton 1998; Stalker 2003; Webb 2006). The essential conundrum for child protection is encapsulated in the pendulum of practice culture (and often public opinion) that oscillates between poles of supportive, prevention-focused family intervention on the one hand, and over-zealous child protection on the other (Driscoll 2009). The latter has often focused on technological approaches to surveillance of at-risk children and young people (Garrett 2005; Munro 2004a; Parton 2009) and child protection is indeed 'risky work' (Stanley 2007). Gillingham and Bromfield attribute 'the fear factor' in child protection to this conundrum: 'On the one hand it is the social construction of blame for the perceived lack of protection afforded by services to children who have died at the hands of their carers. On the other, it is also concerned with those who have been harmed through what is perceived to be over-intervention by child protection services' (Gillingham and Bromfield 2008, p.19). A number of writers have explored the ways in which public inquiries have also contributed to this 'culture of blame' in child protection, creating more risk-averse practices (Connolly and Doolan 2007; Munro 2004b).

Lonne *et al.* (2008) have identified a fundamental change in the culture of social work practice in the past three decades arising from the influence of a risk management approach. The impact of high-profile reviews, common to many countries, also generates a more prescriptive and procedure-focused response. Lonne *et al.* assert that this has resulted in a 'case management' culture, whereby professional discretion has been curtailed in favour of detailed and complex procedural guidance. Caring is replaced by a culture of surveillance' (2008, p.xii). Vigorous debate has questioned the prevailing forensic approach to child welfare, dominated as it is by procedures and risk thinking. Analysis has led to an understanding that this is counterproductive and diminishes social workers' aspiration to provide a more positive engagement in strengthening families. Parton describes the proposed refocusing of child welfare priorities on 'helping parents and children in the community in a supportive way' and to keep 'policing and coercive interventions to a minimum' (Parton 2009, p.716).

As noted earlier in this book, supervision in social work has always been subject to wider influences and has reflected tensions between organisational and professional concerns. Jones described the reconciliation of these tensions in supervision as a 'trade-off' (Jones 2004, p.12) between the new public management ideologies and the professions, 'making it available for appropriation of competing interests' (Jones 2004, p.13). Noble and Irwin agree, suggesting that supervision frequently mirrors practice and, as social work is 'unsettled by the shifts and divergences that have marked the later part of the 20th century' (2009, p.348), it is important 'that the supervisory relationship, like the helping relationship, is built on a trusting, confidential, caring, supportive and empathic experience, which sets the atmosphere for the professional work to be undertaken' (p.347). One major impact of this discourse is the increased focus on computer mediated assessment 'technologies' and the manner in which knowledge is created and used in welfare systems. Parton draws on Howe (1996) in exploring how social workers have become driven by 'performativity' as 'the dominant criterion for knowledge evaluation (Parton 2009, p.716) Risk thinking in practice is now considered to have had a impact on supervision (Beddoe 2010b; Peach and Horner 2007). Significantly, in terms of supervision, in information driven systems the major child welfare role was to collect information in order to manage cases, judge risk and allocate resources information. For Parton a consequence of this is that 'the emphasis on the relationship was thereby stripped of its social, cultural and professional significance. Knowledge was only relevant in so far as it aided the gathering, assessing, monitoring and exchange of information – which became the central focus of the work' (Parton 2009, p.717). In this conceptualisation there is a concomitant danger that supervision becomes surveillance.

Supervision of child welfare practice can thus be stressful and ridden by anxiety and fear, or reduced to checklist approaches which mirror the proceduralised 'informational' approaches to work with families. Taylor, Beckett and McKeigue have noted the complex interaction between social workers' anxieties and those of the wider society and suggest that as such 'social workers are society's defences against anxieties about damage and delinquency' (Taylor *et al.* 2008, p.25). In a climate where there is a preoccupation with risk and low tolerance for public service failure, supervision can be captured by the potential for judgement of how well social work assesses and responds to risk. McLaughlin notes how these attempts to reduce uncertainty can be critiqued for leading to professionals' anxiety and lack of confidence in their abilities to assess and make decisions.

'Failure to follow the correct procedure can leave the worker vulnerable to disciplinary or judicial action if things go wrong' (McLaughlin 2007, p.1264). The proliferation of audits was noted in Chapter 4. Audits and recorded data form 'the visible track record of social workers' attempts to assess and reduce risk – therefore, the social worker's job is less about the 'right decision' and more about a defensible decision' (Pollack 2008, p.12). As Green asserts, 'apprehension about making a mistake, rather than achieving desired outcomes, leads to an increasing focus on the assessment and management of risk, perceived as the primary defence against poor outcomes for the organisation as well as the client' (Green 2007, p.400).

Research by Taylor *et al.* identifies social workers as the 'prime candidates for the projection of society's anxiety in the form of criticism' and yet simultaneously social workers may be characterised as having less expertise in the complex inter-institutional arrangements for child protection. A social worker in Taylor *et al.*'s research said 'I think the courts will look on the doctor, or the psychiatrist or the psychologist's report as having more weight...than the social worker's report. Because doctors are really professional aren't they, it's one of those careers your parents want you to go into whereas social workers...!' (Taylor *et al.* 2008, p.25).

Barry (2007) undertook a major literature review of risk assessment for the Scottish Executive Education Department. In this review she notes that 'supervision is one of the key avenues for practitioners to have the time and capacity to reflect on their practice and to identify, discuss and learn from mistakes. However, the culture of the organisation needs to allow for such dialogue with confidence and trust on the part of both the supervisee and supervisor' (Barry 2007, p.34). Barry cites Stanley's (2005) study of social workers in New Zealand where supervision assisted in the management of risk in child protection, 'but on the assumption that the organisational culture will be welcoming of sharing and learning in supervision, rather than being fearful of reprisals for admissions of failure' (p.34). These tensions create major challenges for supervision.

THE CHILD PROTECTION SYSTEM

The public perception of statutory organisations such as child protection agencies is that they are very powerful, although this power is viewed with some ambivalence. There are of course two kinds of power – that in which acting is powerful and that in which *not* acting has major consequences. In many reviews of practice, inaction or declining to take action has had major consequences for the child protection agency at the centre, although the service staff were frequently not the only people to decline to act in a child protective way. There is a recurring theme of communication failures within and between organisations (Stanley and Manthorpe 2004). Ironically though, as we have noted earlier, child protection social workers, while rightly seen as very powerful by services users, often feel powerless and undervalued in the public domain. As Taylor *et al.* have noted there is also a perception that social workers are less well trained and there is constant challenge to their expertise. 'Medical knowledge is seen as specialized, while social workers' knowledge is in those areas where everybody considers themselves an expert – parenting and family life' (Taylor *et al.* 2008, p.25).

In any human enterprise where emotions, values and belief systems are in interaction with powerful institutions – the state, the courts, the police, the news media – there is inevitably tension, anxiety and potential conflict and a systemic approach is a prerequisite for understanding. As discussed in Chapter 9 we find that a systemic approach is useful to explore the demands of professional practice and the drain on personal emotional resources. In the context of reviewing child deaths Connolly and Doolan (2007) utilise a systems framework to illustrate the four critical sets of relationships in which child protection workers operate: the family system, the worker system, the organisational system and the wider system (Connolly and Doolan 2007, pp.69–70). This systemic analysis also has potential in the context of supervision practice in child protection work.

Figure 11.1, adapted from this work, illustrates the complexity of these systems and relationships and the key components within them, recognising child welfare workers' relationships with the families with which they work; their relationships with colleagues and supervisors; their engagement within the organisational context and last, and significantly often underemphasised, their relationships with other professionals and social systems within the community.

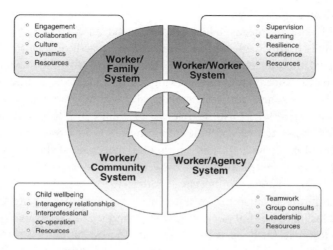

Figure 11.1 The child protection system

Worker–family relationships

Foremost in the child protection system is the worker–family relationship and one of the difficulties for practitioners and supervisors is how to retain hope and positive regard when so often facing the most unpleasant sights and conversations. The supervisor has a vital role in ensuring that practitioners bring a full account of their interactions to the table. In supervision and informal discussions a number of questions can guide the supervisor: 'How is the practitioner presenting both the risk factors and strengths of the family? What cultural and social perspectives are present in the telling of this story? What evidence am I hearing about planning for collaborative approaches? What feelings and fears are stated and what might be ignored or minimised?'

While it is important to seek positive engagement with families, despite fears and challenges, it is frequently unsafe to minimise unpleasant feelings and disturbing thoughts. A balance is needed. Ferguson notes that 'it is quite remarkable how little attention is given to the practitioner's perspective and experience of doing the work' of child protection when referring to the lived experience of child protection workers in conducting home visits (Ferguson 2009, p.473). Ferguson reminds us that practitioners face many challenges when they enter the private worlds of families they encounter. In the worst situations they may have feelings of 'disgust and fears for their own bodily integrity and well-being' and Ferguson notes from his study that these feelings were not mentioned in supervision. The failure to properly discuss such feelings 'meant that they could not be worked through and gone beyond to reach more authentic engagement with the child's life and needs' and this may impact on adequate examination especially in highly neglectful conditions where practitioners may 'distance and detach themselves from abused children' (p.476). The supervisor in such situations needs to encourage full description, for example, 'Tell me about the atmosphere and what reverberates within you about this child/adult/home/family?', trusting that, as we found in Chapter 8, feelings generated in practice can provide rich information in assessment (p.477).

As noted in Chapter 9, there is growing emphasis of the impact of an optimistic stance on relationships between practitioners and service users (Collins 2007, p.264). Collins cites Trotter (1999) and Ryan *et al.* (2004) as highlighting positive dispositions in interactions that feature humour, self-disclosure (p.265). Ryan *et al.* (2004) found that the personal qualities of practitioners such as self-belief, self-efficacy rather than technical knowledge and skills carried through into an optimistic approach to new and challenging situations. A questioning approach and retaining openness to possibilities is vital both to ensure safety and to perceive and acknowledge family strengths; assessments are not truth but part of continuing questioning and theorising (Munro 2004a).

Worker–worker relationships

A participant in a study conducted by Gibbs describes as 'sink or swim' the experience of joining a busy child welfare service and Gibbs notes that 'constant exposure to an action-orientated prescriptive culture means the new recruits will not learn the value of standing back and thinking reflectively about what happened and why' (Gibbs 2009, p.292). Research has consistently identified supervisor support and co-worker support as critical to promoting strong supervisory engagement for child welfare workers. Reasons found for supervisor impact include:

- the provision of guidance (Scannapieco and Connell-Carrick 2007)

- challenge to over-reliance on paperwork and compliance as 'ways of avoiding the emotional challenges of working with dysfunctional and abusive families' (Gibbs 2009, p.293)

- navigation through the demands and responsibilities for child welfare practice (Ellett, Collins-Carmargo and Ellett 2006)

- delivering positive messages to improve workers' self-esteem and self-efficacy (Gibbs 2001)

- a bridge between executive management and frontline workers (Morrison 2001)

- instruction on how to strive for the most effective practice in the face of differing work activities, large volume of work, stress of the daily work and challenges faced in child welfare work (Ellett *et al.* 2006)

- supervisors can definitely create a structure to allow the practice of new skills and encourage an environment of open discussion and support (Gibbs 2009; Yankeelov *et al.* 2009)

- protection against deleterious effects of stress and exposure to harm from professional practice (Mor Barak *et al.* 2009).

Yankeelov highlights awareness that 'supervision is a multi-dimensional construct' and amongst the factors identified (cited in Yankeelov *et al.* 2009, p.549) were: supervisors providing work opportunities to meet practitioners' skill development; supervisors modelling good practices, and strong verbal support to motivate and provide affirming feedback to workers. Further on in this chapter we will examine the potential for group approaches to working with very complex situations. Supervisors may find that group supervision provides excellent, complementary opportunities to model good reasoning, open not closed assessment practices and recognition of the value of listening to feelings.

Worker–agency relationships

Advocacy, negotiation about resources and 'managing up' (Kaiser and Kuechler 2008, p.78) were noted in Chapter 4 as aspects of the supervisory relationship, especially in 'internal' supervision where administrative aspects of supervision are routine. A positive view of administration, conceptualising it as assessing the need for resources, rather than mere compliance, can underpin both support and concern for quality.

Supervision is often allowed to languish in times of great pressure, despite good evidence of the effectiveness of supervision in relation to a number of key factors: retention of staff, as outlined above; mitigation of impact of stress (Mor Barak *et al.* 2009), job satisfaction (Mor Barak *et al.* 2006; Stalker *et al.* 2007) and optimism about the potential for different approaches to supervision to add support for continuing competence, for example from the strengths-based approaches (Presbury *et al.* 1999; Santa Rita 1998) and from positive psychology (Howard 2008).

Retention of employees in the child welfare services is an issue that receives international attention (Chen and Scannapieco 2009; DePanfilis and Zlotnik 2008; Nissly *et al.* 2005; Yankeelov *et al.* 2009). Recent research strongly supports the importance of supervision as a factor in retention in the child welfare workforce, especially when linked to worker confidence in their own abilities. Chen and Scannapieco (2009, p.12) have found that, consistent with findings of prior research, their study 'confirmed the importance of supervisor's support to worker's desire to stay, additionally, the present study further identified the interaction between supervisors' support and worker's self-efficacy and found that the influence of supervisors' support was particularly important to low self-efficacy workers'. The results of an earlier study by Nissly *et al.* had demonstrated that 'embeddedness in a supportive network, consisting of co-workers as well as one's supervisor, can reduce employees' intentions to leave' (Nissly *et al.* 2005, p.96).

Worker–agency–community relationships

The child protection system is made up of many agencies and professionals and the anxiety generated by child abuse underpins much of the conflict and miscommunication. Cahn describes supervisors in child welfare settings as having a key role to 'gain resources, align vision and build stronger connections' (Cahn 2009, p.152) and 'coach workers to represent the agency mandate' and in the wider community to help practitioners 'to navigate the system...in interagency situations' (p.104). Barry suggests that different groups represent three crucial sets of interests: 'the rights of the child, the integrity and rights of the family and the duties and powers of the state' (Barry 2007, p.27) and cites Britner and Mossler who found that 'professional group membership, rather than factors such as age or ethnicity of the child or chronicity of abuse, accounts for different patterns of prioritizing and using information when making decisions' (Britner and Mossler 2002, p.317).

Melissa: the rest of the story

In a vignette in Chapter 6 we considered the problem that Timothy, a health visitor, brought to supervision. Melissa (nine) is a child with multiple, chronic health problems and is being treated by an alternative healer against the advice of the GP and specialist services. On a home visit Timothy found Melissa in pain and deteriorating, and following some heated discussion back in the office, and Timothy's strong opposition, child health nurse Mary has called in the child protection team. We resume the story here.

Vignette – Melissa

Child welfare social worker Rob, a new graduate and his supervisor Kristy meet with Melissa and her family, speak to the health professionals and consult the legal service. Two days later legal intervention is used to obtain orthodox treatment for Melissa. Timothy is very upset about this outcome and relationships are frayed amongst members of the professional system. Timothy is still visiting Melissa and her family but feels that trust has been eroded. Rob meets with Timothy and Mary to work out a longer term plan for teamwork with Melissa's family as she will have long-term needs. The meeting is tense and difficult. Timothy and Mary argue and Rob gets frustrated and walks out. Rob goes to supervision with Kristy and is visibly upset: 'What's the point of it all if even the workers can't get it together and put the child's needs first, instead of their own egos?' Kristy acknowledges Rob's feelings and draws out the issues; they map them on a whiteboard. Rob can see that the tensions are in part due to different ways of seeing the same situation, and that all do have the well-being of the family at heart. Rob is able to re-focus on Melissa's needs and go back to his core role. They plan another meeting and work out how to ensure the plan is indeed developed. Rob and Kristy role play the phone calls he needs to make and he leaves supervision feeling more resolved to get people working together and understanding that these professional relationships are part of the job.

As was noted in Chapter 9, Mor Barak *et al.*'s study suggested that three key supervisory dimensions required attention in assisting child protection workers to remain focused and manage stress: task assistance, social and emotional support, and strong supervisory interpersonal interaction (Mor Barak *et al.* 2009, p.27). A key supervisory task is to promote mastery and independence. In this vignette Kristy demonstrates all these: she is supportive and can contain Rob's strong emotions, she is able to assist him to work out a way forward and is able to facilitate his development, rather than stepping in and taking over his work. However, while she can take a supportive approach and empathise with his strong child advocacy position, Kristy can also model a collaborative inter-agency stance. Some good explorative questions might include: 'What was going on for Timothy and Mary in this situation, what might they have been thinking?' 'Timothy's concern was underpinned by concern for the trust and rapport established with Melissa's family, the health professionals will have a long-term role protecting Melissa, how can we work past this current conflict to support good outcomes for the family, and foster better inter-agency work?'

EFFECTIVE SUPERVISION IN CHILD PROTECTION

There are three major threats to the effectiveness of supervision: the lack of skill and courage to challenge; the domination of 'blame and shame' tactics in contemporary human services, and the weakening of professional values 'in-action' by a focus on technologies of practice. Nowhere are these threats more overt than in the field of child protection.

Supervision was described as 'the cornerstone of good social work practice' in Lord Laming's report into the death of Victoria Climbié (Laming 2003, p.12). Recommendation 45 of this report emphasised regular supervision of frontline children's social workers (p.376). Ruch (2007b) commented that if there was to be more than rhetoric about effective supervision then there was an urgent need to 'propose different and creative support forums for practitioners' (2007b, p.372). Lord Laming's recent review of progress found that inconsistent provision of supervision remained a persistent problem and recommended attention to improvement (Laming 2009, p.30). The Social Work Task Force (Department for Children, Schools and Families 2009b), established to respond to the Laming report, has subsequently reported extensive feedback from frontline social workers about supervision. Practitioners note that 'access to supervision is often threatened or put on hold due to staff shortages and mounting caseloads', and that there was insufficient time to reflect and learn as teams (Department for Children, Schools and Families 2009b, p.20). In addition the task force noted that 'access to supervision can vary significantly between authorities but also within the same authority. In the eyes of frontline staff, supervision tended to be process driven and dominated by case management' (p.20), to the detriment of a supportive and reflective practice environment.

Supervision in child protection requires particular skills. It requires a balance over time of careful oversight of a form of practice in which, as has been explored above, there are both vulnerable children and vulnerable workers and a complex interplay of factors between these two. Of equal importance is the focus on the professional development of supervisees. Two key dimensions of professional development are use-of-self and critical reasoning.

Use-of-self

A clear task of supervision is to support the practitioner in relation to the emotional demands of the work. Increasingly this is understood as how to assist professionals to manage their use-of-self in their work. Mandell (2008, p.235–326) notes the concept of 'use-of-self' has fallen out of favour in recent decades in social work. Self-awareness has long been regarded in popular wisdom as a key attribute of social work and, as supervision educators, the authors have often noted to students, that our 'tools of trade' do not come in a box or a kit but are located in our person. Yip suggests that use-of-self, essential in reflective practice, happens across a number of dimensions in the person of the practitioner where 'self-recall, self-evaluation, self-observation and self-analysis take place within the social worker's mind' (Yip 2006, p.782). Yip argues that practitioners need to find or create time and space in which they can 'distance themselves, to stop and think, to deal with…uncomfortable feelings and to analyse and resolve discrepancies in practice' (p.782). Mandell, however, feels that use-of-self has slipped in favour because of its association with a conceptualisation of countertransference that:

> Does not adequately support structural, anti-oppression or critical social work practice because it has tended to split the individual and the social in ways that reduce social arrangements to manifestations of individual deficit or maladjustment and power to a structural configuration. (Mandell 2008, p 236)

Mandell suggests that writing on use-of-self in 'the mainstream' has not considered how awareness might enhance critical practice (p.236), however, Davis (2002), noting the inherent ambiguity in child protection's dual role as both investigation and support, raised the importance of self-awareness in promoting strengths-based practice with families. Davis notes a number of factors that impede strengths-focused work with families: over-reliance on procedures; a 'shallow conceptual model for understanding the relationships between the families, themselves and the agency's mission' and 'over reliance on personal intuition' (p.187). This latter factor, when 'combined with insufficient self-awareness, can create barriers to searching for families' strengths and lead to more punitive responses' (pp.187–188).

Kondrat, in a seminal article, assists us to sort through the many conceptualisations of 'use-of-self'. She identifies three conceptualisations of self in practice: simple conscious awareness, reflective self-awareness, and reflexive self-awareness (Kondrat 1999, p.452) and describes them as follows:

Simple conscious awareness	'Becoming awake to present realities, noticing one's surroundings, and being able to name perceptions, feelings, and nuances of behavior'. The self can recognise what it is experiencing (p.453).
Reflective self-awareness	Reflective self-awareness turns attention to a self who 'has' the experience. The self's behaviours, affect, cognitive content, and accomplishments become objects of reflection. A 'metaphor of distance' is often used, 'the self steps back to observe and consider its own performance' (pp.453–454).
Reflexive self-awareness	Self-knowledge becomes possible not by creating distance and otherness but by reducing the 'distance' and relying on sameness between 'knower and known' (pp.456–567). Important here is the notion that the self is a 'construct that is continuously emerging within specific social contexts' (pp.459–460).

Kondrat notes that post modernist thinking challenges the notion of a 'self-contained self' able to stand back from experience and observe from a neutral uncontaminated perspective, because our 'knowledge' is constructed in our broad context and thus when considering self-knowledge the problem is intensified by our inescapable insider status (p.456). The work of child protection poses many challenges for the 'critical' practitioner. Not least is the need to remain strongly in tune with the values and commitments that led practitioners to the work in the first place. There is a potential for a focus on the risks of exposure to abuse and the need for self-care to individualise practice and isolate workers rather than build a collective sense of commitment based in teamwork. Profitt (2008, p.159) reminds us that much of the literature that addresses self-care and compassion fatigue focuses on psychological and individual explanations of these problems. Profitt points to the social context of much of what traumatises people, 'the witnessing of social phenomena such as gender violence, hunger and poverty' and the relocation of this to 'the realm of private injury' (p.160). Good supervisory questions might include: 'How do we participate in collaborative opportunities to consider the impact of the work, what do we process at work and what seeps into our personal lives? How can we keep each other safe? What do you need to retain perspective, hope and an understanding of the social inequalities that underpin so much violence and distress?' To avoid such questions risks the depersonalisation and distancing we noted in Chapter 9.

CRITICAL REASONING IN CHILD PROTECTION SOCIAL WORK

A study of public perceptions of social work in the United Kingdom in 2001 found that respondents demonstrated a very poor level of knowledge regarding the qualifications and training required for social work (Research Works 2001). Rather than recognising a career structure, respondents focused on the personal qualities they felt were required, e.g. communication skills, patience, impartiality and inner emotional strength (Research Works 2001, p.5). The majority perceived social work to be a vocation rather than a profession and social workers were 'considered to hold a similar status to broadly equivalent professions such as nursing, teaching and the police' (p.5).

Ruch acknowledges failures of deep thinking in social work and attributes this to the enormous pressure on social workers 'to do something'. 'Concrete manifestations of this emphasis on 'doing' social work abound in the burgeoning of procedures and audit requirements that represent an increasingly technical–rational understanding of practice' (Ruch 2007b, p.371).

Kondrat has suggested that it is within 'reflective self-awareness' that students and new practitioners have been urged to become aware of the potential impact in practice of personal values, needs and biases in order to work consciously and objectively. Prescriptions for increasing objectivity in self-reflection include scrutiny of practice, eliciting feedback from clients, using reflective tools such as audio and video tapes, engaging in supervision, and an examination of the 'cognitive products of the self such as reasoning and judgment, and attending to the practice knowledge assumed to be implicit' in everyday practice (Kondrat 1999, p.455). A challenge for social work in particular is that much practice focuses on the 'everyday' of human life – relationships, families, parenting, sex, religious and political beliefs, values and so forth. There is an assumption that there are truths about all these things that are self-evident and therefore formal knowledge is of questionable value. This is often evident in the belittling of social science by proponents of 'tough love' approaches to social problems. While developing a new social work degree, one of the authors of this book was challenged about why we needed to have courses on sexuality and spirituality – 'Surely these were matters best learned at home?' In the course of professional practice, it is always apparent that what we learn at home about these aspects of human life shapes our thinking (and seeing) but often in ways that are not always helpful to the families we work with. Effective practice requires a theoretical base for practice, the ability to critically analyse the information which underpins decisions as well as a good grasp of the evidence informed 'best practices'. As Munro has noted the novice practitioner 'has to learn to use formal knowledge as well as their pre-existing wisdom…as they become more experienced their use of formal theories becomes absorbed into their intuitive approach' (Munro 2008, p.5).

MAINTAINING HOPE

As we saw in Chapter 9 resilient practitioners maintain hopefulness and optimism and Koenig and Spano (2007) suggest that conscious attention to the fostering of these qualities can be a focus of supervision. Child welfare supervision has a major role to play in safeguarding the supportive engagement of staff, assisting them to manage uncertainty and address the risks at the intersection of the personal and professional experience. These intersections are often where 'dangerousness' may be a fear. Stanford studied social workers' reflections on their interventions and her work supports supervision as providing a place for rekindling of hopefulness:

> Recognition of hope and the possibility of change, alongside a commitment to care therefore need to become directives, as opposed to incidentals, of practice. Supervision is a site in which this orienting framework could be mutually explored and supported by managers and practitioners. Critical reflections of interventions could be used to support this process. (Stanford 2007, p.257)

To retain critically reflective practice, exploration of practitioners' understanding of risk and uncertainty in practice needs to be given a central space in supervision. Moral reasoning and a more nuanced exploration of risk stories can strengthen supervision practice. Profitt (2008, p.161) notes that neither intellectual work (critical analysis) nor the containment of deep feelings alone can 'assuage pervasive feelings such as deep sadness… While sorting out internal boundaries as an act of self care and survival can protect helpers, without a mentor or group of trustworthy colleagues, how do workers protect their human sensibility…?'. Conrad and Kellar-Guenther (2006, p.107) studied the relationship between compassion fatigue (distress experienced by the helper), burnout and 'compassion satisfaction' (fulfilment from helping others and positive relationship with colleagues) for child welfare workers. They found that child welfare workers with high 'satisfaction' had lower levels of compassion fatigue and lower levels of burnout. They suggest that strong social support from colleagues and supervisors may be crucial in buffering workers from their emotionally draining daily work. Shared work builds understanding, draws on different perspectives and knowledge and encourages positive, open and honest team communication, where challenging questions can be asked. Hopefulness requires nurturing to maintain the belief in possibilities.

This highlights the need to develop opportunities to share experience, explore ideas for action, grow confidence in collaborative decision making points to group supervision, structured to meet the particular demands of child protection practice. This need not be uni-professional; indeed it seems likely that well designed group processes involving several disciplines could enhance interprofessional understanding and respect.

BRINGING IT ALL TOGETHER: GROUP SUPERVISION

In the seminal work *Communities of Practice* Wenger argued that 'learning is the engine of practice and practice is the history of that learning' (Wenger 1998, p.96). The 'history of learning' is practice wisdom that develops when there is support and time to learn from success as well as practice mistakes. If thinking space is a scarce resource and absent at the frontline, where is this history formed? Laming regards supervision as critical, as is the provision of 'routine opportunities for peer-learning and discussion. Currently, not enough time is dedicated to this' (Laming 2009, p.32). While individual supervision is a vital component in supporting and developing individual child protection workers, regardless of their profession, there is growing support for a revitalisation of group supervision. This could be in new forms, to address the complex dimensions of assessment and decision making in a field where there are so many challenges at personal, interpersonal, interprofessional, team, organisational and inter-institutional levels. In recent years there has been some questioning of supervision and a reshaping of its application, particularly in child welfare services (Field 2008; Lietz 2008; Strand and Badger 2007). There is a greater focus on critical reasoning and shared decision making (Jones, Washington and Steppe 2007; Munro 2008). Lietz argues that approaches to decision making have been dominated by two styles: the 'practice experience' model and the 'empirically based decision making' model. The former highly values the autonomy of the individual worker to develop expertise and rejects rigid rules and prescriptions for practice (Lietz 2009, pp.192–194). The latter is premised on a critique of the former, where lack of formal guidelines for practice means that decision making can be idiosyncratic and inconsistent. The problem with empirically-based models is that they assume a level of competence in locating and utilising research findings which may be illusory.

Shared decision making

A process in which decision making can be shared (Stevenson 2005) and many minds applied to the development of plans and processes seems to offer much to advance child welfare goals. Shared decision making in group supervision or a group consultation process can incorporate many safeguards and benefits. Space does not allow a full examination of these but the following points provide a summary, with suggestions of relevant material for further exploration:

- Peer review of professional decisions, drawing on both analytical skills (the application of theory in practice and utilisation of empirical evidence) and intuitive capacity (practice wisdom) leading to an improved focus on critical reasoning (Munro 2008).

- Encouragement of a climate where practitioners are questioning, challenging, open about their decision-making process, committed to taking shared responsibility for decisions (Leitz 2009) and which creates a reflective space where practitioners are prepared to challenge each other in the interests of the children and families (Jones and Gallop 2003).

- Protection of human rights. Open discussion contributes to clarity of purpose in making legal interventions and ensuring that no service user's rights are adversely affected (e.g. coming into care) without scrutiny of that decision (Connolly and Ward 2008) and ensures that the perspectives of children, parents and carers have been sought and considered and the most respectful relationships forged (Holland and Scourfield 2004).

- Protection of service users. It ensures that children and young people are not left in unacceptable risk situations on the basis of a single practitioner's assessment or choices, or on unchallenged assumptions (Gibbs 2009).

- Protection of staff. It ensures that practitioners are not put into a position where situations may exceed their knowledge, skills or experience or where they have to manage very stressful emotional or potentially traumatic situations (Davis 2002; Ferguson 2009).

- Maintain and develop an optimistic stance, professional commitment and compassion and preserve hopefulness and morale (Collins 2007; Gibbs 2009; Koenig and Spano 2007).

- Accountability to the agency, the professions and to the public. Professionals are accountable to their agency and to their professional body. Agencies are accountable for the actions of employed practitioners. Shared decision making confirms a commitment to legal, ethical, safe and transparent practice within the framework that has been mandated for the safety of children.

Group processes can 'provide the conditions in which Laming's "respectful uncertainty" and "healthy scepticism" might flourish' (Ruch 2007b, p.373). Wenger's notion of a 'community of practice' is useful to consider in this context (Wenger 1998). The concept recognises the social nature of learning in everyday life, how human beings understand their roles and practices in family, school, community and work, negotiating meaning, identity and power in all the relationships they encounter. Wenger sees learning within all of these communities and alerts us to the complexity of learning within organisations. Wenger notes that 'organisations are social design directed at practice... Communities of practice are thus key to an organisation's competence and to the evolution of that competence' (1998, p.241). Wenger notes, though, that communities of practice differ from organisations in that 'they arise, evolve and dissolve according to their own learning', though they may do so in respect to institutional events and they shape their own boundaries though these may at times may be congruent with institutional boundaries' (1998, p.241). Most importantly, communities of practice are the location of the real work, where 'the official meets the everyday' (p.243) and of course where things are inclined to go wrong. As Wenger points out, policies and procedures can be designed but 'in the end it is practice that produces results', not policies and processes (p.243). The challenge for health and social care practice, especially in high-risk services, is to support 'the knowledgability of practice' while allowing sufficient structure to hold the organisation together as overemphasis on proceduralism is not helpful, serving to support the apparatus, rather than the practice (pp.243–244).

Group consult approach

Finally, we suggest a particular approach to child welfare supervision. We have seen that collaborative approaches to supervision in child protection can offer a solution to the problem of how to organise effective supervision to ensure balanced attention to education, support and administrative aspects. The administrative aspect is here reconceptualised as shared decision making that is not procedure driven but reflective and evidence informed. Educational aspects can be addressed by utilisation of practice frameworks (Connolly 2007) and through engagement in informed critical reflection (Fook and Gardner 2007). Ruch (2007b) exploring how practitioners understood and carried out reflection found that teams were crucial in facilitating reflective practice. Significantly, practices designed to improve communication and collaborative work, such as co-work, consultation forums and case discussions were found to create vital 'spaces where practitioners could stop "doing" and think about their practice' (Ruch 2007b, p.373).

Field describes the introduction of a 'group consult' model which augments supervision in frontline child welfare practice in New Zealand (Field 2008, p.11). This model represents a development which aims to incorporate the three benefits of group supervision described above: support, reflective thinking and shared responsibility. Field notes that the group consult process is based on the 'signs of safety' approach of Turnell and Edwards (1999) and the further development of this work undertaken by Lohrbach and Sawyer (2004). Group consultation has the potential to provide genuine experiential professional development for practitioners as they 'share and critique...pathways, decision-making and practice responses' (Lohrbach 2008, p.20) building practitioner confidence and skill and is kept separate from 'procedural oversight' (p.18). In Olmsted County Minnesota, where this approach was developed it has become the preferred method of supervision; participation is required, consults are held weekly and the model applied to all aspects of child welfare practice. The process is facilitated by one or two supervisors and is active involving use of a consultation template, genograms, eco-maps, written records and a whiteboard to record and process information in the assessment and decision-making process. Discussion of a 'case' is structured around key features: potential danger, safety and protective factors and risk factors (evidence informed), gaps – including incomplete or speculative information, risk statements and next steps (Lohrbach 2008, pp.21–22). The New Zealand group consult model utilises the basic framework of the Lohrbach and Sawyer (2004) model but differs in explicitly linking it to the New Zealand practice frameworks (Connolly 2007) and particular legal and cultural requirements for safe and respectful practice in New Zealand.

Field (2008, p.117) notes that facilitation of the group consult process is highly skilled and that steps need to be taken to manage group dynamics – polarisation, unhelpful roles and 'group think'. We do not advocate the ending of personal individual supervision, rather that this is adjunctive. Lohrbach notes that individual supervision remains accessible for performance evaluation, 'sensitive personal issues', corrective action and in crisis situations (2008, p.20). Support administrative matters and decision making are thus able to be held in creative tension, rather than being seen as inevitably in conflict, and the resources and needs of individuals, practitioners and the agency brought together.

Afterword

Ten years into the new century we have reflected upon that complex process called supervision. We have taken the opportunity in this book to present an overview of our own experiences, to share our developing ideas and to acknowledge the ideas and work of others which have sustained, challenged and inspired us in our 20 years of practising and teaching professional supervision.

The framework established by Hughes and Pengelly's (1997) triangle of functions (Chapter 2), continues to provide, in our opinion, the best definition of the territory of supervision. Whatever approach or model is used in supervision this triangle links supervision practice to its mandate and its, at times conflicting, accountabilities. At its centre stands the supervision relationship (Chapter 3). It is here that the nurture, replenishment and what is sometimes called the 'magic' of supervision occur.

The importance of the overarching culture of the organisation on supervision practice is explored in Chapter 4 and our central belief that supervision is the forum for learning and development is reflected in the Reflective Learning Model described in Chapter 5. Our commitment to providing supervisors with a map for their own journey is highlighted in Chapter 6, where we consider the development of supervisory competence. Chapter 7 and 8 present the 'doing' of supervision, skills and interactions and the role of supervision to respect and work with the emotions generated through the workplace. This is expanded in Chapter 9 where resilience is explored and we consider the role of supervision as a central resource to assist with the stress and distress encountered in the workplace. Our belief that the supervision of students is a parallel, but separate process, is explored in Chapter 10 and, finally, Chapter 11 addresses the role of supervision in care and protection of children.

Our journey with supervision has both delighted us and caused us concern over the 20 years of our teaching and research. Increased acknowledgement from organisations and regulatory bodies of the heavy emotional toll exacted on practitioners at the interface between professional 'people' practitioners and the people themselves has filled us with hope that practices like supervision will be mandated and resourced to provide effective focus and support to practitioners. This hope on many occasions has been cut short when pragmatic responses have inadequately resourced supervision practice and have stolen the process to exact compliance with standards. Yet within this we have witnessed again and again the resilience of professional practitioners from all disciplines who have understood and actualised the potential for supervision to be a truly sustaining practice which provides safety for all.

Inevitably there are areas which we have not covered in this book. We have focused primarily on one-to-one supervision relationships and, apart from Chapter 11, have not addressed the growing literature and research on group supervision. Group supervision, which we believe holds much in common with individual supervision, is nevertheless a separate form of supervision practice. It requires additional skills and competence on the part of the supervisor and we agree with Brown and Bourne (1996, p.155) that it is 'highly context-specific and context-sensitive'. It is not possible to do justice to group supervision in the space we have available in this text. The developing literature and research into spirituality and supervision is another area we have not addressed. Our failure to discuss this explicitly is in no way a reflection of our belief in its importance. 'Spirituality, like supervision, begins with questions and the quest for truth inevitably leads to questions' (Carroll 2001, p.11). Supervision, as we have emphasised in this book, is about asking questions, which in turn lead to more questions. This develops learning, which is not necessarily about answers.

Carroll (2001, p.16) quotes Oscar Wilde: 'Only the shallow know themselves…if you know yourself you have not touched the depths.' The quest for learning and knowing has no destination, only a journey, and it is the quality of that journey which holds the magic, the creativity, the playfulness and the passion of supervision.

We are saddened by the resistance to professional supervision which still exists in some organisations and some professions. Usually, in our opinion, this stems more from a lack of understanding about the process than a dismissal of the purpose. The very name 'supervision' carries its own pejorative meaning and those professions which value independence of judgement and honour the authority of experience have difficulty in isolating and publicly exploring 'unknowing'.

Research continues in supervision and, as each practitioner, supervisor, manager and researcher contributes to the body of knowledge, understanding and possibility increase. 'Wicked spell or magic bullets?' ask Butterworth *et al.* (2008, p.270) in a recent review of the supervision literature: we agree with them that supervision is neither but that it does have the potential to make some practitioners 'uncomfortable'.

Supervision remains for us a vital, sustaining and necessary practice within which we have both delighted in witnessing the growth and development of others and have valued how this has added to our own growth and development. We know the depths of possible exploration of ourselves in supervision and the humility which comes from accompanying another in this journey.

We hope then that this book offers some of our learning and conveys our passion.

References

Adams, R. E., Figley, C. R. and Boscarino, J. A. (2008) 'The compassion fatigue scale: Its use with social workers following urban disaster.' *Research on Social Work Practice 18*, 3, 238–250.

Adamson, C. (1999) 'Towards a social work knowledge base for traumatic events.' *Social Work Review 11*, 1, 29–34.

Adamson, C. (2001) 'The Role of Supervision in the Management of Critical Incidents and Traumatic Events.' In L. Beddoe and J. Worrall (eds) *Supervision from Rhetoric to Reality, Supervision Conference 2000*. Auckland: Auckland College of Education.

Alaszewski, A. and Coxon, K. (2009) 'Uncertainty in everyday life: Risk, worry and trust.' *Health, Risk and Society 11*, 3, 201–207.

Alonso, A. (1985) *The Quiet Profession: Supervisors of Psychotherapy.* New York, NY: Macmillan.

Argyris, C. (1991) 'Teaching smart people how to learn.' *Harvard Business Review 69*, 3, 99–109.

Argyris, C. and Schön, D. (1974) *Theory in Practice: Increasing Professional Effectiveness.* San Francisco, CA: Jossey Bass.

Argyris, C. and Schön, D. (1978) *Organisational Learning.* Reading, MA: Addison Wesley.

Arkin, N. (1999) 'Culturally sensitive student supervision: Difficulties and challenges.' *The Clinical Supervisor 18*, 2, 1–16.

Arndt, J., King, S., Suter, E., Mazonde, J., Taylor, E. and Arthur, N. (2009) 'Socialization in health education: Encouraging an integrated interprofessional socialization process.' *Journal of Allied Health 38*, 1, 18.

Ash, E. (1995) 'Supervision: Taking Account of Feelings.' In J. Pritchard (ed.) *Good Practice in Supervision: Statutory and Voluntary Organisations.* London: Jessica Kingsley Publishers.

Austin, J. and Hopkins, K.M. (2004) (eds) *Supervision as Collaboration in the Human Services: Building a Learning Culture.* Thousand Oaks, CA: Sage.

Baer, R. (2006) *Mindfulness-Based Treatment Approaches: Clinician's Guide to Evidence Base and Applications.* San Diego, CA: Elsevier Academic Press.

Bagnall, R. (1998) 'Professional Codes of Conduct: A Critique with Implications for Continuing Professional Education.' In D. Dymock (ed.) *CPE 98 Meeting the Challenge of Change.* Queensland: University of New England.

Baldwin, M. (2008) 'Promoting and managing innovation: Critical reflection, organizational learning and the development of innovative practice in a national children's voluntary organization.' *Qualitative Social Work 7*, 3, 330–348.

Banks, S. (2008) 'Critical Commentary: Social Work Ethics.' *British Journal of Social Work 38*, 6, 1238–1249.

Barker, P. (1992) 'Psychiatric Nursing.' In T. Butterworth and J. Faugier (eds) *Clinical Supervision and Mentorship in Nursing.* London: Chapman and Hall.

Barretti, M. A. (2009) 'Ranking desirable field instructor characteristics: Viewing student preferences in context with field and class experience.' *The Clinical Supervisor 28*, 1, 47–71.

Barry, M. (2007) *Effective Approaches to Risk Assessment in Social Work: An International Literature Review.* Edinburgh: Education Information and Analytical Services, Scottish Executive.

Baxter, P. (2007) 'The CCARE model of clinical supervision: Bridging the theory–practice gap... (Communication, collaboration, application, reflection, evaluation).' *Nurse Education in Practice 7*, 2, 103–111.

Beck, U. (1992) *Risk Society: Towards a New Modernity.* London: Sage.

Beddoe, L. (2000) 'The Supervisory Relationship.' In L. Cooper and L. Briggs (eds) *Fieldwork in the Human Service.* Sydney: Allen and Unwin.

Beddoe, L. (2003) 'Danger and disdain: Truth or dare in social work education' [Electronic Version]. *Women in Welfare Education (Australia) 6*, 13–25. Available at www.aaswwe.asn.au/wiwe/default.htm, accessed on 16 April 2010.

Beddoe, L. and Davys, A. (2008) 'Revitalizing supervision education through stories of confirmation and difference: The case for interprofessional learning.' *Social Work Now 40*, August, 34–41.

Beddoe, L. (2009) 'Creating continuous conversation: Social workers and learning organizations.' *Social Work Education 28*, 7, 722–736.

Beddoe, L. (2010a) 'Starting out in Supervision.' In K. E. Stagnitti (ed.) *Fieldwork Education for the Health Professions: A Guide to Clinical Learning and Teamwork.* Melbourne: Oxford University Press.

Beddoe, L. (2010b) 'Surveillance or reflection: Professional supervision in the risk society.' *British Journal of Social Work.* Advance published 22 February 2010. DOI:10.1093/bjsw/bcq018.

Beddoe, L. and Davys, A. (1994) 'The status of supervision: Reflections from a training perspective.' *Social Work Review* 6, 5/6, 16–21.

Beddoe, L. and Egan, R. (2009) 'Social Work Supervision.' In M. Connolly and L. Harms (eds) *Social Work: Contexts and Practice*, 2nd edn. Melbourne: Oxford University Press.

Beddoe, L. and Maidment, J. (2009) *Mapping Knowledge for Social Work Practice: Critical Intersections*. Melbourne: Cengage.

Bennett, S. and Deal, K. H. (2009) 'Beginnings and endings in social work supervision: The interaction between attachment and developmental processes.' *Journal of Teaching in Social Work 29*, 1, 101–117.

Bernard, J. M. (2005) 'Tracing the development of clinical supervision.' *The Clinical Supervisor 24*, 1, 3–21.

Bernard, J. M. and Goodyear, R. K. (2009) *Fundamentals of Clinical Supervision*, 4th edn. Upper Saddle River, NJ: Pearson.

Berne, E. (1978) *What Do You Say After You Say Hello?* London: Transworld Publishers.

Bernler, G. and Johnsson, L. (1985) *Handledning i Psykosocialt Arbete*. Stockholm: Natur och Kultur.

Bierema, L. L. and Eraut, M. (2004) 'Workplace-focused learning: Perspectives on continuing professional education and human resource development.' *Advances in Developing Human Resources 6*, 1, 52–68.

Birnbaum, L. (2005) 'Connecting to inner guidance: Mindfulness meditation and transformation of professional self–concept in social work students.' *Critical Social Work 6*, 2. Available at www.criticalsocialwork.com, accessed on 16 April 2010.

Bogo, M. and Dill, K. (2008) 'Walking the tightrope: Using power and authority in child welfare supervision.' *Child Welfare 87*, 6, 141–157.

Bolton, R. (1979) *People Skills: How to Assert Yourself, Listen to Others, and Resolve Conflicts*. New York, NY: Prentice-Hall.

Bond, M. and Holland, S. (1998) *Skills of Clinical Supervision for Nurses*. Buckingham: Open University Press.

Boud, D., Keogh, R. and Walker, D. (eds) (1985) *Reflection: Turning Experience into Learning*. London: Kogan Page.

Bower, S. A. and Bower, G. H. (1991) *Asserting Yourself: A Practical Guide for Positive Change*. Cambridge, MA: Peresus Books.

Bradley, G. and Hojer, S. (2009) 'Supervision reviewed: reflections on two different social work models in England and Sweden.' *European Journal of Social Work 12*, 1, 71–85.

Bradley, J., Jacob, E. and Bradley, R. (1999) 'Reflections on culturally safe supervision, or why Bill Gates makes more money than we do.' *Te Komako III Social Work Review 11*, 4, 3–6.

Britner, P. and Mossler, D. (2002) 'Professionals' decision making about out-of-home placements following instances of child abuse.' *Child Abuse and Neglect 26*, 4, 317–332.

Brookfield, S. (1995) *Becoming a Critically Reflective Teacher*. San Francisco, CA: Jossey-Bass.

Brookfield, S. (2009) 'The concept of critical reflection: Promises and contradictions.' *European Journal of Social Work 12*, 3, 293–304.

Brown, A. and Bourne, I. (1996) *The Social Work Supervisor*. Buckingham: Open University Press.

Burke, R. J. (2001) 'Workaholism in organizations: The role of organizational values.' *Personnel Review 30*, 5/6, 637.

Busse, S. (2009) 'Supervision between critical reflection and practical action.' *Journal of Social Work Practice: Psychotherapeutic Approaches in Health, Welfare and the Community 23*, 2, 159–173.

Butler, J. (1996) 'Professional development: Practice as text, reflection as process, and self as locus.' *Australian Journal of Education 40*, 3, 265–283.

Butterworth, T. (1994) 'Preparing to take on clinical supervision.' *Nursing Standard 8*, 52, 32–34.

Butterworth, T. (2001) 'Clinical Supervision and Clinical Governance for the Twenty-First Century: An End or Just the Beginning.' In J. Cutcliffe, T. Butterworth and B. Proctor (eds) *Fundamental Themes in Clinical Supervision*. New York, NY: Routledge.

Butterworth, T., Bell, L., Jackson, C. and Pajnkihar, M. (2008) 'Wicked spell or magic bullet? A review of the clinical supervision literature 2001–2007.' *Nurse Education Today 28*, 3, 264–272.

Cahn, K. (2009) 'The World beyond the Unit.' In C. C. Potter and C. R. Brittain (eds) *Child Welfare Supervision: A Practical Guide for Supervisors, Managers and Administrators*. New York, NY: Oxford University Press.

Carroll, M. (2001) 'The spirituality of supervision.' In L. Beddoe and J. Worrall (eds) *Supervision: From Rhetoric to Reality*. Auckland: Auckland College of Education.

Carroll, M. (2007) 'One more time: What is supervision?' *Psychotherapy in Australia 13*, 3, 34–40.

Carroll, M. (2009) 'Supervision: Critical reflection for transformational learning, Part One.' *The Clinical Supervisor 28*, 2, 210–220.

Carroll, M. and Gilbert, M. C. (2005) *On Being a Supervisee: Creating Learning Partnerships*. London: Vukani Press.

Carroll, M. and Tholstrup, M. (eds) (2001) *Integrative Approaches to Supervision*. London: Jessica Kingsley Publishers.

Carver, C., Scheier, M. and Weintraub, J. (1989) 'Assessing coping strategies: A theoretically based approach.' *Journal of Personality and Social Psychology 56*, 2, 267–283.

Casey, C. (2003) 'The learning worker, organizations and democracy.' *International Journal of Lifelong Education 22*, 6, 620–634.

Cassedy, P., Epling, M., Williamson, L. and Harvery, G. (2001) 'Providing Cross Discipline Supervision to New Supervisors.' In J. Cutcliffe, T. Butterworth and B. Proctor (eds) *Clinical Supervision*. London: Routledge.

Chang, C. Y., Hays, D. G. and Milliken, T. F. (2009) 'Addressing social justice issues in supervision: A call for client and professional advocacy.' *The Clinical Supervisor 28*, 1, 20–35.

Chen, S.-Y. and Scannapieco, M. (2009) 'The influence of job satisfaction on child welfare worker's desire to stay: An examination of the interaction effect of self-efficacy and supportive supervision.' *Children and Youth Services Review*. Advance published. DOI:10.1016/j.childyouth.2009.10.014.

Clare, B. (2007) 'Promoting deep learning: A teaching, learning and assessment endeavour.' *Social Work Education 26*, 5, 433–446.

Clare, M. (2001) 'Operationalising professional supervision in this age of accountabilities.' *Australian Social Work 54*, 2, 69–79.

Clarke, N. (2006) 'Developing emotional intelligence through workplace learning: Findings from a case study in healthcare.' *Human Resource Development International 9*, 4, 447–465.

Claxton, G. (2005) 'Mindfulness, learning and the brain.' *Journal of Rational-Emotive and Cognitive-Behavior Therapy 23*, 4, 301–314.

Clouder, L. and Sellars, J. (2004) 'Reflective practice and clinical supervision: An interprofessional perspective.' Journal of Advanced Nursing 46, 3, 262–269.

Cole, B. and Wessel, J. (2008) 'How clinical instructors can enhance the learning experience of physical therapy students in an introductory clinical placement.' *Journal Advances in Health Sciences Education 13*, 2, 163–179.

Collins, S. (2007) 'Social workers, resilience, positive emotions and optimism.' *Practice: Social Work in Action 19*, 4, 255–269.

Collins, S. (2008) 'Statutory social workers: Stress, job satisfaction, coping, social support and individual differences.' *British Journal of Social Work 38*, 6, 1173–1193.

Connolly, M. (2007) 'Practice frameworks: Conceptual maps to guide interventions in child welfare.' *British Journal of Social Work 37*, 5, 825–837.

Connolly, M. and Doolan, M. (2007) *Lives Cut Short: Child Death by Maltreatment*. Wellington: Dunmore Press.

Connolly, M. and Ward, T. (2008) *Morals, Rights and Practice in the Human Services: Effective and Fair Decision-Making in Health, Social Care and Criminal Justice*. London and Philadelphia: Jessica Kingsley Publishers.

Conrad, D. and Kellar-Guenther, Y. (2006) 'Compassion fatigue, burnout and compassion satisfaction among Colorado child protection workers.' *Child Abuse and Neglect 30*, 10, 1071–1080.

Cooper, A. (2001) 'The state of mind we're in: Social anxiety, governance and the audit society.' *Psychoanalytic Studies 3*, 3–4, 349–362.

Cooper, L. (2000) 'Organisational Changes and Social Work Supervision: Analysis and Reconstruction.' In L. Beddoe and J. Worrall (eds) *Supervision: From Rhetoric to Reality*. Auckland: Auckland College of Education.

Cooper, L. (2006) 'Clinical supervision: Private arrangement or managed process?' *Social Work Review 18*, 3, 21–30.

Cooper, L. and Anglem, J. (2003) *Clinical Supervision in Mental Health*. Adelaide: Australian Centre for Community Services Research (ACCSR).

Cornelius, H. and Faire, S. (2006) *Everyone Can Win: Responding to Conflict Constructively*, 2nd edn. Sydney: Simon and Schuster.

Cox, T. and Griffiths, A. (1996) *Work-Related Stress in Nursing: Controlling the Risk to Health*. Geneva: International Labour Office. Available at www.ilo.org/public//english/protection/condtrav/pdf/wc-cgc-96.pdf, accessed on 16 April 2010.

Davies, E. J., Tennant, A., Ferguson, E. and Jones, L. F. (2004) 'Developing models and a framework for multiprofessional clinical supervision.' *British Journal of Forensic Practice 6*, 3, 36–42.

Davis, B. (2002) 'Group supervision as a learning laboratory for the purposeful use of self in child protection work.' *Journal of Teaching in Social Work 22*, 1, 183–198.

Davys, A. (2001) 'A Reflective Learning Process for Supervision.' In L. Beddoe and J. Worrall (eds) *Supervision: From Rhetoric to Reality*. Auckland: Auckland College of Education.

Davys, A. (2002) 'Perceptions through a prism: Three accounts of good social work supervision.' Unpublished MSW thesis. Palmerston North: Massey University.

Davys, A. (2005a) 'At the heart of the matter: Culture as a function of supervision.' *Social Work Review 17*, 1, 3–12.

Davys, A. (2005b) 'Supervision: Is What We Want What We Need?' In L. Beddoe, J. Worrall and F. Howard. *Supervision Conference, 2004: Weaving Together the Strands of Supervision. Conference Proceedings*. Auckland: University of Auckland.

Davys, A. (2007) 'Active Participation in Supervision: A Supervisee's Guide.' In D. Wepa (ed.) *Clinical Supervision in Aotearoa/New Zealand: A Health Perspective*. Auckland: Pearson Education.

Davys, A. and Beddoe, L. (2000) 'Supervision of Students: A Map and a model for the decade to come.' *Social Work Education 19*, 5, 483–449.

Davys, A. and Beddoe, L. (2008) 'Interprofessional learning for supervision: Taking the blinkers off.' *Learning in Health and Social Care 8*, 1, 58–69.

Davys, A. M. and Beddoe, L. (2009) 'The Reflective Learning Model: Supervision of social work students.' *Social Work Education 28*, 8, 919–993.

Deal, K. H. (2004) 'The relationship between critical thinking and interpersonal skills.' *The Clinical Supervisor 22*, 2, 3–19.

Deal, K. H. and Pittman, J. (2009) 'Examining predictors of social work students' critical thinking skills.' *Advances in Social Work 10*, 1, 87–102.

Dekel, R. and Baum, N. (2009) 'Intervention in a shared traumatic reality: A new challenge for social workers.' *British Journal of Social Work.* Advance published 24 November 2009. DOI: 10.1093/bjsw/bcp137.

DePanfilis, D. and Zlotnik, J. L. (2008) 'Retention of front-line staff in child welfare: A systematic review of research.' *Children and Youth Services Review 30*, 9, 995–1008.

Department for Children, Schools and Families (2009a) *The Protection of Children in England: Action Plan. The Government's Response to Lord Laming.* London: HM Stationery Office.

Department for Children, Schools and Families (2009b) *Facing up to the Task – The Interim Report of the Social Work Task Force.* London: HM Stationery Office.

de Shazer, S. (1985) *Keys to Solution in Brief Therapy.* New York, NY: Norton.

Dewey, J. (1998) 'Analysis of reflective thinking.' *How We Think* (1933). In L. A. Hickman and T. M. Alexandra (eds) *The Essential Dewey, Ethics, Logic, Psychology* (vol. 2). Bloomington, IN: Indiana University Press.

Dirkx, J. M., Gilley, J. W. and Gilley, A. M. (2004) 'Change theory in CPE and HRD: Towards a holistic view of learning and change in work.' *Advances in Developing Human Resources 6*, 1, 35–51.

Dolgoff, R. (2005) *An Introduction to Supervisory Practice in Human Services.* Boston, MA: Pearson Education.

Down, G. (2000) 'Supervision in a Multicultural Context.' In G. Gorrell-Barnes (ed.) *Systemic Supervision: A Portable Model for Supervision Training.* London: Jessica Kingsley Publishers.

Driscoll, J. J. (2009) 'Prevalence, people and processes: A consideration of the implications of Lord Laming's progress report on the protection of children in England.' *Child Abuse Review 18*, 5, 333–345.

Duggleby W., Cooper D. and Penz K. (2009) 'Hope, self-efficacy, spiritual well-being and job satisfaction.' *Journal of Advanced Nursing 65*, 11, 2376–2385.

Dwyer, S. (2007) 'The emotional impact of social work practice.' *Journal of Social Work Practice 21*, 1, 49–60.

Edwards, J. K. and Chen, M. W. (1999) 'Strength-based supervision: Frameworks, current practice and future directions.' *Family Journal: Counselling and Therapy for Couples and Families 7*, 4, 349–357.

Ellett, A., Collins-Camargo, C. and Ellett, C. (2006) 'Personal and organizational correlates of outcomes in child welfare: Implications for supervision and continuing professional development.' *Professional Development 9*, 2/3, 44–53.

Elston, M. A., Gabe, J., Denney, D., Lee, R. and O'Beirne, M. (2002) 'Violence against doctors: A medical(ised) problem? The case of National Health Service general practitioners.' *Sociology of Health and Illness 24*, 5, 575–598.

Elston, M., Gabe, J. and O'Beirne, M. (2006) 'A "Risk of the Job"? Violence against Nurses from Patients and the Public as an Emerging Policy Issue.' In P. Godin (ed.) *Risk and Nursing Practice.* Basingstoke: Palgrave Macmillan.

Eraut, M. (1994) *Developing Professional Knowledge and Competence.* London: Falmer.

Eraut, M. (2004) 'Sharing practice: Problems and possibilities.' *Learning in Health and Social Care 3*, 4, 171–178.

Eraut, M. (2006) 'Editorial.' *Learning in Health and Social Care 5*, 3, 111–118.

Eruera, M. (2007) 'He Korero Korari.' In D. Wepa (ed.) *Clinical Supervision in Aotearoa/New Zealand: A Health Perspective.* Auckland: Pearson Education.

Facione, R. A. (1998) *Critical Thinking: What it is and Why it Counts.* Millbrae, CA: California Academic Press.

Farmer, S. S. (1988) 'Communication competence in clinical education/supervision – Critical notes.' *The Clinical Supervisor 6*, 2, 29–46.

Fawcett, B. (2009) 'Vulnerability: Questioning the certainties in social work and health.' *International Social Work 52*, 4, 473–484.

Ferguson, H. (2009) 'Performing child protection: Home visiting, movement and the struggle to reach the abused child.' *Child and Family Social Work 14*, 4, 471–480.

Ferguson, K. (2005) 'Professional Supervision.' In M. Rose and D. Best (eds) *Transforming Practice through Clinical Education, Professional Supervision and Mentoring.* Edinburgh: Elsevier Churchill Livingstone.

Feudtner, C., Santucci, G., Feinstein, J. A., Snyder, C. R., O'Rourke, M. T. and Kang, T. I. (2007) 'Hopeful thinking and level of comfort regarding providing pediatric palliative care: A survey of hospital nurses.' *Pediatrics 119*, 1, e186–e192.

Field, J. (2008) 'Rethinking supervision and shaping future practice.' *Social Work Now 40*, August, 11–18.

Fish, D. and Twinn, S. (1999) *Quality Clinical Supervision in the Health Care Professions.* Oxford: Butterworth Heinemann.

Fook, J. and Askeland, G. A. (2007) 'Challenges of critical reflection: Nothing ventured, nothing gained.' *Social Work Education 26*, 5, 520–533.

Fook, J. and Gardner, F. (2007) *Practising Critical Reflection: A Resource Handbook.* Maidenhead: Open University Press.

Ford, K. and Jones, A. (1987) *Student Supervision.* London: BASW Macmillan.

Fox, R. (1989) 'Relationship: The cornerstone of clinical supervision.' *Social Casework 70*, 3, 146–152.

Franks, V. (2004) 'Evidence-based uncertainty in mental health nursing.' *Journal of Psychiatric and Mental Health Nursing 11*, 1, 99–105.

Freeman, E. M. (1985) 'The importance of feedback in clinical supervision – Implications for direct practice.' *The Clinical Supervisor 3*, 1, 5–26.

Freeth, D., Hammick, M., Reeves, S., Koppel, I. and Barr, H. (2006) *Effective Interprofessional Education Development*. Oxford: CAIPE and Blackwell.

Freshwater, D. (2005) 'Exploring "field dynamics" in the supervisory relationship.' Inaugural Australian Counselling and Supervision Conference, Brisbane.

Froggett, L. (2000) 'Staff supervision and dependency culture: A case study.' *Journal of Social Work Practice 14*, 1, 27–35.

Furedi, F. (2008) 'Fear and security: A vulnerability-led policy response.' *Social Policy and Administration 42*, 6, 645–661.

Furedi, F. (2009) 'Fear and security: A vulnerability-led policy response.' In D. Denney (ed.) *Living in Dangerous Times: Fear, Insecurity, Risk and Social Policy*. Chichester: Wiley Blackwell.

Gabe, J. and Elston, M. (2008) '"We don't have to take this": Zero tolerance of violence against health care workers in a time of insecurity.' *Social Policy and Administration 42*, 6, 691–709.

Gardiner, D. (1989) *The Anatomy of Supervision: Developing Learning and Professional Competence for Social Work Students*. Milton Keynes: Society for Research on Higher Education and Open University Press.

Gardner, F. (2009) 'Affirming values: Using critical reflection to explore meaning and professional practice.' *Reflective Practice: International and Multidisciplinary Perspectives 10*, 2, 179–190.

Garratt, B. (1986) *The Learning Organisation: The Need for Directors Who Think*. London: Harper Collins.

Garrett, K. J. and Barretta-Herman, A. (1995) 'Moving from supervision to professional development.' *The Clinical Supervisor 13*, 2, 97–110.

Garrett, P. M. (2005) 'Social work's "electronic turn": Notes on the deployment of information and communication technologies in social work with children and families.' *Critical Social Policy 25*, 4, 529–553.

Gazzola, N. and Theriault, A. (2007) 'Super- (and-not-so-super) vision of counsellors-in-training: Supervisee perspectives on broadening and narrowing processes.' *British Journal of Guidance and Counselling 35*, 2, 189–204.

Gelman, C. R. and Baum, N. (2009) 'Social work students' pre-placement anxiety: An international comparison.' *Social Work Education: The International Journal*. Advance published 1 July 2009. DOI: 10.1080/02615470903009007.

Gibbs, J. (2009) 'Changing the cultural story in child protection: Learning from the insider's experience.' *Child and Family Social Work 14*, 3, 289–299.

Gibbs, J. A. (2001) 'Maintaining front-line workers in child protection: A case for refocusing supervision.' *Child Abuse Review 10*, 5, 323–335.

Giddens, A. (1999) *Risk: Runaway World Series*. Lecture 2 Reith Lectures. London: BBC. Available at www.bbc.co.uk/radio4/reith1999, accessed 16 April 2010.

Gilbert, M. and Evans, K. (2000) *Psychotherapy Supervision in Context: An Integrative Approach*. Buckingham: Open University Press.

Gilbert, T. (2001) 'Reflective practice and clinical supervision: Meticulous rituals of the confessional.' *Journal of Advanced Nursing 36*, 2, 199–205.

Gillingham, P. (2006) 'Risk assessment in child protection: Problem rather than solution.' *Australian Social Work 59*, 1, 86–98.

Gillingham, P. and Bromfield, L. (2008) 'Child protection, risk assessment and blame ideology.' *Children Australia 33*, 1, 18–24.

Goddard, C. and Tucci, J. (1991) 'Child protection and the need for the appraisal of the social worker-client relationship.' *Australian Social Work 44*, 2, 3–10.

Goleman, D. (1995) *Emotional Intelligence: Why it can Matter More than IQ.* New York, NY: Bantam Books.

Goleman, D. (1996) *Emotional Intelligence: Why It Can Matter More than IQ.* London: Bloomsbury.

Goleman, D. (2005) *Emotional Intelligence*, 10th Anniversary edn. New York, NY: Bantam Books.

Gould, N. and Baldwin, M. (eds) (2004) *Social Work, Critical Reflection and the Learning Organization*. Aldershot: Ashgate.

Gould, N. and Harris, N. (1996) 'Student imagery of practice in social work and teacher education: A comparative research approach.' *British Journal of Social Work 26*, 2, 223–237.

Gould, N. and Taylor, I. (1996) (eds) *Reflective Learning for Social Work: Research, Theory and Practice*. Aldershot: Arena Ashgate.

Grauel, T. (2002) 'Professional Oversight: The Neglected Histories of Supervision.' In M. McMahon and W. Patton (eds) *Supervision in the Helping Professions A Practical Approach*. Frenchs Forest, NSW: Prentice Hall.

Green, D. (2007) 'Risk and social work practice.' *Australian Social Work 60*, 4, 395–409.

Green Lister, P. and Crisp, B.R. (2005) 'Clinical Supervision in Child Protection for Community Nurses.' *Child Abuse Review 14*, 1, 57–72.

Hair, H. J. and O'Donoghue, K. (2009) 'Culturally relevant, socially just social work supervision: Becoming visible through a social constructionist lens.' *Journal of Ethnic and Cultural Diversity in Social Work 18*, 1, 70–88.

Hall, P. (2005) 'Interprofessional teamwork: Professional cultures as barriers.' *Journal of Interprofessional Care 19*, 2, Suppl. 1, 188–196.

Hawkins, P. and Shohet, R. (1989) *Supervision in the Helping Professions*. Maidenhead: Open University Press.

Hawkins, P. and Shohet, R. (2000) *Supervision in the Helping Professions*, 2nd edn. Buckingham: Open University Press.

Hawkins, P. and Shohet, R. (2006) *Supervision in the Helping Professions*, 3rd edn. Maidenhead: Open University Press.

Healy, K. and Meagher, G. (2004) 'The reprofessionalization of social work: Collaborative approaches for achieving professional recognition.' *British Journal of Social Work 34*, 2, 243–260.

Healy, K., Meagher, G. and Cullin, J. (2009) 'Retaining novices to become expert child protection practitioners: Creating career pathways in direct practice.' *British Journal of Social Work 39*, 2, 299–317.

Heath, H. and Freshwater, D. (2000) 'Clinical supervision as an emancipatory process: Avoiding inappropriate intent.' *Journal of Advanced Nursing 32*, 5, 1298–1306.

Heid, L. (1997) 'Supervisor development across the professional lifespan.' *The Clinical Supervisor 16*, 2, 139–152.

Heron, J. (2001) *Helping the Client: A Creative Practical Guide*. London: Sage.

Hess, A. K. (1986) 'Growth in Supervision: Stages of Supervisee and Supervisor Development.' In F. W. Kaslow (ed.) *Supervision and Training: Models, Dilemmas and Challenges*. New York, NY: Haworth.

Holland, S., and Scourfield, J. (2004) 'Liberty and respect in child protection.' *British Journal of Social Work 34*, 1, 21–36.

Horney, K. (1970) *Neurosis and Human Growth: The Struggle towards Self-realization*. New York, NY: W. W. Norton and Company, Norton Library.

Howard, F. (1997) 'Supervision.' In H. Love and W. Whittaker (eds) *Practice Issues for Clinical and Applied Psychologists in New Zealand*. Wellington: New Zealand Psychological Society.

Howard, F. (2008) 'Managing stress or enhancing wellbeing? Positive psychology's contributions to clinical supervision.' *Australian Psychologist 43*, 2, 105–113.

Howe, D. (1996) 'Surface and depth in social work practice.' In N. Parton (ed.) *Social Work Theory, Social Change and Social Work*. London: Routledge.

Howe, D. (2008) *The Emotionally Intelligent Social Worker*. New York, NY: Palgrave Macmillan.

Hughes, L. and Pengelly, P. (1997) *Staff Supervision in a Turbulent Environment: Managing Process and Task in Front-Line Services*. London: Jessica Kingsley Publishers.

Hunter, M. (2009) 'Whatever happened to supervision?' *Community Care* (April). Available as 'Poor supervision continues to hinder child protection practice' at www.communitycare.co.uk/Articles/2009/04/22/111327/poor–supervision–continues–to–hinder–child–protection.html, accessed on 16 April 2010.

Inskipp, F. and Proctor, B. (1993) *Making the Most of Supervision: A Professional Development Resource for Counsellors, Supervisors and Trainees*. Twickenham: Cascade.

Ivey, A. E. (1988) *Intentional Interviewing and Counselling: Facilitating Client Development*, 2nd edn. Pacific Grove, CA: Brooks/Cole.

Johns, C. (2001) 'Depending on the intent and emphasis of the supervisor, clinical supervision can be a different experience.' *Journal of Nursing Management 9*, 3, 139–145.

Johns, C. (2005) 'Expanding the Gates of Perception.' In C. Johns and D. Freshwater (eds) *Transforming Nursing Through Reflective Practice*, 2nd edn. Oxford: Blackwell.

Johns, C. and Freshwater, D. (eds) (2005) *Transforming Nursing through Reflective Practice*. Oxford: Blackwell.

Jones, A. (1997) 'Clinical supervision in moderating organisational conflict and preserving effective working relationships.' *International Journal of Palliative Nursing 3*, 5, 293–295.

Jones, A. (2006) 'Clinical supervision: What do we know and what do we need to know? A review and commentary.' *Journal of Nursing Management 14*, 8, 577–585.

Jones, A. (2008) 'Clinical supervision is important to the quality of health-care provision.' *International Journal of Mental Health Nursing 17*, 5, 379–380.

Jones, J. and Gallop, L. (2003) 'No time to think: Protecting the reflective space in children's services.' *Child Abuse Review 12*, 2, 101–106.

Jones, J. L., Washington, G. and Steppe, S. (2007) 'The role of supervisors in developing clinical decision-making skills in child protective service (CPS).' *Journal of Evidence-Based Social Work 4*, 3/4, 103–116.

Jones, M. (2004) 'Supervision, Learning and Transformative Practices.' In N. Gould and M. Baldwin (eds) *Social Work, Critical Reflection and the Learning Organisation*. Aldershot: Ashgate.

Jones, S. and Joss, R. (1995) 'Models of Professionalism.' In M. Yelloly and M. Henkel (eds) *Learning and Teaching in Social Work: Towards Reflective Practice*. London: Jessica Kingsley Publishers.

Juhnke, G. A. (1996) 'Solution focused supervision: Promoting supervisee skills and confidence through successful solutions.' *Counsellor Education and Supervision 36*, Sept, 48–57.

Kadushin, A. (1976) *Supervision in Social Work*. New York, NY: Columbia University Press.

Kadushin, A. and Harkness, D. (2002) *Supervision in Social Work*, 4th edn. New York, NY: Columbia University Press.

Kaiser, T. L. and Kuechler, C. F. (2008) 'Training supervisors of practitioners: Analysis of efficacy.' *The Clinical Supervisor 27*, 1, 76–96.

Kalliath, T. and Beck, A. (2001) 'Is the path to burnout and turnover paved by a lack of supervisory support? A structural equations test.' *New Zealand Journal of Psychology 30*, 2, 72–78.

Kane, R. (2001) 'Supervision in New Zealand Social Work.' In M. Connolly (ed.) *New Zealand Social Work: Contexts and Practice.* Auckland: Oxford University Press.

Karpman, S. (1968) 'Fairy tales and script drama analysis.' *Transactional Analysis Bulletin 7,* 26, 39–44.

Karpman, S. (2007) 'The New Drama Triangles.' USATAA/ITAA Conference lecture. Available at Karpman Drama Triangle on 25 February 2010 at www.karpmandramatriangle.com/pdf/thenewdramatriangles.pdf, accessed on 16 April 2010.

Kerlinger, F. N. (1986) *Foundations of Behavioural Research* (3rd edn). New York, NY: Holt, Rinehart and Winston.

Kilminster, S. M. and Jolly, B. C. (2000) 'Effective supervision in clinical practice settings: A literature review.' *Medical Education 34,* 10, 827–840.

King, L. A., Jackson, M. T., Gallagher, A., Wainwright, P. and Lindsay, J. (2009) 'Towards a model of the expert practice educator – interpreting multi-professional perspectives in the literature.' *Learning in Health and Social Care 8,* 2, 135–144.

Koenig, T. and Spano, R. (2007) 'The cultivation of social workers' hope in personal life and professional practice.' *Journal of Religion and Spirituality in Social Work: Social Thought 26,* 3, 45–61.

Kofman, F. and Senge, P. (1993) 'Communities of commitment: The heart of learning organizations.' *Organizational Dynamics 22,* 2, 5–23.

Kolb, D. (1984) *Experiential Learning as the Source of Learning and Development.* Englewood Cliffs, NJ: Prentice Hall.

Kondrat, M. E. (1992) 'Reclaiming the practical: Formal and substantive rationality in social work practice.' *Social Service Review* (June 1992), 237–255.

Kondrat, M. E. (1999) 'Who is the "self" in self-aware: Professional self-awareness from a critical theory perspective.' *Social Service Review 73,* 4, 451–477.

Koppes, L. L. (2008) 'Facilitating an organization to embrace a work–life effectiveness culture: A practical approach.' *Psychologist-Manager Journal 11,* 1, 163–184.

Krause, A. and Allen, G. J. (1988) ‚Perceptions of counsellor supervision: An examination of Stoltenberg's model from the perspective of supervisor and supervisee.' *Journal of Counseling Psychology 35,* 1, 77–80.

Ladany, N., Ellis, M. V. and Friedlander, M. L. (1999) 'The supervisory working alliance, trainee self-efficacy, and satisfaction.' *Journal of Counseling and Development 77,* 4, 447–455.

Laming, Lord (2003) *The Victoria Climbié Inquiry: Report of an Inquiry by Lord Laming.* London: Stationery Office.

Laming, Lord (2009) *The Protection of Children in England: A Progress Report.* London: Stationery Office.

Lau, M., Bishop, S., Segal, Z., Buis, T. *et al.* (2006) 'The Toronto mindfulness scale: Development and validation.' *Journal of Clinical Psychology 62,* 12, 1445–1467.

Lave, J. and Wenger, E. (1991) *Situated Learning: Legitimate Peripheral Participation.* Cambridge: Cambridge University Press.

Le Maistre, C., Boudreau, S. and Pare, A. (2006) 'Mentor or evaluator? Assisting and assessing newcomers to the professions.' *The Journal of Workplace Learning 18,* 6, 344–354.

Leonard, K. and Weinstein, J. (2009) 'Interprofessional Practice Education and Learning.' In M. Doel and S. Shardlow (eds) *Educating Professionals: Practice Learning in Health and Social Care.* Farnham: Ashgate.

Lietz, C. A. (2008) 'Implementation of group supervision in child welfare: Findings from Arizona's supervision circle project.' *Child Welfare 87,* 6, 31–48.

Lietz, C. A. (2009) 'Critical theory as a framework for child welfare decision-making: Some possibilities.' *Journal of Public Child Welfare 3,* 2, 190–206.

Lindahl, B. and Norberg, A. (2002) 'Clinical group supervision in an intensive care unit: A space for relief, and for sharing emotions and experiences of care.' *Journal of Clinical Nursing 11,* 6, 809–818.

Littlechild, B. (2008) 'Child protection social work: Risks of fears and fears of risks – Impossible tasks from impossible goals?' *Social Policy and Administration 42,* 6, 662–675.

Lizzio, A. and Wilson, K. (2002) 'The Domain of Learning Goals in Professional Supervision.' In M. McMahon and W. Patton (eds) *Supervision in the Helping Professions: A Practical Approach.* Frenchs Forest, NSW: Pearson Education.

Lizzio, A., Stokes, L. and Wilson, K. (2005) 'Approaches to learning in professional supervision: Supervisee perceptions of processes and outcome.' *Studies in Continuing Education 27,* 3, 239–256.

Lizzio, A., Wilson, K. and Que, J. (2009) 'Relationship dimensions in the professional supervision of psychology graduates: Supervisee perceptions of processes and outcome.' *Studies in Continuing Education 31,* 2, 127–140.

Loganbill, C., Hardy, E. and Delworth, U. (1982) 'Supervision: A conceptual model.' *The Counseling Psychologist 10,* 1, 3–42.

Lohrbach, S. (2008) 'Group supervision in child protection practice.' *Social Work Now 40,* August, 19–24.

Lohrbach, S. and Sawyer, R. (2004) 'Creating a constructive practice: Family and professional partnership in high-risk child protection case conferences.' *Protecting Children 20,* 2 and 3, 78–92.

Lombardo, C., Milne, D., and Proctor, R. (2009) 'Getting to the heart of clinical supervision: A theoretical review of the role of emotions in professional development.' *Behavioural and Cognitive Psychotherapy 37,* 02, 207–219.

Lonne, B., Parton, N., Thomson, J. and Harries, M. (2008) *Reforming Child Protection.* London: Routledge.

Low, H. and Weinstein, J. (2000) 'Interprofessional Education.' In R. Pierce and J. Weinstein (eds) *Innovative Education and Training for Care Professionals.* London: Jessica Kingsley Publishers.

Luthans, F. (2002) 'The need for and meaning of positive organizational behavior.' *Journal of Organizational Behavior* 23, 6, 695–706.

Luthans, F., Youssef, C. M. and Avolio, B.J. (2007a) *Psychological Capital.* New York, NY: Oxford University Press.

Luthans, F., Avolio, B.J., Avey, J. B. and Norman, S. M. (2007b) 'Positive psychological capital: Measurement and relationship with performance and satisfaction.' *Personnel Psychology* 60, 3, 541–572.

Lynch, L., Hancox, K., Happell, B. and Parker, J. (2008) *Clinical Supervision For Nurses.* Chichester: Wiley Blackwell.

Mafile'o, T. and Su'a-Hawkins, A. (2005) 'A case for cultural supervision: Reflections on experiences of Pasifika cultural supervision.' In L. Beddoe, J. Worrall and F. Howard (eds) *Weaving Together the Strands of Supervision: Proceedings of the 2004 Conference,* Auckland, New Zealand. Auckland: Faculty of Education, University of Auckland.

Mandell, D. (2008) 'Power, care and vulnerability: Considering use of self in child welfare work.' *Journal of Social Work Practice* 22, 2, 235–248.

Marris, P. (1974) *Loss and Change.* London: Routledge and Kegan Paul.

Marsh, P. (2006) 'Promoting children's welfare by inter-professional practice and learning in social work and primary care.' *Social Work Education* 25, 2, 148–160.

Marsick, V. J. and Watkins, K. E. (2002) 'Envisioning New Organisations for Learning.' In F. Reeve, M. Cartwright and R. Edwards (eds) *Supporting Lifelong Learning Vol. 2. Organizing Learning.* London: Routledge Falmer.

Marton, F. and Saljo, R. (1976) 'On qualitative difference in learning: Outcome and process.' *British Journal of Educational Psychology* 46, 2, 4–11.

Maslach, C. (1978) 'Job burnout: How people cope.' *Public Welfare* 36, 1, 56–58.

McCann, D. (2000) 'From Here to Eternity and Back Again: Developing a Supervisory Relationship with Training Family Therapists.' In G. G. Barnes, G. Down and D. McCann (eds) *Systemic Supervision: A Portable Guide for Supervision Training.* London: Jessica Kingsley Publishers.

McLaughlin, K. (2007) 'Regulation and risk in social work: The General Social Care Council and the Social Care Register in context. *British Journal of Social Work* 37, 7, 1263–1277.

McNamara, Y., Lawley, M. and Towler, J. (2007) 'Supervision in the context of youth and community work training.' *Youth and Policy* 97/98, 73–90.

Mezirow, J. (1991) *Transformative Dimensions of Adult Learning.* San Fransisco, CA: Jossey-Bass.

Middleman, R. and Rhodes, G. (1980) 'Teaching the practice of supervision.' *Journal of Education for Social Work* 16, 3, 51–59.

Milne, D., Aylott, H., Fitzpatrick, H. and Ellis, M. V. (2008) 'How does clinical supervision work? Using a "best evidence synthesis" approach to construct a basic model of supervision.' *The Clinical Supervisor* 27, 2, 170–190.

Moffatt, K. (1996) 'Teaching Social Work as a Reflective Process.' In N. Gould and I. Taylor (eds) *Reflective Learning for Social Work.* Aldershot: Arena.

Mor Barak, M. E., Levin, A., Nissly, J. A. and Lane, C. J. (2006) 'Why do they leave? Modeling child welfare workers' turnover intentions.' *Children and Youth Services Review* 28, 5, 548–577.

Mor Barak, M. E., Travis, D. J., Pyun, H. and Xie, B. (2009) 'The impact of supervision on worker outcomes: A meta-analysis.' *Social Service Review* 83, 1, 3–32.

Morrison, T. (1996) *Staff supervision in Social Care.* Brighton: Pavilion.

Morrison, T. (1997) 'Emotionally Competent Child Protection Organisations: Fallacy, Fiction or Necessity.' In J. Bates, R. Pugh and N. Thompson (eds) *Protecting Children: Challenges and Changes.* Aldershot: Arena.

Morrison, T. (2001) *Staff supervision in social care: Making a real difference for staff and service users.* Brighton: Pavilion.

Morrison, T. (2007) 'Emotional intelligence, emotion and social work: Context, characteristics, complications and contribution.' *British Journal of Social Work* 37, 2, 245–263.

Munro, E. (2004a) 'A simpler way to understand the results of risk assessment instruments.' *Children and Youth Services Review* 26, 9, 873–883.

Munro, E. (2004b) 'The Impact of Child Abuse Inquiries since 1990.' In N. Stanley and J. Manthorpe (eds) (2004) *The Age of the Inquiry: Learning and Blaming in Health and Social Care.* London: Routledge.

Munro, E. (2008) 'Improving reasoning in supervision.' *Social Work Now 40,* August, 3–10.

Munson, C. E. (1993) *Clinical Social Work Supervision,* 2nd edn. New York, NY: Haworth Press.

Neukrug, E. (2008) *Theory Practice and Trends in the Human Services: An Introduction,* 4th edn. Melbourne: Thomson/ Brooks/Cole.

Nissly, A., Mor Barak, M. and A. Levin. (2005) 'Stress, social support, and workers' intentions to leave their jobs in public child welfare.' *Administration in Social Work* 29, 1, 79–100.

Noble, C. and Irwin, J. (2009) 'Social work supervision: An exploration of the current challenges in a rapidly changing social, economic and political environment.' *Journal of Social Work 9,* 3, 345–358.

Nordentoft, H. M. (2008) 'Changes in emotion work at interdisciplinary conferences following clinical supervision in a palliative outpatient ward.' *Qualitative Health Research* 18, 7, 913–927.

Northcott, N. (2000) 'Clinical Supervision: Professional Development or Management Control.' In J. Spouse and L. Redfern (eds) *Successful Supervision in Health Care Practice.* London: Blackwell Science.

Nye, C. (2007) 'Dependence and independence in clinical supervision: An application of Vygotsky's developmental learning theory.' *The Clinical Supervisor* 26, 1, 81–98.

Nzira, V. and Williams, P. (2009) *Anti–Oppressive Practice in Health and Social Care.* London: Sage.

O'Donoghue, K. (2003) *Re-storying Social Work Supervision.* Palmerston North: Dunmore Press.

O'Donoghue, K. (2004) 'Uniprofessional, multiprofessional, field of practice, discipline: Social workers and cross-disciplinary supervision.' *Social Work Review 16,* 3, 2–7.

O'Neill, O. (2002) 'A question of trust: Lecture One "Spreading Suspicion".' Paper presented at the 2002 Reith Lecture Series, BBC. Available at www.bbc.co.uk/radio4/reith2002/lecture1.shtml, accessed 16 April 2010.

Owen, D. (2008) 'The Ah-Ha Moment: Passionate Supervision as a Tool for Transformation and Metamorphosis.' In R. Shohet (ed.) *Passionate Supervision.* London: Jessica Kingsley Publishers.

Pack, M. (2009a) 'Clinical supervision: An interdisciplinary review of literature with implications for reflective practice in social work.' *Reflective Practice: International and Multidisciplinary Perspectives 10,* 5, 657–668.

Pack, M. (2009b) 'Supervision as a liminal space: Towards a dialogic relationship.' *Gestalt Journal of Australia and New Zealand 5,* 2, 60–78.

Page, S. and Wosket, V. (1994) *Supervising the Counsellor: A Cyclical Model.* London: Routledge.

Papell, C. P. (1996) 'Reflections on Issues in Social Work Education.' In N. Gould and I. Taylor (eds) *Reflective Learning for Social Work: Research, Theory and Practice.* Aldershot: Arena.

Parton, N. (ed.) (1996) *Social Theory, Social Change and Social Work.* London: Routledge.

Parton, N. (1998) 'Risk, advanced liberalism and child welfare: The need to rediscover uncertainty and ambiguity.' *British Journal of Social Work 28,* 1, 5–27.

Parton, N. (2009) 'Challenges to practice and knowledge in child welfare social work: From the "social" to the "informational"?' *Children and Youth Services Review 31,* 7, 715–721.

Parton, N., Thorpe, D. and Wattam, C. (1997) *Child Protection: Risk and the Moral Order.* Basingstoke: Macmillan.

Patton, M. J. and Kivlighan, D. M. (1997) 'Relevance of the supervisory alliance to the counseling alliance and to treatment adherence in counselor training.' *Journal of Counseling Psychology 44,* 1, 108–115.

Payne, M. (1994) 'Personal Supervision in Social Work.' In A. Connor and S. E. Black (eds) *Performance Review and Quality in Social Care.* London: Jessica Kingsley Publishers.

Peach, J. and Horner, N. (2007) 'Using Supervision: Support or Surveillance.' In M. Lymbery and K. Postle (eds) *Social Work: A Companion to Learning.* London: Sage.

Pettes, D. (1967) *Supervision in Social Work.* London: George Allen and Unwin.

Pollack, S. (2008) 'Labelling clients "risky": Social work and the neo-liberal welfare state.' *British Journal of Social Work,* BJSW Advance published 30 May 2008. DOI:10.1093/bjsw/bcn079.

Presbury, J., Echterling, L. G. and McKee, J. E. (1999) 'Supervision for inner vision: Solution-focused strategies.' *Counsellor Education and Supervision 39,* 2, 146–156.

Proctor, B. (2001) 'Training for the supervision alliance attitude, skills and intention.' In J. R. Cutcliffe, T. Butterworth and B. Proctor (eds) *Fundamental Themes in Clinical Supervision.* New York, NY: Routledge.

Profitt, N. J. (2008) 'Who cares about us? Opening paths to a critical, collective notion of self-care.' *Canadian Social Work Review 25,* 2, 146–167.

Rains, E. (2007) 'Interdisciplinary supervisor development in a community health service.' *Social Work Review 19,* 3, 58–65.

Redmond, B. (2004) *Reflection in Action: Developing Reflective Practice in Health and Social Services.* Aldershot: Ashgate.

Reich, A. (2002) 'Learning organisations and child protection agencies: Post-Fordist techniques?' *Studies in Continuing Education 24,* 2, 219–232.

Research Works (2001) *Perceptions of Social Work and Social Care: Report of Findings.* Study carried out for Department of Health, UK. London: COI Communications, Department of Health.

Rich, P. (1993) 'The form, function and content of clinical supervision: An integrated model.' *The Clinical Supervisor 11,* 1, 137–178.

Richards, M. and Payne, C. (1991) *Staff Supervision in Child Protection Work.* London: National Institute for Social Work.

Richmond, D. (2009) 'Using multi-layered supervision methods to develop creative practice.' *Reflective Practice: International and Multidisciplinary Perspectives 10,* 4, 543–557.

Roche, A. M., Todd, C. L. and O'Connor, J. (2007) 'Clinical supervision in the alcohol and other drugs field: An imperative or an option?' *Drug and Alcohol Review 26,* 3, 241–249.

Ruch, G. (2002) 'From triangle to spiral: Reflective practice in social work education, practice and research.' *Social Work Education 21,* 2, 199–216.

Ruch, G. (2007a) 'Reflective practice in contemporary child-care social work: The role of containment.' *British Journal of Social Work 37,* 4, 659–680.

Ruch, G. (2007b) '"Thoughtful" practice: Child care social work and the role of case discussion.' *Child and Family Social Work 12,* 4, 370–379.

Ryan, M., Merighi, J., Healy, B. and Renouf, N. (2004) 'Belief, optimism and caring: Findings from a cross national study of expertise in mental health social work.' *Qualitative Social Work 3,* 4, 411–429.

Ryan, S. (2004) *Vital Practice: Stories from the Healing Arts: The Homeopathic and Supervisory Way.* Portland, Dorset: Sea Change.

Santa Rita, E. (1998) 'Solution–focused supervision.' *The Clinical Supervisor 17,* 2, 127–139.

Santoro, N. and Allard, A. (2008) 'Scenarios as springboards for reflection on practice: Stimulating discussion.' *Reflective Practice 9*, 2, 167–176.

Satymurti, C. (1981) *Occupational Survival.* Oxford: Pergamon.

Scaife, J. (2001) *Supervision in Mental Health Professions.* Philadelphia, PA: Brunner Routledge.

Scaife, J. (2009) *Supervision in Clinical Practice: A Practitioner's Guide,* 2nd edn. London: Routledge.

Scannapieco, M. and Connell-Carrick, K. (2007) 'Child welfare workplace: The state of the workforce and strategies to improve retention.' *Child Welfare 86*, 6, 31–52.

Schein, E. H. (1996) 'Three cultures of management: The key to organizational learning.' *Sloan Management Review 38*, 1, 9–20.

Schindler, N. J. and Talen, M. R. (1996) 'Supervision 101: The basic elements for teaching beginning supervisors.' *The Clinical Supervisor 14*, 2, 109–120.

Schön, D. (1983) *The Reflective Practitioner.* London: Temple Smith.

Schön, D. (1987) *Educating the Reflective Practitioner.* San Francisco, CA: Jossey-Bass.

Schön, D. (1991) *The Reflective Practitioner: How Professionals Think in Action.* Aldershot: Ashgate.

Shulman, L. (1999) *The Skills of Helping: Individuals and Groups.* Itasca, Il: Peacock.

Schutte, N. S., Malouff, J. M., Bobik, C., Coston, T. D. *et al.* (2001) 'Emotional intelligence and interpersonal relations.' *Journal of Social Psychology 141*, 4, 523–536.

Scourfield, J. and Welsh, I. (2003) 'Risk, reflexivity and social control in child protection: New times or same old story?' *Critical Social Policy 23*, 3, 398–420.

Senge, P. (1990) *The Fifth Discipline: The Art and Practice of the Learning Organisation.* New York, NY: Doubleday.

Skills for Care and Children's Workforce Development Council (2007) *Providing Effective Supervision.* London: Skills for Care.

Sloan, G. (1999) 'Good characteristics of a clinical supervisor: A community mental health nurse perspective.' *Journal of Advanced Nursing 30*, 3, 713–722.

Sloan, G. (2006) *Clinical Supervision in Mental Health Nursing.* Chichester: Wiley.

Smith, M. (2000) 'Supervision of fear in social work: A re-evaluation of reassurance.' *Journal of Social Work Practice 14*, 1, 17–26.

Smith, M. (2006) 'Too little fear can kill you: Staying alive as a social worker.' *Journal of Social Work Practice 20*, 1, 69–81.

Smith, R. and Anderson, L. (2008) 'Interprofessional learning: Aspiration or achievement? *Social Work Education: The International Journal 27*, 7, 759–776.

Smythe, E. A., MacCulloch, T. and Charmley, R. (2009) 'Professional supervision: Trusting the wisdom that "comes".' *British Journal of Guidance and Counselling 37*, 1, 17–25.

Snyder, C. R. (2000) *Handbook of Hope: Theory, Measures and Applications.* San Diego, CA: Academic Press.

Sprengel, A. and Job, L. (2004) 'Reducing student anxiety by using clinical peer mentoring with beginning nursing students.' *Nurse Educator 29*, 6, 246–250.

Stalker, C. A., Mandell, D., Frensch, K. M., Harvey, C. and Wright, M. (2007) 'Child welfare workers who are exhausted yet satisfied with their jobs: How do they do it?' *Child and Family Social Work 12*, 2, 182–191.

Stalker, K. (2003) 'Managing Risk and Uncertainty in Social Work: A Literature Review.' *Journal of Social Work 3*, 2, 211–233.

Stanford, S. (2007) 'The operations of risk: The meaning, emotion and morality of risk identities in social work practice.' Unpublished PhD thesis, University of Tasmania, Launceston.

Stanley, J. and Goddard, C. (2002) *In the Firing Line: Violence and Power in Child Protection Work.* Chichester: John Wiley and Sons.

Stanley, N. and Manthorpe, J. (eds) (2004) *The Age of the Inquiry: Learning and Blaming in Health and Social Care.* London: Routledge.

Stanley, T. (2005) 'Making decisions: Social work processes and the construction of risk(s) in child protection work.' PhD thesis. Canterbury, New Zealand: University of Canterbury.

Stanley, T. (2007) 'Risky work: Child protection practice.' *Social Policy Journal of New Zealand 30*, March, 163–177.

Stevenson, J. (2005) 'Professional supervision in social work.' Unison, City of Edinburgh Branch. Available at: www.unison-edinburgh.org.uk/socialwork/supervision.html, accessed on 16 April 2010.

Stoltenberg, C. D. and Delworth, U. (1987) *Supervising Counselors and Therapists: A Developmental Approach.* San Francisco, CA: Jossey-Bass.

Strand, V. and Badger, L. (2007) 'A clinical consultation model for child welfare supervisors.' *Child Welfare 86*, 1, 79–96.

Swain, G. (1995) *Clinical Supervision: the Principles and Process.* London: Health Visitors Association.

Taylor, H., Beckett, C. and Mc Keigue, B. (2008) 'Judgements of Solomon: Anxieties and defences of social workers involved in care proceedings.' *Child and Family Social Work 13*, 1, 23–31.

Thomas, C. and Davis, S. (2005) 'Bicultural Strengths Based Supervision.' In M. Nash, R. Munford and K. O'Donoghue (eds) *Social Work Theories in Action.* London: Jessica Kingsley Publishers.

Thomas, T., Dickson, D., Broadbridge, J., Hopper, L. *et al.* (2007) 'Benefits and challenges of supervising occupational therapy fieldwork students: Supervisors' perspectives.' *Australian Occupational Therapy Journal 54*, S1, S2–S12.

Thompson, N. (2009) 'Stress.' In N. Thompson and J. Bates (eds) *Promoting Workplace Well-being.* London: Palgrave Macmillan.

Toasland, J. (2007) 'Containing the container: An exploration of the containing role of management in a social work context.' *Journal of Social Work Practice 21,* 2, 197–202.

Townend, M. (2005) 'Interprofessional supervision from the perspectives of both mental health nurses and other professionals in the field of cognitive behavioural psychotherapy.' *Journal of Psychiatric and Mental Health Nursing 12,* 5, 582–588.

Trotter, C. (1999) *Working with involuntary clients: A guide to practice.* Sage: Sydney.

Tsui, M. S. and Ho, W. S. (1997) 'In search of a comprehensive model of social work supervision.' *Clinical Supervisor 16,* 2, 181–205.

Tugade, M. and Frederickson, B. (2004) 'Resilient individuals use positive emotions to bounce back from negative emotional experiences.' *Journal of Personality and Social Psychology 86,* 2, 320–333.

Turnell, A. and Edwards, S. (1999) 'Signs of safety: A solution and safety oriented approach.' New York, NY: Norton.

Ungar, M. (2006) 'Practicing as a postmodern supervisor.' *Journal of Marital and Family Therapy 32,* 1, 59–71.

Urdang, E. (1999) 'Becoming a field instructor: A key experience in professional development.' *The Clinical Supervisor 18,* 1, 85–103.

Valkeavaara, T. (1999) 'Sailing in calm waters doesn't teach: Constructing expertise through problems in work.' *Studies in Continuing Education 21,* 2, 177–196.

van Heugten, K. (2009) 'Bullying of social workers: Outcomes of a grounded study into impacts and interventions.' *British Journal of Social Work.* Advance published. DOI: 10.1093/bjsw/bcp003.

van Kessel, K. and Haan, D. (1993) 'The Dutch concept of supervision: Its essential characteristics as a conceptual framework.' *The Clinical Supervisor 11,* 1, 5–27.

van Ooijen, E. (2003*) Clinical Supervision Made Easy: The 3-Step Method.* London: Churchill Livingstone.

Warner, J. (2008) 'Community Care, Risk and the Shifting Locus of Danger and Vulnerability.' In A. Petersen and I. Wilkinson (eds) *Risk Health and Vulnerability.* London: Routledge.

Watkins, C.E. (1997) 'The ineffective psychotherapy supervisor: some reflections about bad behaviour, poor process and offensive outcomes.' *The Clinical Supervisor 16,* 1, 163–180.

Webb, S. A. (2006) *Social Work in a Risk Society: Social and Political Perspectives.* New York, NY: Palgrave Macmillan.

Webber–Dreadon, E. (1999) 'He Taonga Mo o Matou Tipuna (A gift handed down by our ancestors): An indigenous approach to social work supervision.' *Te Komako III Social Work Review 11,* 4, 7–11.

Wenger, E. (1998) *Communities of Practice: Learning, Meaning and Identity.* Cambridge: Cambridge University Press.

Westheimer, I. (1977) *The Practice of Supervision in Social Work – A Guide for Staff Supervisors.* London: Ward Lock Educational.

White, E., Butterworth, T., Bishop, V., Carson, J., Jeacock, J. and Clements, A. (1998) 'Clinical supervision: Insider reports of a private world.' *Journal of Advanced Nursing 28,* 1, 185–192.

Williams, L. and Irvine, F. (2009) 'How can the clinical supervisor role be facilitated in nursing: A phenomenological exploration.' *Journal of Nursing Management 17,* 4, 474–483.

Worthington, E. L. (1987) 'Changes in supervision as counselors and supervisors gain experience: A review.' *Professional Psychology: Research and Practice 18,* 3, 189–208.

Wright, T. A. and Quick, J. C. (2009) 'The emerging positive agenda in organizations: Greater than a trickle, but not yet a deluge.' *Journal of Organizational Behavior 30,* 2, 147–159.

Yankeelov, P. A., Barbee, A. P., Sullivan, D. and Antle, B. F. (2009) 'Individual and organizational factors in job retention in Kentucky's child welfare agency.' *Children and Youth Services Review 31,* 5, 547–554.

Yegdich, T. (1999a) 'Clinical supervision and managerial supervision: Some historical and conceptual considerations.' *Journal of Advanced Nursing 30,* 5, 1195–1204.

Yegdich, T. (1999b) 'Lost in the crucible of supportive clinical supervision: Supervision is not therapy.' *Journal of Advanced Nursing 29,* 5, 1265–1275.

Yegdich, T. and Cushing, A. (1998) 'An historical perspective on clinical supervision in nursing.' *Australian and New Zealand Journal of Mental Health Nursing 7,* 1, 3, 3–24.

Yip, K. (2006) 'Self reflection in reflective practice: A note of caution.' *British Journal of Social Work 36,* 5, 777–788.

Subject Index

Author Index